W9-CTW-439

DATE DUE

DEMCO 38-296

The Jurisprudential Vision
of Justice Antonin Scalia

Studies in American Constitutionalism
General Editors: Gary J. Jacobsohn and Richard E. Morgan

In Defense of the Text: Democracy and Constitutional Theory
by Leslie Friedman Goldstein
Our Peculiar Security: The Written Constitution and Limited Government
edited by Eugene W. Hickok Jr., Gary L. McDowell, and Philip J. Costopoulos
Madison on the "General Welfare" of America: His Consistent
Constitutional Vision
by Leonard R. Sorenson
The Jurisprudential Vision of Justice Antonin Scalia
by David A. Schultz and Christopher E. Smith

The Jurisprudential Vision
of Justice Antonin Scalia

David A. Schultz
&
Christopher E. Smith

ROWMAN & LITTLEFIELD PUBLISHERS, INC.

ROWMAN & LITTLEFIELD PUBLISHERS, INC.

Published in the United States of America
by Rowman & Littlefield Publishers, Inc.
4720 Boston Way, Lanham, Maryland 20706

3 Henrietta Street
London WC2E 8LU, England

Copyright © 1996 by Rowman & Littlefield Publishers, Inc.

British Cataloging in Publication Information Available

Library of Congress Cataloging-in-Publication Data

Schultz, David Andrew.
The jurisprudential vision of Justice Antonin Scalia / David A. Schultz &
Christopher E. Smith.
p.   cm.
Includes bibliographical references and index.
1. Scalia, Antonin.   2. United States. Supreme Court.   3. Judicial process—United
States.   4. United States—Constitutional law—Interpretation and construction.
5. Conservatism—United States.   I. Smith, Christopher E.   II. Title
KF8745.S33S38   1996   347.73'26—dc20   95-47518   [347.30735]   CIP

ISBN 0-8476-8131-9 (cloth : alk. paper)
ISBN 0-8476-8132-7 (pbk. : alk. paper)

Printed in the United States of America

For Helene and Charlotte

Contents

Acknowledgments

There are many individuals whom we would like to thank and acknowledge as helpful in our endeavors to prepare this book.

Thomas R. Hensley and Scott Patrick Johnson of Kent State University and Joyce Baugh of Central Michigan University deserve recognition for assistance with previous work on the Supreme Court that contributed to our thinking about Scalia.

In addition, there are many other individuals who at one time or another commented on early portions of this book when the chapters were presented as conference papers at the American, Midwest, Southern, Southwestern, Northeastern, and New York State Political Science Association annual conventions over the last few years. These individuals include: Daniel Lowenstein of UCLA Law School; John Shockley of Western Illinois University; Bruce Auerbach of Albright College; Kent Rissmiller of Worcester Polytechnic Institute; Henry Abraham of the University of Virginia; Steve Wasby and Martin Edelman of Albany University; Stephen Gottlieb of Albany Law School; and Roy Shotland of Georgetown Law School.

Special acknowledgment also goes to Richard Brisbin Jr., of West Virginia University. His work on Justice Scalia has influenced our thinking in many ways.

Portions of chapter 3 contain some material that originally appeared in Christopher E. Smith, "Justice Antonin Scalia and the Institutions of American Government," *Wake Forest Law Review*, volume 25, 1988. Chapter 7 contains some material that originally appeared in Christopher E. Smith, "Justice Antonin Scalia and Criminal Justice Cases," *Kentucky Law Journal*, volume 81, 1992–93, and in Christopher E. Smith, "The Constitution and Criminal Punishment: The Emerging Visions of Justices Scalia and Thomas," *Drake Law Review*, volume 43, 1994. We are grateful for the cooperation of these journals in permitting material to be incorporated into the book.

Finally, our wives, Helene Levy Schultz and Charlotte Smith, and the Smith children, Alicia and Eric, deserve our eternal gratitude for tolerating with good humor our preoccupation with Justice Scalia.

Introduction

An individual justice cannot control decision making on the United States Supreme Court. By casting only one of the nine votes that define the law and determine the outcomes of cases, the formal power possessed by each individual justice is quite limited. Although the chief justice possesses special authority to recommend which cases should be discussed and then to lead discussions after oral arguments, the Court's titular leader nevertheless casts only one vote among the other equal votes when it is time to make a decision. The apparent equality of the justices' power when it comes to casting votes does not mean that the justices are equally influential in shaping the Court's decisions. If the equality of each justice's formal power translated into equality of influence, there might be little reason to study intensively the work of any individual justice. Yet there are significant differences in the impact of various justices upon legal doctrines and case outcomes, and these differences provide the justification for seeking to understand the behavior and impact of selected justices.

Some justices follow the lead of others or react to each case in an ad hoc fashion. These justices may be influential by casting deciding votes in close cases, but they do not steer the Court in any planned direction. In order to aspire to steer the Court, a justice must have *vision* and must enunciate that vision in a manner that seeks to persuade his or her colleagues to cast their votes in a manner that moves the Court down a designated path. What makes a justice recognizable as one who possesses a jurisprudential vision? Such a visionary justice must have strongly held and articulated views on the values embodied in the Constitution, the proper methods for judicial interpretation, and the Supreme Court's role in the governing system. The visionary justice must aspire to achieve coherence in advancing and applying these elements, although scholars are well aware that even the most apparently single-minded justice will inevitably show signs of inconsistency. Even a visionary justice may permit a fixed view of a particular constitutional phrase to produce an apparent deviation from the vision's coherence with respect to certain issues. The visionary's defining characteristic is not absolute consistency, but rather the persistent articulation of distinctive themes that address enduring questions about the judiciary's proper role in interpreting the Constitution and shaping public policy.

The possession and advancement of a jurisprudential vision does not guarantee that a justice will be sufficiently influential to shape legal doctrines and case outcomes. The Warren Court's Justice John Harlan was an articulate visionary of a restraintist judicial perspective, yet he was frequently outvoted by the liberal activists who surrounded him during his era of judicial service. That Harlan found himself dissenting in a number of key cases does not mean, however, that his influence can be dismissed. Indeed, Judge Robert Bork (1990) viewed Harlan's interpretive approach as sufficiently prominent to require singling out Harlan as the one "conservative" justice deserving of detailed analysis and criticism in his best-selling book, *The Tempting of America: The Political Seduction of the Law*.

Harlan, like some other justices, continues to receive attention after his death because the influence of a judicial visionary need not be limited to the cases in which the justice participated. A judicial visionary may lay a foundation of opinions for future judges to revive and apply in later eras. For example, Justice Harlan's grandfather, John Marshall Harlan, who served on the Supreme Court from 1877 to 1911, provided dissenting opinions on the incorporation of the Bill of Rights and equal protection for African Americans that helped to provide the foundation for majority decisions of the Warren Court in the 1950s and 1960s.

Among the justices on the Rehnquist-era Supreme Court, one individual stands out as a judicial visionary with firmly held and staunchly advocated views: Justice Antonin Scalia. When Antonin Scalia was elevated from judge on the U.S. Court of Appeals to justice on the U.S. Supreme Court in 1986, conservatives hoped he would become the dynamic conservative leader of President Reagan's judicial counterrevolution. Appointed to fill Justice Rehnquist's seat after the Court's most outspoken conservative was selected to replace Warren Burger as Chief Justice, Scalia was described as the "intellectual lodestar who would pull the Court to the right by the force of his brilliance" (Mauro 1990: 10).

Although Scalia did not fulfill his supporters' fervent desire for him to transform the Supreme Court, he quickly became an important and powerful figure on the high court. As his sharp intellect and unique judicial philosophy became increasingly evident with each strident opinion, he became a magnet for scholarly attention. Because he arrived on the Court at age fifty as a relatively youthful justice, commentators from across the political spectrum recognized that Scalia possesses the potential to place a significant imprint on constitutional law and statutory interpretation, whether or not he succeeds in gaining majority support among the contemporary justices for each of his opinions. As Linda Greenhouse (1990: B8) observed, Scalia's "willingness to discard accepted rules and refashion them in light of his own constitutional vision makes his impact greater than his rather low success rate might suggest." This is not to say that Scalia's opinions and decisions are always consistent. A visionary's coherence does not imply absolute consistency. Instead, it means that Scalia is a forceful advocate of recurring themes that illuminate a specific, unique conception of constitutional law and the judicial branch's proper place in the governing system. If the Court's future compositional changes move in directions favorable to Scalia's viewpoints, whether or not he is still on the Court, his many opinions will be available to provide arguments and reasoning that advance a unique jurisprudential vision.

In analyzing Scalia's jurisprudential vision, this book is neither a judicial biography nor an encyclopedia of Scalia's opinions. It is meant to be an assessment of Scalia's jurisprudence, not an evaluation of his life and works. Scalia had great importance in the historical moment in which he arrived at the Court as the anticipated leader of a conservative counterrevolution. Although the Court's composition has subsequently shifted away from its peak of conservatism with the addition of Democratic appointees Justices Ruth Bader Ginsburg and Stephen Breyer, as well as the liberalizing drift of Justice David Souter's opinions (Smith, Baugh, Hensley, and Johnson 1994), Scalia remains important. His importance lies in the words and reasoning that constitute his vision, and that vision, when placed in the enduring form of a written opinion, has the potential to shape doctrines and decisions in the near and distant future.

Scalia's Background

The roots of the impressive intellect and strident conservatism that Scalia brought to his judicial career can be found in his background and experiences. Antonin Scalia was born in 1936. He grew up in New York City, where his father was a professor of Romance languages at Brooklyn College. Some commentators have pointed to Scalia's religious upbringing and his religion-based education at Xavier High School, a Catholic military academy in Manhattan, and Georgetown University as a basis for his conservatism and approaches to legal interpretation. According to George Kannar

(1990: 1309), Scalia's "frequent use of particularly strong language in his opinions, even against his fellow 'conservatives,' suggests that his commitment to his methodology and his faith in the correctness of his views arises from sources in his character running deeper than his specifically political convictions." This is not to say that Scalia's opinions are guided by specific religious doctrines. No evidence suggests that he seeks to follow his church's doctrines when deciding legal cases, as can be seen in his support for capital punishment. Instead, both his underlying values and approaches to the meaning of texts may be influenced by his upbringing. In Kannar's (1990: 1313) words, "[l]earning Catholic doctrine concerning moral matters— which Justice Scalia surely did during the 1950s at the Catholic military high school he attended and as an undergraduate at Georgetown—may not be what counts. What counts may be the habit of mind he acquired in the course of learning it."

After graduating first in his class at Georgetown, Scalia attended Harvard Law School. Subsequent to his graduation from law school, he practiced law with a prominent Cleveland firm for eight years, then became a law professor at the University of Virginia. He became an attorney in the Justice Department during the Nixon administration, and he served as an assistant attorney general in the Office of Legal Counsel during the Ford administration. During the Democratic Carter administration, Scalia taught law at the University of Chicago and served as a frequent commentator on administrative law as editor of the American Enterprise Institute's journal, *Regulation* (Smith 1993b: 26). President Reagan appointed Scalia to the U.S. Court of Appeals for the District of Columbia Circuit in 1982.

Even before his elevation to the Supreme Court, Scalia had established a reputation as an articulate spokesperson for right-wing positions. Scalia's record on the court of appeals seemed to indicate that he would be a reliably conservative appointment to the high court. Wilson (1986) examined Judge Scalia's voting record on the court of appeals, along with the records of other prominent Reagan appointees, including Judges Robert Bork on the District of Columbia Circuit, Richard Posner and Frank Easterbrook on the Seventh Circuit, and Ralph Winter on the Second Circuit. After surveying Scalia's voting record (along with those of the other four judges) on access to the courts, the First Amendment, procedural due process, equal protection, and governmental structure, Wilson concluded that, "President Reagan must be pleased with these men, who to varying degrees, have made major creative contributions to emerging right-wing jurisprudence. They have aggressively applied traditional conservative techniques: increasing judicial deference to other branches of government and imposing new limits on federal court jurisdiction" (Wilson 1986a: 1173).[1] Specifically, Wilson noted that in twenty-three decisions involving criminal defendants, media defendants, and civil plaintiffs, Scalia ruled against the claims of rights twenty times (Wilson 1986a: 1178). In contrast to the other Reagan judges, Scalia did not seek to build elaborate constitutional theories. He apparently eschewed theory-building in favor of reaching pragmatic results (Wilson 1986a: 1175).[2]

Presidents Reagan and Bush sought to appoint judges who would use their decisions to advance a conservative policy agenda. In pursuit of this goal, they attempted to screen judicial appointees carefully to ensure that new federal judges shared certain conservative values and policy preferences (Schwartz 1988). They observed this practice in naming appointees to the Supreme Court, including Justices Sandra Day O'Connor, Anthony Kennedy, David Souter, and Clarence Thomas. They were also applied to the appointment of other federal judges, including the 268 lower federal court judges appointed by Reagan and the 185 judges appointed by Bush (Goldman 1989; Goldman 1993). Although presidents cannot control legislative activity to ensure passage of their preferred laws and policies, they can have an enduring impact on law and policy through the appointment of life-tenured federal judges. Thus, the Reagan and Bush judicial appointees, by constituting a majority of the federal judiciary, were positioned to usher in a new era of judicial policy. Political conservatives hoped that the new judges, and especially the new justices on the Supreme Court, would alter and reverse liberal Warren and Burger Court precedents related to crime and civil rights, as well as other controversial opinions, including *Roe v. Wade* (1973), the famous abortion decision (Moore 1992).

Presidents cannot predict with complete accuracy how judicial appointees will perform (Smith and Beuger 1993). For example, in spite of President Nixon's best efforts to create a conservative Supreme Court during the 1970s, the Burger Court has been described as the counterrevolution that "wasn't" (Blasi 1983). Although presidents cannot achieve all of their legal policy goals through judicial appointments, as Lawrence Baum indicates (1989: 41), "[M]ost justices do turn out to be ideologically compatible with the presidents who appoint them." Thus, Scalia's appointment raised the expectations of political conservatives. His appointment to the Supreme Court was assumed to guarantee that this time, the conservatives would succeed in redirecting the focus of the federal courts toward a more conservative agenda.

Scalia's Performance

Scalia's performance and achievements on the Supreme Court have proven to be more ambiguous than political conservatives had hoped. He clearly has supported many outcomes that follow a conservative agenda. Indeed, empirical examinations of his voting behavior would classify him as a "consistent conservative" because he supports the government in two-thirds or more of cases concerning constitutional claims by individuals (see, e.g., Baugh, Smith, Hensley, and Johnson 1995). In addition, his votes follow a conservative agenda with respect to many issues. For example, his judicial votes and opinions oppose a right of choice with respect to abortion (i.e., *Webster v. Reproductive Health Services* [1989], *Rust v. Sullivan* [1991], and *Planned Parenthood v. Casey* [1992]). Consistent with his outspoken opposition to affirmative action as a law professor (Scalia 1979), he has opposed such policies when they are challenged before the Supreme Court (i.e., *Johnson v. Transportation Agency, Santa Clara County* [1987], *City of Richmond v. Croson Co.* [1989], and *Metro Broadcasting v. Federal Communication Commission* [1990]). In other examples, he has endorsed the constitutionality of the death penalty, including its application to juvenile offenders (*Stanford v. Kentucky* [1989]), and has sought limits on standing and access of environmental groups to the federal courts (*Lujan v. Defenders of Wildlife* [1992]).

Despite his consistently conservative performance, Scalia has also surprised observers, including the political interests who advocated his appointment, by joining the liberal justices in cases concerning specific rights. Scalia provided a crucial vote for the five-member majority that recognized burning the American flag as a protected form of political expression (*Texas v. Johnson* [1989]). He objected to detaining arrestees in jail for forty-eight hours before holding probable cause hearings (*County of Riverside v. McLaughlin* [1991]). He also opposed random drug testing of Customs Service employees as a violation of the Fourth Amendment's prohibition against unreasonable searches and seizures (*National Treasury Employees Union v. Von Raab* [1989]).

The apparent difficulty in interpreting Scalia's impact and developing legacy on the Supreme Court stems not only from his periodic defections from his conservative colleagues. Scalia's judicial style has also diminished his ability to achieve the expectations of his supporters who anticipated an overhaul of liberal judicial precedents. Scalia's often acerbic opinions, bitter dissents, and well-known refusal to compromise have often alienated him from other justices and thereby affected his role in key cases (Greenhouse 1989; Taylor 1990). He has a penchant for attacking his usual allies as well as his regular opponents if they disagree with him in individual cases. This mixture of independence and combativeness has been most evident when Scalia has voted alone or with Justice Clarence Thomas in many cases. As a result, he has not successfully fulfilled the original expectations that he would have a leadership role and significant influence on the Court.

Scalia's capacity to alienate other justices has been credited with prompting the emergence of a relatively centrist bloc of justices (i.e., Kennedy, Souter, and O'Connor) who, despite their conservative credentials, upheld liberal precedents concerning abortion and prayer in school (Greenhouse 1992; Smith and Johnson 1993). For example, as fellow conservatives Chief Justice William Rehnquist and Justices Byron White and Anthony Kennedy attempted to cultivate and persuade Justice O'Connor to provide the needed fifth vote to overturn the right of abortion choice established in *Roe v. Wade* (1973), Scalia launched a strident attack on O'Connor in a concurring opinion (*Webster v. Reproductive Health Services* [1989]). In the next major abortion decision, a centrist block of Justices O'Connor, Kennedy, and Souter rejected Scalia's position—perhaps repelled by his strident attacks on O'Connor—lauded the importance of precedent, and protected basic abortion rights in *Planned Parenthood v. Casey* (1992). Scalia's confrontational role on the Court may also explain Souter's ascendence as his chief intellectual rival on the Court (Garrow 1994; Barrett 1993). Scalia's outspoken opinions have effectively raised a challenge to many precedents and doctrines, and Souter has risen to the task of analyzing and rebutting some of Scalia's claims.

Research on Justice Scalia

Throughout Scalia's tenure on the Supreme Court, there have been many efforts to explain his judicial behavior. In many respects, Scalia's jurisprudence has received more sustained analysis than that of most other justices, including many with longer tenure on the high court. By 1991, *Cardozo Law Review* had already devoted an entire issue to Scalia's opinions. Long-serving justices, such as White and Stevens, have never received the same level of attention. Scalia, in fact, attracted much scholarly attention even before he was appointed to the Supreme Court (Wilson 1986a; Nagareda 1987).

Overall, scholarly analyses of Scalia characterize him as a brilliant yet opinionated justice. He is regarded as a justice who favors a strict and aggressively enforced conception of separation of powers, limited access to the courts, and deference to members of Congress and, especially, the President. These analyses, while noting his conservative political views, generally did not emphasize his ideology as the controlling factor over his jurisprudence. Instead, scholars placed emphasis upon his legal pragmatism, his democratic vision of American society, and most importantly, his interpretive methodology as crucial to the decisions he reaches. The emphasis on interpretive methodology as the guiding influence over his opinions implies that Scalia may be more neutral or principled than his colleagues who, typical of Supreme Court justices, use their decisions to advance their values and policy preferences (Segal and Spaeth 1993). Given how attractive Scalia is to scholars and his importance on the Court, it is useful to look at the kinds of studies that have generated these conclusions.

In studies of Scalia, scholars have examined whether he displayed characteristics of the so-called freshman effect that bewilders new justices and impedes the immediate development of confident opinions (Heck and Hall 1981). Thea F. Rubin and Albert P. Melone reviewed Scalia's decisions during his first years on the Supreme Court and found that while he wrote fewer than his fair share of decisions, he nevertheless appeared comfortable with his new role as justice and quickly established his generally conservative voting pattern (Rubin and Melone 1988: 101–102). Thus, in their opinion, no real freshman effect occurred. In addition, studies by Michael Patrick King (1988) and Richard A. Brisbin Jr. (1990) of Scalia's first-year decisions concluded that his conservative "decisions suggest long-term influence on constitutional doctrine and the high court" (King 1988: 5–6). Both studies concluded that the justice's conservatism demonstrates constitutional and political values that place him in the restraintist tradition of Justice Felix Frankfurter and Yale Law Professor Alexander Bickel and thus, he fulfills the role of a "Reagan Justice" (Brisbin 1990: 28).

After his first year on the Court, studies of Scalia turned in three directions. One focus was on the impact of his judicial style and behavior, as illustrated by his increasingly vocal and often acrimonious opinions and dissents that included belittlement of other justices' opinions. One primary thesis is that Scalia's strident behavior has diminished his ability to persuade other justices to join his opinions (Smith 1993b).

Second, a set of articles examined his interpretive method and the sources of his disagreement with other conservative members of the Court (Pear 1991). George Kannar, for example, sought to understand Scalia's approach to reading the Constitution (Kannar 1990). Kannar located Scalia's rejection of appeal to authors' or Founders' intent in the justice's pre-Vatican II Catholicism. Kannar further argued that Scalia's father's professorial background in Romance literature provided the justice's essential approach to reading statutes and the Constitution in terms of the plain meaning that the words convey (Kannar 1990: 1299, 1316). Daniel Farber and Philip Frickey, on the other hand, located Scalia's interpretive approach in the justice's general distrust of legislative politics and his questioning of judges' ability to ascertain legislative intent from the committee reports and comments of particular legislators (Farber and Frickey 1991: 89–95).

They also agreed with other studies that Scalia's methodology is important to his approach to the law. (Farber and Frickey 1991: 89–91). Similarly, Arthur Stock noted Scalia's unwillingness to defer to legislative intent and other extratextual evidence when interpreting Congressional statutes (Stock 1991: 160–161). However, Scalia is willing to defer to extratextual evidence such as the *Federalist Papers* when interpreting the Constitution (Stock 1991: 180). Stock argued that this interpretive strategy is "inconsistent" and is meant to limit legislative power in order to benefit executive and judicial power (Stock 1991: 160–161, 190–191).

Jean Morgan Meaux, Richard Nagareda, and Jay Schlosser saw Scalia's interpretive strategies, including his skepticism towards legislative intent and history, as important to his jurisprudence in the areas of executive and administrative authority (Meaux 1987: 227), the First Amendment (Nagareda 1987: 722), and church/state issues (Schlosser 1988: 387). Finally, Daniel Reisman contended that the justice's interpretive method was not strictly a textual approach but rather appeals to extratextual values, including a belief in a strong executive government. (Reisman 1988: 49). Hence, Scalia's jurisprudence and appeal to a neutral methodology actually masked his commitment to executive power and his depreciation of congressional authority. (Reisman 1988: 92–93; Strauss 1991: 1716; Tushnet 1991: 1740).

A third line of scholarship concentrated on Scalia's definition of the Court's role in American society, his attitude toward the other major branches of government, and his views on substantive doctrinal issues such as the First Amendment. Christopher E. Smith argued that the justice's "strong views on separation of powers and the institution of the Supreme Court place him at odds with his colleagues" (Smith 1990: 785). Moreover, Smith claimed that Scalia's commitment to separation of powers has given him the role as "stalwart guardian of American government institutions" (Smith 1990: 809). Brisbin reached a similar conclusion (Brisbin 1990: 25–28). He also concluded that Scalia's deference to Congress and the Presidency as the primary policy-making institutions was important to the Justice's conception of American politics (Brisbin 1990: 5–6). Both authors agreed with other observers that Scalia's willingness to place limits on standing and deny access to the federal courts was an attempt to preserve the federal judiciary and, especially, the Supreme Court, as an elite institution in American politics (Smith 1990: 794- 795; Brisbin 1990: 6–9; Meaux 1987: 246; Schlosser 1988: 385; Schwartz 1990: 226–227; Scatena 1987, 1235, 1254).

Overall, various scholarly explanations have been set forth for Scalia's decision-making behavior and impact on the Court. Some articles have located the key to his opinions as residing in his commitment to separation of powers (Reisman 1988), his political conservatism (Brisbin 1990), his Catholicism (Kannar 1990), and his specific interpretative methodology (Wildenthal 1991; Brisbin 1991; Newland 1994), among other factors. These conclusions have been based on studies examining Scalia's decisions in specific areas of law, including religion (Brisbin 1992b; Schlosser 1988), speech (Schultz 1993), criminal justice (Smith 1992–93), and property and land use decisions (Schultz 1995; Bosselman 1993; Freitag 1994; Levitt 1993). Thus far, no comprehensive, integrative analysis has examined his jurisprudence to determine if patterns discerned in one area reveal similar patterns elsewhere in his legal thinking. As this book will discuss, for example, analysis of Scalia's views on constitutional interpretation, judicial review, the legislative process, patronage, and campaign finance-reform suggests that Scalia's image as a neutral, principled decisionmaker is illusory. In fact, certain ideological values and policy preferences take precedence over any putative interpretive methodology.

Seeking a Comprehensive Analysis

The failure of scholars to consider seemingly disparate areas of the law simultaneously within a single analysis, such as property law and civil rights law, has inadvertently resulted in the failure of the Scalia scholarship to find or search for overriding, fundamental changes that may be occurring in Scalia's jurisprudence. While Scalia has invoked Emerson's admonition that "Consistency is the hobgoblin of little minds" (Scalia 1989–90: 587), Scalia's jurisprudence is not simply a scattered mix of opinions that lacks focus and consistency. There is a logic to Scalia's opinions, and while his jurisprudence may not approach the ideals of the neutral-principles tradition advocated by Herbert Wechsler, Alexander Bickel, and Robert Bork (Wechsler 1959; Bickel 1986; Bork 1990), clear themes are evident in Scalia's jurisprudence that span traditional doctrinal boundaries.

The goal of this book is to explicate these patterns, indicate how they influence his decision-making, and suggest how they might change. We seek to examine Scalia's jurisprudence and offer an explanation of those values that seem most influential in illustrating how and why the justice decides his cases.

The scope of the book's analysis encompasses Scalia's opinions on the Supreme Court through the end of the 1993 term. Because Scalia is one of the Court's most prolific opinion authors, his first eight terms on the Court provide a wealth of information about his jurisprudential vision. In addition, we will look at some prior opinions issued while he was still on the

U.S. Court of Appeals for the District of Columbia Circuit, some recent opinions as they reinforce or reflect jurisprudential trends, and also his scholarly and off-bench writings and speeches. Examination of these sources will help to clarify aspects of Scalia's views, and will also permit us to look for consistency and contradictions.

We argue that clear patterns are discernible in Scalia's jurisprudence. Other analyses point to one or two variables or themes that dominate Scalia's jurisprudence; we adopt a perspective similar to those presented in comprehensive studies of justices such as William Rehnquist (Davis 1989). Specifically, we argue that several values that structure and guide Scalia's judicial decision-making. These values are neither simply political nor solely jurisprudential, but rather a combination of substantive political, methodological, and interpretive values that influence his thought. Hence, the book departs from the claims of Segal and Spaeth (1993), who argued that a political, policy, or outcome model can adequately explain a justice's opinions. The analysis here also departs from positivist or legalist models that would contend simply that legalistic values and a neutral methodology determine Scalia's decisions. Instead, we seek an integrated approach that recognizes the influence of both political and legal factors.

Many values are important to Scalia and operative in his jurisprudence. As others have noted, Scalia consistently advocates deference to executive authority, respect for the majoritarian process, skepticism towards legislative politics, and rejection of the role of the Court as a social arbiter and protector of all types of minority interests. These elements reflect important values that motivate Scalia's opinions. While Scalia often seems to respect and wish to defer to the majoritarian political process for authoritative decision making, Scalia does not ignore protection of traditional guarantees contained within the Bill of Rights. When Scalia sees the Constitution's words and intentions as providing a clear meaning for the Supreme Court to follow, he will subordinate his majoritarian orientation and his deference to the elected branches of government. Thus, Scalia has supported expansive interpretations of some provisions within Bill of Rights protections, such as those to protect property rights. In making these decisions and others, Scalia's opinions also reveal influential methodological and interpretive strategies, such as deference to the framers in reading the Constitution, and to the use of the plain English meanings when reading statutes.

We argue that Scalia's jurisprudence, as is characteristic of any justice, is an attempt to reconcile several competing values and goals (Cardozo 1969). In Scalia's case, we see an effort to step outside of the current dominant patterns of decision-making among contemporary justices. Scalia's opinions advance the creation of what we shall call a post-*Carolene Products* jurisprudence. We take this label from the famous Supreme Court case *United States v. Carolene Products* (1938), in which the Court repudiated economic due process and signaled, in Justice Stone's footnote number four, a new role for the Supreme Court in protecting individual rights while granting legislatures broad discretion to enact economic regulation. Scalia's jurisprudence does adopt many assumptions of post-1937 legal thinking, such as general deference to legislatures to regulate the economy, increased judicial scrutiny towards protection of Bill of Rights guarantees, and support for New Deal-style administrative reorganization of the economy and polity (Sunstein 1987; Ely 1980). However, Scalia's jurisprudence also reorders and apparently rejects some basic claims of the contemporary paradigm of Supreme Court decision-making, advancing a different hierarchy of values or pattern of assumptions.

Scalia's jurisprudence is not a flat rejection of post-1937 jurisprudence, and he has even stated that it would be impossible and perhaps undesirable to return to the assumptions of pre-1937 doctrine (Scalia 1987: 33–4). Yet Scalia's views include opposition to the property/personal rights dichotomy that, since 1937, has led to a two-tier system or disparate levels of scrutiny for property and personal rights. Scalia's jurisprudence, for example, seems determined to give greater deference to legislatures to regulate individual rights, as his death penalty and religious-freedoms opinions suggest. By contrast, in affirmative action and in land use regulatory cases, Scalia's skepticism towards legislative politics, as well as his political and legal concerns for protection of ownership claims, have led him to give greater levels of scrutiny to actions of legislatures.

Moreover, in departing from the logic of Justice Stone's footnote number four in *United States v. Carolene Products*, Scalia deviates from several accepted doctrines that have dominated judicial decision-making in recent decades. For example, Scalia is often willing to allow legislatures to regulate politics to protect the integrity of the electoral process, even if it disadvantages some third-party candidates (*Norman v. Reed* [1991]). At the same time, Scalia has also been willing to join opinions that turn white voters into discrete and insular minorities needing protection in the political process (*City of Richmond v. Croson* [1989]). In addition, Scalia rejects portions of the New Deal compromise on delegation, as is evidenced by his opinions on the special prosecutor (*Morrison v. Olson* [1988]) and the Gramm-Rudman-Hollings Act on balancing the budget (*Synar v. United States* [D.D.C 1986]). Such opinions seem to harken back to the restrictive pre- or early New Deal cases that stand in sharp contrast to the post-*Schechter Poultry v. United States* (1935) jurisprudence which permitted broad delegation of power and broke down traditional separation-of-powers principles.

In short, the value hierarchy to which Scalia is committed includes respect for the majoritarian process, protection of property, use of a specific political methodology, and a qualified respect for judicial defense of traditional Bill-of-Rights claims. All of these commitments are influenced and bracketed by a generally conservative ideology that shapes the trade-offs the justice makes among these four values. Scalia's efforts to integrate, articulate, and assert these values are not simply a rejection of the logic of *Carolene Products* jurisprudence or specific aspects of this approach that have dominated a half-century of constitutional law. Instead, Scalia seeks both to rethink what rights and persons are substantively protected under the *Carolene Products* logic, and even how the logic of footnote number four is interpreted. In doing this, Scalia endeavors to persuade, lead, push, hector, and embarrass the other justices into joining his new vision for constitutional law and the judiciary's role. Thus, Scalia's persistent advocacy of specific themes that deviate from recent traditions constitutes the development and advocacy of a post-*Carolene Products* jurisprudence.

Unquestionably, many of Scalia's commitments are consistent with Reagan's or other conservative political agendas. Previous studies by Henry Abraham and others tell us that, generally, the opinions of justices do not significantly depart from those of the appointing president (Abraham 1992). Yet simply to argue that politics controls Scalia's opinions ignores the possible legitimate jurisprudential reasons for many of his claims. Evidence suggests that a complex mixture of influences shapes justices' decisions. In examining case selection, for example, Perry (1991) notes both an outcome and jurisprudential mode that structure how a justice selects cases. By that, he means that if a justice cares about the outcome of a case, one set of logical and decision-making rules appears to influence how the justice selects a case. If, however, the justice is indifferent to the outcome of the case, more jurisprudential or legalistic criteria obtain. We think the same is true for Scalia. To state the argument most simplistically, Scalia's opinions may reflect a more outcome-oriented approach when they concern issues he cares about, such as in the case of abortion or property. Yet sometimes, more of a jurisprudential mode may dominate when the issue is not as important to him. The jurisprudential and outcome modes are not clearly separable since both factors undoubtedly influence cases to some degree. Scalia's opinions shift along a spectrum between these two modes, with most opinions displaying discernible elements of both political and legalistic factors.[3] Although specific modes visibly dominate in the contexts of specific cases and issues, the challenge is to gain an integrated understanding of how these elements shape Scalia's jurisprudential vision and judicial decision-making.

The various chapters in the book seek to demonstrate how different values compromise and shape Scalia's jurisprudence. Chapter one examines Scalia's cases on economic regulation, property rights, and land use. Here we find Scalia's influence perhaps at its greatest, as he authors two important majority opinions. It is in his property-rights decisions, juxtaposed to his civil rights and liberties opinions, that we see the clearest indication of Scalia's move towards a post-*Carolene Products* jurisprudence. This analysis of Scalia's approach to property and civil rights defines many of the themes important to the justice's post-*Carolene Products* jurisprudence, and lays the foundation for the remainder of the book.

Chapters two through four address constitutional and statutory interpretation, as well as Scalia's vision of the basic structure of the political process. Here we seek to define Scalia's political philosophy. By political philosophy, we mean the justice's view on the basic order of how the political process should operate, the duties of the different branches of the government, and the Court's approach to its duties. Chapter two examines the issue of constitutional interpretation and the political process, seeking to clarify how Scalia understands what the Founders were doing when they designed our political system. Chapter three turns to statutory interpretation and construction, seeking to show how a methodology of interpretation here reinforces his views about how the political process should operate as well as vice versa. Chapter four focuses on separation of powers and the political authority of the different branches of government, including the issue of federalism. In these chapters, topics such as affirmative action, abortion, and the death penalty are discussed because in Scalia's dicta we find important observations about his views of the political process, the relative divisions of labor among the different branches of government, and his use of an interpretative methodology to support his political philosophy. Overall, Scalia's understanding and rethinking of the logic of *Carolene Products* dominates his views on interpretation and how the institutions of American government should operate and what values should be given priority. Finally, these chapters demonstrate also that Scalia has not convinced the Court to adopt his interpretative strategies. He has been unsuccessful in getting others to accept his views on separation of powers and the distribution of institutional responsibility for deciding policy issues, such as abortion.

Chapters five through eight are more substantive, examining some specific issues of law. Chapter five examines freedom of religion; chapters six and seven analyze First Amendment expressive freedoms, including free speech, press, and association claims; and chapter eight looks at criminal justice issues, including the death penalty, search and seizure, and self-incrimination. These four chapters analyze some of the major civil rights and liberties cases in which Scalia has participated. They demonstrate that the justice is unsympathetic to most traditional criminal due process and civil libertarian claims, and that this indifference, along with his views towards property rights, separation of powers, and other issues, provides evidence that Scalia is seeking to reorder the basic canons of jurisprudence that have dominated constitutional law since the New Deal. Moreover, we also find that in these cases, Scalia's record of influence is mixed. In some issues, such as the Eighth Amendment, Scalia has written for the majority of justices, but in others, such as in free speech or religion, he has infrequently spoken for the Court. However, instead of simply arguing that his opposition is political, we seek to clarify of the different legal and political variables that influence his decisions.

Chapter nine is a conclusion, summing up the analysis, clarifying the main lines of Scalia's jurisprudence, and offering some observations about Scalia's views and future role on the Court. Clearly, no justice's opinions remain static. Thus, predictions about how Scalia's jurisprudence will evolve are inherently uncertain, especially in light of changes in Court personnel, party control over the Congress and the Presidency, and other changes in the economy.

Notes

1. B. Schwartz, *The New Right and the Constitution: Turning Back the Legal Clock*, 223–231 (1990), similarly includes Scalia among those Reagan appointees whom he considers leaders of the "new right" legal movement seeking to overturn the more liberal post-New Deal and Warren Court decisions.

2. Compare this claim to J. M. Meaux, "Justice Scalia and Judicial Restraint: A Conservative Resolution of Conflict Between Individual and the State," *Tulane Law Review* 62 (1987): 227.

3. This might suggest that there is a coherence between his political values and methods, with them mutually reinforcing one another, such that to seek to distinguish interpretative strategies from substantive values is, if not futile, an inappropriate approach Scalia's jurisprudence. Gadamer (1986) is one of several to note how ostensibly neutral rules or methods of interpretation actually embody the biases and values of the interpreter.

Chapter 1

Property Rights and the Emergence of a Post-*Carolene Products* Jurisprudence

Since his elevation to the Supreme Court in 1986, Antonin Scalia has been an outspoken and important defender in the Rehnquist Court's revival of landowner rights (Schwartz 1990: 73–137). During his tenure on the Court, Scalia has participated in nine cases directly addressing land use and property rights questions, voting in favor of the property owner in eight of the nine cases or eighty-nine percent of the time. This voting record affirming property owner's claims is by far the most supportive and consistent among all justices sitting on the Supreme Court since 1986, locating Scalia among the leaders on the Court in its effort to limit land use regulation and affirm property claims. The one possible exception to this claim is that Justice Powell voted for the property owner in all five of the cases he participated in from 1986 until his retirement.

The holding in *Dolan v. City of Tigard* (1994), which affirmed property owners' rights over government regulation illustrates Scalia's and the Rehnquist Court's effort to reinvigorate property rights (Coyle 1987). The case represents the confluence of several different yet overlapping lines of constitutional jurisprudence regarding property rights; it also helps to crystalize the assertion that Scalia has been a major Court influence in land use cases and in fashioning a post-*Carolene Products* judicial philosophy that seeks to reorder some of the basic assumptions on property and individuals rights that the judiciary has shared since the New Deal. On one level, *Dolan* grows out of a line of regulatory-takings jurisprudence that can be traced backed to *Pennsylvania v. Mahon* (1922), in which Holmes sought to distinguish police power land use regulation from an eminent domain taking by that saying the difference between the two was a "question of degree." *Dolan*, like cases subsequent to *Pennsylvania v. Mahon*, such as *Euclid v. Ambler*

Realty (1926), *Goldblatt v. Town of Hempstead* (1962), and *Penn Central Company v. City of New York* (1978), sought to clarify when the line has been crossed from regulation to a taking.

On a second level, *Dolan* addresses one of the most enduring dichotomies in constitutional jurisprudence, i.e., the contrasting levels of judicial scrutiny given to property and civil rights (otherwise known as the property rights/civil rights dichotomy). In the period approximately between the late nineteenth century and the New Deal, known as the *Lochner* era, the Supreme Court decided cases such as *Lochner v. New York* (1905) and *Allgeyer v. Louisiana* (1897) in which it articulated the doctrine of substantive or economic due process. Although the Court did affirm most economic regulation during that period (Ely 1994). It also often demanded a greater level of legislative justification for economic regulation than would be required for legislation curtailing individual rights. Along with these cases, decisions such as *Plessy v. Ferguson* (1896) and *Bradwell v. Illinois* (1873), demonstrated judicial willingness and broad deference to legislatures, allowing them to adopt legislation that restricted many civil rights or liberties. Other decisions such as the *Civil Rights Cases* (1883) suggested limits that the Court would place upon Congress's ability to protect civil rights when those rights conflicted with the economic privileges of others.

Yet cases affirming New Deal legislation such as *West Coast Hotel v. Parrish* (1937) and most importantly, *U.S. v. Carolene Products* (1938) brought an end to the *Lochner* era and ushered in what could be called the *Carolene Products* era. In *Carolene Products*, especially footnote number four, the Court stated that economic regulation would be subject to rational basis tests, while legislation that affected discrete and insular minorities or that otherwise impacted upon Bill of Rights protections would be subject to a higher level of scrutiny. As a result of a *Carolene Products* logic, Warren and Brennan transformed the Court to protect individual rights more vigorously than property rights. In many ways, the *Carolene Products* era reversed the *Lochner* era relationship between property and individual rights.[1]

Yet the Reagan and Bush presidencies brought a much more conservative Supreme Court and federal judiciary, both committed to limiting government regulation and addressing the "takings" issue (Lazarus 1993: 1413–14). Their appointments produced a judiciary more supportive of property rights and less sympathetic towards individual rights than was characteristic of the Warren Court and *Carolene* Products era (Schwartz 1990, 73–137). *Dolan* fits in here as one the clearest indications yet that the current Supreme Court, with Scalia leading, is moving towards a post-*Carolene Products* approach to adjudicating property and civil rights. Under Rehnquist and Scalia, the Supreme Court has moved toward placing both property and civil rights under a level of judicial scrutiny that both resembles and differs from the levels of analysis found in previous periods of the Court's jurisprudential history.

Finally, on a third level, *Dolan* clarifies the direction that Justice Scalia is headed in his views on property rights. Although Rehnquist wrote *Dolan*, the intellectual roots for this decision reside in *Nollan v. California Coastal Commission* (1987) and *Lucas v. South Carolina Coastal Commission* (1992), both of which were Scalia opinions invalidating coastal regulations that limited property owner's rights. These early Scalia opinions laid the precedent for *Dolan*. Overall, while nine cases may not be a large sample, *Dolan* and the other eight property rights cases that Scalia participated in do reveal definite jurisprudential patterns and themes, especially when these cases are compared to his views on other individual-rights claims.

This chapter examines Scalia's views on property rights, demonstrating how the justice has been important to, if not the leader in the current rethinking of takings and land use jurisprudence (Fisher 1993: 1393–4) as well as a more comprehensive reevaluation of the jurisprudence of the *Carolene Products* era that is transpiring both off and on the Court.[2] While previous works have examined Rehnquist's and the Rehnquist Court's views on property (Davis 1989; Massey 1984; Schwartz 1990; Schultz 1992), there is no comprehensive discussion that addresses Scalia's views on property rights.[3] To rectify this, the chapter will first offer an examination of Scalia's views on property rights in light of his scholarly writings and Court decisions. Next, the chapter draws upon statistics to be developed in later chapters and contrasts Scalia's property-rights decisions with his voting record on selected civil rights/liberties issues. The purpose of this contrast is to show how *Dolan* represents an effort on the part of Scalia and the Rehnquist Court to rethink the relative relationship between property and civil rights and, in the process, articulate what appears to be a post-*Carolene Products* jurisprudence that reconceptualizes the property rights/civil rights dichotomy.

Scalia's Philosophical Views on Property Rights Statistical Analysis

One way to examine Scalia's support for property rights is to look at the percentage of time that he has voted in favor of property-owner claims. Since Scalia joined the Court in 1986, nine cases directly address these land use or property owners' claims. Scalia has supported the property owner in eight cases, or eighty-nine percent of the time. Table I compares the voting records of all the justices on property claims since 1986.

TABLE I
Supreme Court Voting Record on Property Rights Claims
1986–1993 Terms

Justice Total Property Opinions		Total votes/percentage for Property Owner
Powell	5	5 (100%)
Scalia	9	8 (89%)
Rehnquist	9	6 (67%)
O'Connor	9	6 (67%)
Kennedy	3	2 (67%)
Thomas	3	2 (67%)
White	8	5 (63%)
Court	9	5 (56%)
Marshall	6	2 (33%)
Brennan	6	2 (33%)
Stevens	9	2 (22%)
Blackmun	9	1 (11%)
Souter	3	0 (0%)
Ginzberg	1	0 (0%)

No justice on the Court from the 1986–1993 terms has cast more votes for property owners than has Scalia and, with the exception of Powell, no justice has a voting percentage that better supports such claims. However, for the sake of comparison, when we examine Scalia's voting record on other Bill of Rights or civil rights/liberties issues, a different pattern emerges. For example, Table II, which was drawn from cases discussed in chapters five and six, reviews Scalia's voting pattern on First Amendment free speech, press, and association claims from 1986 through the 1993 term.

As will be argued in chapters six and seven, in expressive-freedom claims arising under the First or Fourteenth Amendments, Scalia has supported these claims only forty-one percent of the time. Moreover, if we include his expressive freedom decisions from when he was an appellate court judge, then we find that he has supported these claims in only twenty-one of sixty-six decisions or thirty-eight pcercent of the time.

Finally, Table III examines Scalia's support for criminal due process issues.

Scalia's support is weak for criminal due process claims that arise out of the Bill of Rights; he supports such claims only nineteen percent of the time. This presents an interesting contrast within Scalia's voting record. Although Scalia has stated that property rights are related to other human or civil rights (Scalia 1987: 31–2), and that relationship might suggest simi-

TABLE II
Supreme Court Support for First Amendment
Free Speech, Press, and Association: 1986 through 1993 Terms

Justice Total Expressive Freedom Votes		*Total Votes/Percentage for Expressive Freedom*
Rehnquist	56	18 (32%)
Thomas	17	07 (41%)
Scalia	56	23 (41%)
O'Connor	55	26 (47%)
White	51	25 (49%)
Ginzburg	05	03 (60%)
Court	**56**	**34 (61%)**
Stevens	56	38 (63%)
Souter	25	16 (64%)
Kennedy	41	27 (66%)
Blackmun	55	42 (76%)
Brennan	31	28 (90%)
Marshall	36	33 (92%)

TABLE III
Percentage of Justices' Decisions Against Individuals in Criminal Justice Cases, 1986–1993 (includes 4th Amendment, 5th Amendment, 6th Amendment, 8th Amendment, Death Penalty, and Habeas Corpus)

Justice Total Criminal Due Process Votes		*Total Votes/Percentage Against Criminal Due Process Claims*
Thomas	24	21 (88%)
Rehnquist	139	121 (87%)
Scalia	139	113 (81%)
Powell	26	21 (81%)
Kennedy	109	82 (75%)
O'Connor	138	102 (74%)
White	139	101 (73%)
Souter	45	24 (56%)
Blackmun	138	48 (35%)
Stevens	139	30 (22%)
Brennan	92	07 (08%)
Marshall	111	03 (03%)

lar treatment of both types of rights, his voting pattern reveals otherwise. He appears to be more supportive of property than other personal rights, supporting them eighty-nine percent of the time compared to forty-one percent and nineteen percent for expressive freedom and criminal due process claims, respectively. If we also consider his religious freedom cases, we see clear patterns in Scalia's treatment property and civil rights.

Philosophical Views

Scattered throughout Scalia's academic writings and legal opinions are various statements about property rights and their relationship to other rights. His views are characteristic of the views shared by many politically conservative writers who advocate more support for property-rights claims at the expense of environmental regulation. In "Economic Affairs as Human Affairs," the justice advocates renewed judicial and cultural support for economic liberties. Scalia states that "I know of no society, today or in any era of history, in which high degrees of intellectual and political freedom have flourished with a high degree of state control over the relevant citizen's economic life" (ibid.: 32). In addition, Scalia eschews contemporary distinctions that separate property and civil rights. Such a distinction for Scalia

> is a pernicious notion, though it represents a turn of mind that characterizes much American political thought. It leads to the conclusion that economic rights and liberties are qualitatively distinct from, and fundamentally inferior to, other noble human values called civil rights, about which we should be more generous . . . On closer analysis, however, it seems to me that the difference between economic freedom and what are generally called civil rights turns out to be a difference of degree rather than of kind . . . In any case, in the real world a stark dichotomy between economic freedoms and civil rights does not exist (ibid.: 31–2).

Scalia depicts economic freedoms as important as other political freedoms, contending that economic freedoms are linked to and the basis of other political freedoms:

> Human liberties of various types are dependent on one another, and it may well be that the most humble of them is indispensable to the others—the firmament, so to speak, upon which the high spires of the most exalted freedoms ultimately rest . . . The free market, which presupposes relatively broad economic freedom, has historically been the cradle of broad political freedom,

and in modern times the demise of economic freedom has been the grave of political freedom as well (ibid.: 31–2).

For Scalia, political freedoms such as free speech and association appear linked to the free market and respect for economic autonomy (ibid.: 32). The marketplace of ideas and the economic marketplace are connected, with protection of the latter as the surest way to protect the former. Protecting our society against excessive economic regulation and defending property interests appear to be a surer way for Scalia to support civil liberties than would it be for the judiciary to single out political freedoms of speech, press, and assembly alone. Constitutional protections do not seem to be enough to protect political liberties. Some institutions or forces, such as property rights, are needed to sustain these liberties.

Beyond his own view that property rights are as important to political liberties, Scalia hints that the framers of the Constitution also thought property rights were important. In the "The Two Faces of Federalism," Scalia states that the framers intended to limits the ability of states to engage in economic regulation (ibid.: 20). In *Austin v. Michigan Chamber of Commerce* (1990), Scalia dissented from the six-person majority which held that corporations, even some nonprofit ones such as the Michigan Chamber of Commerce, could constitutionally be prohibited from using direct corporate treasury funds for independent expenditures to support or oppose candidates for office. In his dissent, Scalia held, among other points, that the Michigan law interfered with the First Amendment rights of the Chamber, which he presumably labeled a voluntary political association (ibid.: 1416).

Scalia defends the Michigan Chamber of Commerce as more like a voluntary political association, as described by the Alexis de Tocqueville in *Democracy in America*. Suppressing these voluntary associations, according to Scalia, is destructive:

> To eliminate voluntary associations—not only including powerful ones, but *especially* (Scalia's emphasis) including powerful ones—from the public debate is either to augment the always dominant power of government or to impoverish public debate (ibid.: 1416).

The Michigan legislation, for Scalia, is clearly a form of censorship, inconsistent with the First Amendment, the intent of Madison and Jefferson, as well as the observations of de Tocqueville on the need for free speech and voluntary associations in society. Scalia's dicta here, although not conclusive, arguably intimates that the framers would be willing to protect property interests, even powerful ones, because such rights are linked to rights of speech and association.

Yet despite his respect for constitutional originalism, Scalia argues against constitutionalizing property rights for two reasons.[4] The first is that this would require judicial intervention into the economy and economic policy (Scalia 1987: 34). Involvement in these areas not only would raise the question of the competence of the courts to act (ibid.: 35), but would also lead to an activist Court, thus violating principles of judicial restraint and separation of powers. The benefits of judicial restraint far outweigh any damage done to property rights by not constitutionalizing them (ibid.: 34). The second is that the framer support for property rights, "[T]he social consensus as to what the limited, 'core' economic rights are does not exist today as it once perhaps did" (ibid.: 36). What has happened, according to Scalia, is that the underlying social consensus necessary to make property rights worthy of significant legal and constitutional protection is missing. He suggests, "[I]f you are interested in economic liberties, then the first step is to recall the society to that belief in their importance which (I have no doubt) the founders of the republic shared" (ibid.: 37).

Protection of property rights necessitates that society take the lead in demanding that they need renewed support, presumably through legislative action. Even though some conservative critics call for a return to pre-New Deal legal assumptions regarding property rights (Epstein 1985: 281), Scalia rejects a return to the *Lochner* doctrines that gave the Court broad authority to create and protect economic rights (Scalia 1987: 33–4). The tone of his arguments does suggest that some judicial support for economic rights against the government is important (ibid.: 33, and Scalia notes that the judiciary does protect many of economic rights and liberties) if we are to maintain political liberty and limit governmental authority. The belief in property rights is an important value in our society, worthy of respect and defense; this belief suggests one possible reason why Scalia supports property rights more often than many other constitutional claims, i.e., because he views them as more important and instrumental to the maintenance of a free society than perhaps any other type of rights.

Given Scalia's relative support for property claims and his relative lack of sympathy for expressive freedom, criminal due process, and religious claims, the question becomes: where is Scalia's jurisprudence headed on this issue? Review of Scalia's land use cases help clarify the answer to this question.

Scalia's Property Rights Cases

Unlike other areas of law—religion or criminal due process—Scalia was quick to define his own views on property rights. Several cases during the

1986–87 term early on defined Scalia both as an important defender of property-rights claims and as seeking to clarify and narrow the distinction between valid land use regulation and regulatory takings.

The first case is *California Coastal Commission v. Granite Rock Company* (1987). At issue here was whether a company with an unpatented mining claim on federal land in California had to obtain a state permit for mining operations in the state. In 1981, Granite Rock Company had obtained approval from the National Forest Service for a five-year mining operation. Subsequently California, pursuant to the California Coastal Act, contended that the company needed a permit for any mining in the federal lands that Granite Rock undertook. In an O'Connor majority opinion, the Court held that neither Forest Service regulations nor any other federal law preempted the state from mandating a permit requirement.

Dissenting, Scalia argued that the question of whether a state environmental law is preempted by federal law is immaterial in this case (ibid.: 1438). He reached out and redefined the issue as a property-rights and land use case, describing the permit requirement as a land use control (ibid.: 1439), purporting to exercise land use authority over federal property (ibid.: 1441). Instead of necessarily seeing this case as a question of federal environmental preemption, he saw it as a case of federal preemption of state regulation of federal lands. The tone of Scalia's opinion demonstrated that he saw this case more as a question of whether a governmental entity could impose land use controls upon another owner, even though in this case that owner was the federal government. For Scalia, if the government can place limits upon a landowner to such an extent that she loses control over her property, that regulation is extensive.

Nollan v. California Coastal Commission (1986) was Scalia's second Supreme Court land use decision and, more than *Granite Rock*, it immediately demonstrated Scalia views on property and ownership rights. In *Nollan*, the Nollans had a contract to purchase beachfront property, and then they planned totear down the existing structure, and replace it with a three-bedroom house. The Nollans sought a construction permit and were granted it, provided they left a narrow public easement along their property, thus allowing people to walk to the public beach. Similar easements had been required for other houses along the beach. The commission justified the easement as necessary to inform the public that the beach was public. A house, obstructing the view of the water, would lead the public to think the beach was private. The Nollans objected to the requirement and brought suit claiming the easement was an uncompensated taking.

The Supreme Court agreed. Scalia's majority opinion examined the stated purpose of the California Coastal Act and the zoning regulation, which was to prevent obstruction of the public's view of the waterfront (ibid.: 3147–8). The Act stated that a wall of houses would "psychologically" prevent or block the public from viewing and visiting a coast that they had every right to visit. Scalia argued that the vertical easement would not further this goal (ibid.: 3148–9). The houses would still block a view of the beach, and the public access would not rectify that problem.

Scalia also contended that the Nollans were being asked by the commission to give up part of their property for the public good. Scalia did not see how this loss of land would further the aesthetic good mentioned above. While the access might or might not have diminished the value of their property, the real question was one of the basic rights of ownership. Here, the right to exclude others, an important "stick" in the bundle of rights associated with property ownership, was taken away from the Nollans (ibid.: 3145). The building permit was not simply regulation, but "leveraging" on the part of the commission to force owners to give away part of their land in return for certain uses (ibid.: 3148 n. 5). This permit requirement did not serve the objectives of the act but instead constituted an uncompensated taking.

Brennan's dissent indicated that Scalia's opinion "imposed a standard of precision for the exercise of a State's police power that has been discredited for the better part of this century" (ibid.: 3151). According to Brennan, Scalia's opinion even offered judicial notice of what constituted reasonable regulation to fulfill the stated objects. The majority did not grant wide deference to the legislature, but had questioned the reasonableness and substance of the statute. Brennan, following up on his views in *Penn Central Company v. City of New York* (1978), saw the act here as furthering a substantial public purpose, and believed that it did not involve a unilateral government action denying use of the property (ibid.: 3156). The easement requirement only took effect when a building permit was obtained and even then the permit would only require the easement under certain conditions (ibid.: 3155–6). No taking had occurred because no preexisting investment-backed expectations were damaged.

In 1986–87 term Scalia also supported property-rights claims in two other cases. The first was *First English Evangelical Lutheran Church of Glendale v. the County of Los Angeles* (1986, hereinafter "First Lutheran"). First Lutheran owned buildings that were destroyed by a flood; subsequent to the flood, the County of Los Angeles declared a temporary and total construction ban on properties in the plane. First Lutheran was thus temporarily denied any use of its property. In a majority opinion that included Rehnquist, Scalia, White, Brennan, Marshall, and Powell, the temporary but total ban on property use was ruled a taking. For the time the ban was in effect total use of the property was enjoined, so preventing a previous use and a return on an investment. The second case was *Keystone Coal Association v. DeBenedictis* (1986). This case involved a Pennsylvania coal mining and subsidence act. Sections 4 and 6 of the act required companies to leave fifty percent of the coal in the ground to prevent the soil from flattening and depression. The act noted the devastating effects of subsidence on the soil and on structures on the surface and the fifty percent rule allowed for enough subsurface soil structure to support structures the act aimed to protect. Keystone Coal Association filed suit, claiming this act, specifically sections 4 and 6, which dealt with the fifty percent rule, was an unconstitutional taking without compensation and that it was also a violation of the contract clause because their leases from other private persons, which gave them the rights to mine, had been destroyed by this act. The association's argument was that this case was no different from *Pennsylvania v. Mahon*, and that the fifty percent requirement denied them of substantial investment-backed expectations.

The majority ruled against the association, distinguishing the case from *Mahon* (ibid.: 1240–42). In *Mahon*, only one private building was to be saved by the Kohler Act and it was questionable even in Holmes's mind whether the law served a substantial public purpose. In *Keystone*, many structures, including cemeteries were involved, thus saving them served a significant public interest. The second difference concerned the degree of the regulation. In *Mahon*, the act denied all use of the property for mining. The present act did not do that; it still allowed for a fifty percent mining (ibid.: 1246–48). Stevens noted that even without the fifty percent rule companies never extracted all the coal. Much of it was needed to support the mine tunnels. (ibid.: 1248–49) The question then became whether the fifty percent rule served a reasonable public purpose, and whether the rule had a substantial impact on the value of the property as a whole. The majority answered yes to the first and no to the second, thus ruling that no taking had occurred

Rehnquist, Powell, O'Connor, and Scalia agreed with the Association that *Mahon* was controlling. The regulation here and in *Mahon* served public purposes, but both had placed substantial burdens on private property such that a taking had occurred (ibid.: 1254–5). Using what appeared to be a strict scrutiny test that inquired into the nature of the regulation and state interest involved (ibid.: 1256–7), the dissenters declared that the fifty percent rule denied Association members significant "investment-backed expectations" (ibid.: 1257–9), and thus was not regulation but a regulatory taking that required compensation. Implicit in the dissenting opinion was the foreshadowing of a return to judicial scrutiny of legislation affecting property rights. A return to a stricter scrutiny for economic legislation would mean that the line between regulation and eminent domain would be subject to more acute analysis. This is exactly what had happened in *Nollan*, and appeared to be the direction Scalia was headed towards in subsequent decisions.

In *Pennell v. San Jose* (1988), Scalia concurs with and dissents from a majority that held a rent-control ordinance that allowed a hearing officer to consider the hardship to the tenant when reviewing rent increase proposals. In the majority ruling, the Court held that the ordinance did not violate either the equal protection or due process clauses of the Fourteenth Amendment, and that it was premature to consider whether the hardship provision violated the Fifth Amendment takings clause. In his dissent, Scalia agreed with the arguments about the equal protection and due process clauses, but also ruled on the merits of the Fifth Amendment claim and contended that the tenant hardship provision did effect an uncompensated takings (ibid.: 859).

According to Scalia, this provision violates the Constitution for two reasons. First, it does not advance a legitimate state interest (ibid.: 859–60). Second, the provision imposes a special public burden upon individual landlords when that burden should rightly be shared more collectively by society (ibid.: 860). To support these claims, Scalia first cites *Armstrong v. United States* (1960), in which the Court said that the purpose of the takings clause was to "bar Government from forcing some people alone to bear public burdens which, in all fairness and justice, should be borne by the public as a whole" (ibid.: 862, quoting *Armstrong* at 49). What rent control does, specifically this tenant hardship-provision, is to make particular landlords subsidize individuals who are poor by accepting less financial return than they might otherwise obtain. Such a subsidy is not the traditional manner in which American society addresses the problem of poverty. Instead, more traditional (acceptable?) routes to transfer wealth include food stamps, welfare, etc. (ibid.: 863). This rent-control policy, instead, hides the subsidy and circumvents the "normal democratic process"—raising taxes and paying for programs to help the poor—by placing the burden on particular landlords to help specific tenants (ibid.: 863). The City of San Jose is not really engaging in the valid state interest of land use regulation; it is engaging in an illegitimate transfer of wealth by using a tenant-hardship provision without availing itself of the proper democratic channels to undertake this transfer. It is asking a few individuals to use their property to benefit society. Such a regulation of property is, for Scalia, a violation of the Fifth Amendment.

Critical to Scalia's claims here is the belief that valid forms of land use regulation exist, not only invalid regulations. Scalia distinguishes more traditional land use policies as those that: (1) do not totally destroy the economic use of the property and (2) link some cause and effect between the proposed regulation and the evil or remedy that the regulation addresses (ibid.: 862). As demonstrated in *Nollan*, without a reasonably tight fit or nexus between a regulation and the problem the regulation seeks to address, Scalia will not support the regulation. Scalia examines land use regulation with some level of scrutiny beyond some simply means/end or rational basis test that gives legislatures broad authority to regulate property. Sustaining and distinguishing a land use regulation from a regulatory takings requires a tighter fit between means and ends or cause and effect (in Scalia's words).

Despite striking down a tenant-hardship provision in one rent control ordinance, in *Yee v. City of Escondido* (1992) Scalia joined an O'Connor majority opinion upholding a variety of rent control provisions that affected mobile homes. As in *Pennell*, the owners raised the claim that the rent control provisions raised a regulatory takings issue (ibid.: 169). The Court declined to address the takings issue, arguing that the petitioners (the property owners) failed to raise the regulatory takings issue in their certiorari petition, therefore, the Court would leave this issue to the state court (ibid.: 172). Although it is difficult to extrapolate Scalia's own views from an opinion written by someone else, it is nevertheless curious that he did not reach out and seek to address the takings claim, much as he did in *Pennell*. Perhaps the failure of the owners to raise this claim in their petition was crucial in making *Yee* the only vote Scalia has thus far cast against a property owner while on the Supreme Court. Had this claim been raised, Scalia might have ruled in *Yee* much as he did in *Pennell* and thus offered a clearer view on whether he thinks all rent control are forms of regulatory takings.

Perhaps Scalia's most important land use decision is *Lucas v. South Carolina Coastal Commission* (1992), which builds upon many of the frames of analysis Scalia laid down in *Granite Rock*, *Nollan*, and *Pennell*. In some ways, *Lucas* is similar to *Nollan*. In *Lucas*, a state law existed declaring certain coastal land as a "critical area," requiring a permit from the state coastal commission before the owner could change the use of the property. Lucas had purchased two pieces of beachfront property in the designated critical area, and he intended to build houses there. Subsequently, another state law was passed banning the construction of any occupiable structures beyond a designated area into the beach. This law prohibited Lucas from constructing his homes, and he challenged the ordinance in court, claiming that the law was a regulatory taking that deprived him of all value of his property. Eventually, Lucas appealed to the Supreme Court, where Scalia authored a majority opinion sustaining the owners' claims.

Scalia opened his legal analysis in *Lucas* by noting that prior Court decisions initially indicated that the takings clause was invoked only when the government engaged in a direct appropriation of property (ibid.: 812). However, in *Pennsylvania v. Mahon*, the Court argued that mere physical appropriation of land alone did not invoke the takings clause; instead, there may be points at which regulation goes too far and thus effects a taking. In seeking to clarify when the regulation becomes expropriation, Scalia noted that the Court has stated that regulation goes too far when either the owner suffers a physical invasion of his property, or when the regulation "[D]enies all economically beneficial or productive uses of land" (*Lucas* 812–3). This denial of all economically viable use happened to Lucas.

The South Carolina Coastal Commission contended that in denying Lucas the permit to build where he wished to came within the well-established principle that governments may prevent "noxious uses" without paying compensation (ibid.: 817).[5] Scalia acknowledged this exception, stating that it generated the requirement that a land use regulation must substantially advance a legitimate interest to be valid (ibid.: 817–8). But the question for Scalia is how to distinguish a state interest that clearly prevents a harm versus conferring a benefit (ibid.: 817–8). Some land use regulation, in denying the right to use property in a certain way, does not prevent a real harm, but instead seeks to confer a benefit upon another party. Using Scalia's example, we may view the limits on Lucas's land development as either aiming to prevent a harm that the construction would entail or as a means of conferring a benefit upon the South Carolina coast (ibid.: 818). In the first instance, the building of a house is a harm in itself; in the latter instance, the building of the house is not a harm in itself, but denying construction is a way to preserve or protect something else, i.e., the beach ecology. Those regulations that are truly preventing a harm are a species of the noxious-use exception to regulation, would not implicate the takings clause, and would not necessitate compensation. Conversely, regulations that confer a benefit do invoke the takings clause and would require compensation.

Scalia stated that specifying that when a use or state interest is truly harm-preventing or benefit-conferring is often ambiguous, necessitating some rule to clarify what type of state interest or regulation is involved (ibid.: 819). He clarifies that distinction thus:

> the State seeks to sustain regulation that deprives land of all economically beneficial use, we think it may resist compensation only if the logically antecedent inquiry into the nature of the owner's estate shows that the proscribed use interests were not part of his title to begin with (ibid.: 820).

For a state to be able to deny someone total economic use of his property without paying compensation, the state must show that the person never had the right to use her property as she desired. If a person lacked a right to use that property in a certain way, denying the use would not diminish the value of the property and would not require compensation; the denied use had never conferred value to the property. States need to show a preexisting list of common law nuisances or prohibited uses that limit the owner's titled use of property. In Lucas's case, since building on the beach beyond a certain line was not among the prohibited uses when he acquired title to his property, the state interest in denying the building permit was clearly meant to be benefit-conferring, thus invoking the takings clause and compensation.[6]

In *Nollan* and *Lucas*, Scalia wrote majority opinions that stated several important propositions about property rights. The first is the right to exclude, one of the important rights that property ownership entails; to deny that right would invoke a taking under certain circumstances. Second, Scalia suggests that state interests in regulation must directly aim at denying harms and not seek to use regulation to achieve other social goods that should be awarded compensation or determined in other decision-making forums. Third, unless certain uses of property are excluded from the owner's titled uses of his property, the owner may use the property in any way unless the state seeks to compensate her for uses that it denies. Fourth, the government generally needs more than a reasonable relationship between regulations and their goals if the Court is to hold that legislation was a valid exercise of the police power and not a regulatory taking. Exactly what that relationship is and how much judicial analysis the judiciary should give to state regulations, however, was left unclear until *Dolan v. City of Tigard* (1994).

In *Dolan*, at issue was whether the City of Tigard could issue a permit to expand a building on the condition the owners dedicate part of their property located in a flood plain to the city for a public greenway and pedestrian and bicycle pathway. In a 5–4 opinion that was joined in by Scalia, and clearly influenced by his views in *Nollan* and *Lucas*, the Court said no.

Rehnquist wrote for the Court and built upon Scalia's earlier land use decisions. He stated that this decision resolved ". . . a question left open by our decision in *Nollan v. California Coastal Commission*, of what is the required degree of connection between the exactions imposed by the city and projected impacts of the proposed development" (*Dolan* 311). Rehnquist turned to the examples of different states to answer this question. First, Rehnquist specifically rejected as too lax the state standards that merely require some type of ". . . generalized statements as to the necessary

connection between the required dedication and the proposed development" (ibid.: 319). Such a standard merely asks for a reasonable relationship between the regulation and the state interest. Conversely, Rehnquist
also rejected state tests that mandate a "very exacting correspondence"
between the regulation and state interest (ibid.: 319). According to Rehnquist, such a standard and level of scrutiny are not mandated by the Constitution (ibid.: 319).

Rehnquist turned to states that had adopted a species of intermediate
level of analysis (ibid.: 319), and found this level closer to what is constitutionally mandated (ibid.: 320). In putatively following some state case-law
analysis,[7] Rehnquist argued that while no precise mathematical rule is available to clarify the level of analysis, the intermediate level of scrutiny that
he adopts requires a "rough proportionality" between the goals and the
regulations (ibid.: 320). Such a rough proportionality and an intermediate
level of analysis seems to flow both from Scalia's arguments and from the
levels of analysis in *Nollan* and *Lucas*, where an emphasis was developed on
establishing and clarifying the nexus or causality between state interests
and land use regulations.

Dolan is significant in part because the Court mandated a stricter level
of analysis when examining the impact of regulations on property than had
been the norm for the last fifty or so years. Stevens, in dissent, contended
that the majority does not really derive its standard of analysis from state
precedent but from resurrecting substantive due process claims (ibid.: 329).
He chastised the majority opinion for ". . . abandoning the traditional presumption of constitutionality and imposing a novel burden of proof on the
City" (ibid.: 329) that is "essentially the doctrine of substantive due process" (ibid.: 332). For Stevens, the majority applies "heightened scrutiny to
a single strand—the power to exclude—in the bundle of rights" (ibid.: 332).

Dolan's importance becomes more evident in Rehnquist's statement that
"We see no reason why the Takings Clause of the Fifth Amendment, as
much a part of the Bill of Rights as the First and Fourth Amendments,
should be relegated to the status of poor relation" (ibid.: 321). This statement appears to indicate that the takings clause of the Fifth Amendment
and, with it, property rights claims, should occupy the same position as
other types of civil rights claims arising under the Bill of Rights. Such a
claim by Rehnquist foreshadowed and endorsed by Scalia, represents a significant challenge to contemporary *Carolene Products* jurisprudence. The
nature of the challenge can be understood in light of the Court's previous
approach to the distinction between property and civil rights claims.

The Property Rights-Civil Rights Dichotomy
Property Rights and the *Lochner* Era

One of the most enduring dichotomies in constitutional jurisprudence is the contrasting levels of judicial scrutiny given to property and civil rights. The federal judiciary has a long history of protecting property rights (Ely: 1992). In a period approximately between the late nineteenth century and the New Deal, known as the *Lochner* era, the Supreme Court decided cases such as *Lochner v. New York* (1905) and *Allgeyer v. Louisiana* (1897) where it articulated the doctrine of substantive or economic due process.[8] Although the Court during this period sustained most state and federal economic regulation, in many cases it demanded a greater level of legislative justification for economic regulation than it would have required for legislation curtailing individual rights. Despite some historical exaggeration or mischaracterization of what the Court did during this era, *Lochner v. New York* or the *Lochner* era have often been used as shorthand references to a legal ideology that involved active use of judicial power to protect property rights at the expense of Bill of Rights claims.

State precedent exists for substantive due process; *Wynehamer v. New York* (1856) appears to be the earliest state court decision to invoke substantive due process to limit state property regulation. The first Supreme Court case to invoke this doctrine came in 1872 with the *Slaughterhouse Cases* (1872). These cases involved a Louisiana law that granted an exclusive charter for a slaughterhouse to operate in New Orleans. All other slaughterhouses were required to cease operation, and the butchers who became unemployed due to this statute filed suit contending that it violated the Thirteenth and Fourteenth Amendments. Although the Supreme Court upheld this statute and affirmed the police power of the state, the Court made several points in both the majority and dissenting opinions that were important for the development of substantive due process.

The first is that the majority rejected claims made by the defendants that the Louisiana law violated the Privileges and Immunities clause of the Fourteenth Amendment. The Court extensively reviewed the meaning of this clause and stated that these were the same privileges and immunities found in section two, article four of the Constitution which applied to the rights of citizens with respect to the federal government. The clause did not create any new rights of citizens. Rather privileges and immunities refers to those rights that are

. . . fundamental; which belong of right to the citizens of all free governments, and which have at all times been enjoyed by citizens of the several States which compose this Union, from the time of their becoming free, independent, and sovereign. What these fundamental principles are, it would be more tedious than difficult to enumerate (ibid.: 76).

The privileges and immunities clause simply affirmed preexisting rights; it added nothing to the rights citizens enjoyed against the state.

The second point made in the majority decision limited federal enforcement of this clause. The majority stated that Congress did not have the power to intervene on behalf of citizens against their state to enforce their rights.

And where it is declared that Congress shall have the power to enforce that article, was it intended to bring within the power of Congress the entire domain of civil rights hithertofore belonging exclusively to the States? . . . We are convinced that no such results were intended by the Congress which proposed these amendments, nor by the legislatures of the States which ratified them (ibid.: 77–8).

The majority effectively read the Privileges and Immunities Clause out of the Constitution. Neither did the clause create new rights, nor did it allow for federal intervention to enforce the rights that might have been covered by this clause. The implication of this argument was to create three distinct spheres, one belonging to the states, one to national government, and one to the individual. Even the majority opinion established a zone of individual freedom that states could not violate. All that was necessary to create substantive due process was to show that that zone included economic rights. The dissents here paved that way for that inclusion.

Justice Field disagreed with the majority, relying on the Privileges and Immunities clause to argue that this clause did protect the ". . . natural and inalienable rights which belong to all citizens." What rights were those? Field refers to the 1866 Civil Rights Act, which lists, among other rights, the rights

to make and enforce contracts, to sue, be parties and give evidence, to inherit, purchase, lease, sell, hold, and convey real and personal property, and to full and equal benefit of all laws and proceedings for the security of person and property (ibid.: 96–7).

Field also cited *Corfield v. Coryell* (1823) in which Justice Washington, seeking to interpret the meaning of the Privileges and Immunities Clause of article IV, section 2 of the Constitution, states that the clause protects, among other things, the right to acquire and possess property and to pass through or reside in a state for the purposes of engaging in a trade or profession. This clause did have a substantive meaning, and it included the protection of economic rights.[9] Disagreeing with the majority, Field claimed that the federal government had the authority to enforce these economic rights against state interference. Justice Bradley agreed and argued that

> [The] right to choose one's calling is an essential part of that liberty which it is the object of government to protect; and a calling, when chosen, is a man's property and right. Liberty and property are not protected when these rights are arbitrarily assailed (ibid.: 116).

Bradley thus held that the Louisiana law violated the Due Process clause of the Fourteenth Amendment, which protected certain fundamental rights such as the right to property and freedom from government interference in following an economic calling.

Four years later, in *Munn v. Illinois* (1876), the Court again refused to strike down a state regulation, this time a law establishing maximum rates for grain stored in elevators. Again as in *Slaughterhouse*, both the majority and dissenting opinions tended to defend economic due process. The majority, relying upon a common-law rule of Judge Hale's, held regulation of private interests is justified only when the private property is affected with a public interest.

The majority distinction between private and public interests meant that only the latter could be regulated. The implication was that truly private (economic) interests were beyond the scope of regulation. Field again dissented along the same lines as in *Slaughterhouse*. He again affirmed the right of property and to pursue a calling and would have found this law a violation of both the due process and privileges and immunities clauses.

The majority and minority opinions declared that certain rights of individuals were beyond the encroachment of the state. However, the opinions disagreed on two fronts. The majority did not necessarily see these rights as economic or property rights, and they did not see it as a role for the courts to second guess the reasonableness of legislative action involving property regulation. The minority argued the opposite, and their position might have remained a minority view had that the personnel and attitude of the entire Court not changed in the next several years. Evidence of the new attitude of the Court can be seen in *Mugler v. Kansas* (1887). The Court, in upholding a Kansas prohibition law, stated:

> It does not follow that every statute enacted ostensibly for the promotion of these ends is to be accepted as a legitimate exertion of the police powers of

the state. There are, of necessity, limits beyond which legislation cannot rightfully go. While every possible presumption is to be indulged in favor of the validity of the statute, the courts must obey the Constitution rather than the law-making department of the government, and must, upon their own responsibility, determine whether, in any particular case, these limits have been passed . . . The courts are not bound by mere forms, nor are they to be misled by mere pretenses. They are at liberty—indeed, are under a solemn duty—to look at the substance of things, whenever they enter upon the inquiry whether the legislature has transcended the limits of its authority (ibid.: 297).

The implications of the *Mugler* dicta were that the courts were obliged to scrutinize economic regulation particularly hard. The courts could review regulations to determine whether they were reasonable or encroached upon private economic rights, and strike down encroachments of the former if unreasonable. This heightened scrutiny of economic regulation led to the doctrines of liberty of contract and substantive due process.

Over the course of the next fifty years numerous state statutes were struck down as violations of substantive due process (Wright 1942, 154). While the Court did affirm most state regulation, it also extended substantive due process to protect many property rights. Doctrinal development of substantive due process included application of the Fourteenth Amendment to corporations, holding them in *Santa Clara County v. Southern Pacific R.R. Co.* (1886) to be persons under the due process and equal protection clauses. The court also set limits upon rate-fixing for railroads unless hearings were held (*Chicago M. & St. P.R. Co. v. Minnesota* [1890]); limited Louisiana's practice of preventing individuals from using the mail to conduct certain businesses with companies not licensed in that state (*Allgeyer v. Louisiana* (1897)); prohibited certain manufacturing materials (*Weaver v. Palmer Bros. Co.* (1926)); and ruled on cases involving maximum work hours, minimum wage, yellow dog contracts, and wage settlements in labor disputes (*Lochner v. New York* [1905], *Adkins v. Children's Hospital* [1923], *Coppage v. Kansas* [1915], and *Wolff Packing v. Court of Industrial Relations* [1923]).

Even those cases in which the Court affirmed regulation that supported judicial scrutiny of legislative activity by judging its reasonableness according to substantive due process. The most famous cases of this era, such as *Lochner v. New York* (1905) affirmed individual economic liberties, limits upon state police power, and the general right of the court to protect property by reviewing state legislation. During the substantive due process era, the Court protected laissez-faire capitalism by invalidating many federal commerce and taxation statutes. An exhaustive review of taxation and commerce clause cases would constitute a book in itself, but among the key cases were *Hammer v. Dagenhart* (1918, child labor); *The Shreveport Case* (1914, interstate commerce); *U.S. v. E.C. Knight* (1895, antitrust); and *Pollack v. Farmers Loan & Trust Co.* (1895, income tax).[10]

The peak of substantive due process as a legal doctrine is hard to identify. The New Deal ended whatever strength the Fourteenth Amendment had in protecting property rights and economic interests. The Court reversed itself for multiple reasons. Perhaps changes in Court personnel, the FDR Packing plan, changes in public opinion, were factors; perhaps the explanation lay elsewhere. (Pritchett 1969). Regardless of the reasons, the Court from 1937 on reversed itself and (re)affirmed state and federal police, regulatory, commerce, and taxation power in cases such as *National Labor Relations Board v. Jones & Laughlin* (1937); *U.S. v. Darby* (1941); *Wickard v. Filburn* (1942); *Mulford v. Smith* (1939); and *Steward Machine v. Davis* (1937), as cases effectively overruling those articulated during the *Lochner* era. But *West Coast Hotel Co v. Parrish* (1937) and *U.S. v. Carolene Products* (1938) were important in ending substantive due process and judicial protection of property rights.

West Coast contested the constitutionality of a Washington State minimum wage statute. An employee of West Coast Hotel, paid below the minimum wage, sued her employer to be paid at least this state minimum. West Coast Hotel, following precedent set in *Adkins v. Children's Hospital* (1923) where the Court struck down a similar minimum wage statute for Washington D.C., claimed this law was a limitation of their liberty and in violation of the Fourteenth Amendment. In a 5-4 decision Justice Hughes wrote for the majority affirming the *West Coast* statute. In reaching their decision the Court rejected *Adkins* as ill-considered and a departure from ". . . the true application of principles governing the regulation by the state of the relation of employer and employed." Further, Hughes inquired into the meaning of liberty of contract:

> What is this freedom? The Constitution does not speak of freedom of contract. It speaks of liberty and prohibits the deprivation of liberty without the due process of law . . . But the liberty safeguarded is liberty in a social organization which requires the protection of law against the evils which menace the health, safety, morals, and welfare of the people. Liberty under the Constitution is thus necessarily subject to the restraints of due process, and regulation which is reasonable in relation to its subject and is adopted in the interests of the community is due process (ibid.: 391).

In *West Coast Hotel* Hughes departed from precedent in previous cases and affirmed the constitutionality of minimum-wage regulations. First,

Hughes referred to standards in previous due process cases to show that the state regulation was reasonable. Second, noting that this case involved a woman paid a subminimum wage, Hughes expanded upon previous regulation that had sustained laws affecting the working conditions of women, i.e., *Muller v. Oregon* (1908). Third, liberty of contract was effectively read out of the due process clause by redefining liberty in terms of those ends furthered by the police power of the state. Finally, the definition of reasonableness was changed from the existing standard—not impinging one's economic rights—to a new standard—does the statute further the health, safety, morals, and welfare of the community? Half of *Mugler* was overruled here by changing the standard of reasonableness the Court would use. All that was left to do was overturn the rest of *Mugler* and return to the legislature the right to judge the reasonableness of regulation. This is what happened in *United States v. Carolene Products*.

Carolene Products involved a federal law regulating and prohibiting the interstate shipment of doctored or adulterated skim milk. Carolene Products Company contested this commerce regulation as a violation of the Fifth Amendment Due Process clause. In affirming the regulation as a proper exercise of federal commerce power, the Court's ruling also affirmed both congressional and state legislative authority to regulate and use their discretion to determine if the facts of a situation merit legislation.

> [T]he existence of facts supporting the legislative judgment is to be presumed, for regulatory legislation affecting ordinary commercial transactions is not to be pronounced unconstitutional unless in light of the facts made known or generally assumed it is of such a character as to preclude the assumption that it rests upon some rational basis within the knowledge and experience of the legislators (ibid.: 152).

According to Justice Stone, the judiciary generally should not second-guess the wisdom of any legislation, but especially economic legislation. If legislation contains some reasonableness or rational basis, the courts should affirm the regulation. *West Coast* and *Carolene Products* together heralded the end of judicial determinations of legislation to protect property interests. Stone denied that any special or heightened scrutiny would be used by the courts to judge economic regulation. Scrutiny of this type of legislation would presume its constitutionality unless shown contrary.

Individual Rights and the *Carolene Products* Era

During the *Lochner* era, the Supreme Court and the federal judiciary scrutinized more carefully legislation that sought to regulate the economy. At the same time that special protection was afforded to economic rights, other Bill of Rights claims during the *Lochner* era were given short shrift, at least when judged by post-1937 standards. In cases such as *Plessy v. Ferguson* (1896) and *Bradwell v. Illinois* (1873), among others, the judiciary indicated willingness and broad deference to let legislatures adopt legislation that restricted many civil rights, while in the *Civil Rights Cases* (1883) the Court invalidated legislation protecting civil rights in order to protect the economic privileges of private businesses. Hence, one legacy of the *Lochner* era was to create a property rights/civil rights dichotomy, whereby the former occupied greater constitutional status and protection than did the latter.

United States v. Carolene Products (1938) ended the special status given to economic legislation. This case also planted the seed for a reversal of the property rights-civil rights dichotomy, and also instigated a new role for the Supreme Court by suggesting, in Justice Stone's footnote number four, that:

> There may be narrower scope of operation of the presumption of constitutionality when legislation appears on its face to be within a specific prohibition of the Constitution, such as those of the first ten Amendments . . .
>
> . . . it is unnecessary to consider now whether legislation which restricts those political processes which can ordinarily be expected to bring about repeal of undesirable legislation, is to be subjected to more exacting judicial scrutiny . . . than most other types of legislation . . .
>
> . . . Nor need we enquire whether similar considerations enter into the review of statutes directed . . . against discrete and insular minorities may be a special condition, which tends seriously to curtail the operation of those political processes ordinarily to be relied upon to protect minorities, and which may call for a correspondingly more searching judicial scrutiny (ibid.: 152, n. 4).

Implied in this footnote was a definition of a judicial role and review aimed at the promotion of individual liberty, the limiting of legislative power, and the protection of powerless minorities against intrusive and tyrannical majorities. It is a role that the Court subsequently adopted most enthusiastically in the Warren Court.

A good description of the Warren Court's approach to the *Carolene Products* footnote is found in John Hart Ely's arguments about judicial review in *Democracy and Distrust*. Ely argues that the role of the Supreme Court should be to keep the channels of political change open and to facilitate the representation of minorities in the political process (ibid.: 135–181). Relying upon Justice Stone's footnote number four in *Carolene Products*, Ely describes the job of the courts not as second-guessing the substance of legislation, but as helping discrete and insular minorities protect their interests in the political process (ibid.: 75–6). When certain interests are denied access to the political process, or when the representative system ignores or fails to represent a minority out of prejudice, hostility, or an incompatibility of interests, the political process has "malfunctioned" (ibid.: 102–3). The role of the judiciary is not to substitute a legislature's policy judgment with its own, but to take steps to ensure that unrepresented and unprotected interests and groups receive a fair and adequate opportunity to be heard in the political process. The judiciary's role is one of broadening and strengthening the democratic political process by striking down legislation that limits the access or ability of certain groups to protect themselves in the political process.

Ely's comments, as well as the Court's interpretation of footnote number four of *Carolene Products*, were directed in support of intervention to protect Blacks and women, among others, who either lacked adequate political representation or who were the targets of prejudice and discrimination. The logic of *Carolene Products* jurisprudence, as interpreted by the Warren Court, was to incorporate Bill of Rights protections through the Due Process clause of the Fourteenth Amendment to apply to the states and to otherwise give strict or heightened scrutiny to legislation affecting suspect or semi-suspect racial or gender classifications (*Korematsu v. United States* (1944); *Mississippi v. Hogan* (1982)), or other fundamental rights such as interstate travel (*Shapiro v. Thompson* (1969)), or the right to procreate (*Skinner v. Oklahoma* (1942)). Unlike the logic of the *Lochner* Era, the jurisprudence of the *Carolene Products* Era did not generally give economic legislation greater constitutional scrutiny than legislation affecting other individual rights or Bill of Rights claims. The *Carolene Products* jurisprudence reversed the logic of the *Lochner* era and instead gave greater protection to civil rights claims than it would to property rights and economic claims. The *Carolene Products* era continued to perpetuate the property rights/civil rights dichotomy, only it now reversed their priority. Hence, while in the *Lochner* era the judiciary generally deferred to legislatures and the political process to regulate civil rights, it did not always trust the political process to regulate the economy. Conversely, in the *Carolene Products* era, the judiciary generally deferred to legislatures and the political process to regulate the economy; it did not always trust the political process to protect civil rights.

Scalia and the Emergence of a Post-*Carolene Products* Jurisprudence

Given the Court's approach to addressing property and civil rights claims has changed over time, *Nollan*, *Lucas*, and *Dolan* take on a different meaning and now represent an effort by Scalia and Rehnquist to reverse, in part, the generally lax attitude and level of protection the Court has given to property rights claims since 1937. Much as Justices Bradley and Fields launched a judicial revolution in the nineteenth century through their dissents defending property rights and their vision of American politics, Scalia has attempted another revolution with his opinions on the Rehnquist Court.

Despite Scalia's claim that the Court lacks the competence to address economic affairs, Scalia has taken it upon himself and the Court to decide how legislatures can appropriately address economic inequalities in our society. In *Pennell v. San Jose*, Scalia argues that rent control is not a legitimate way to redistribute wealth and that only taxation and direct welfare payments constitute "normal" ways to effect transfers of wealth (ibid.: 863). Scalia's comments suggest his willingness to substitute his opinion in place of a legislature's determination of the best way to address economic inequalities in our society. This questioning of legislative discretion regarding the economy seems more characteristic of the *Lochner* era than of *Carolene Products* jurisprudence.

Next, recall Rehnquist's dicta in *Dolan* where he stated: "We see no reason why the Takings Clause of the Fifth Amendment, as much a part of the Bill of Rights as the First and Fourth Amendments, should be relegated to the status of poor relation." Viewed in the context of the property rights/ civil rights dichotomy, such dicta reveals a break or disagreement with the sentiments of the *Carolene Products* era jurisprudence. Rehnquist's call in *Dolan* for an intermediate level of scrutiny to ascertain the nexus between regulation and state interests, as well as uses of some type of heightened scrutiny by Scalia in *Nollan* and *Lucas*, similarly break with the use of rational basis tests to review economic and land use regulation in the *Carolene Products* era.

Documenting increased support for property rights claims tells only part of the story. Recall the data presented in Tables I-III of this chapter. They indicate that Scalia and Rehnquist have voting records that strongly support property claims while, at the same time, their voting records do not indicate strong support either for First Amendment expressive claims or for criminal due process arguments. Such a voting record indicates that Rehnquist and Scalia have changed their mind regarding how they view their role and the role of the Court in protecting property versus civil rights claims.[11] Their voting record indicates some rethinking of the *Carolene Products* era jurisprudence, prompting one to ask if Scalia and Rehnquist are prepared to weaken the level of protection and scrutiny they give civil rights against the political process. This rethinking also appears to be the case. Richard Brisbin and Edward Heck argue, based on a study of the Rehnquist Court's decisions on the First Amendment, equal protection, and substantive due process, that the Rehnquist Court is accepting the use of "means-end scrutiny as a model for resolving conflicts between individual rights and governmental power" (Brisbin and Heck 1992: 1101). Other decisions by the Rehnquist Court also support this conclusion. In the death penalty case *Payne v. Tennessee* (1991), Rehnquist states:

> *Stare decisis* is not an inexorable command; rather it is a principle of policy and not a mechanical formula of adherence to the latest decision' . . . This is particularly true in constitutional cases, because in such cases 'correction through legislation action is practically impossible' . . . Considerations in favor of *stare decisis* are at their acme in cases involving property and contract rights, where reliance interests are involved . . . and the opposite is true in cases such as the present one involving procedural and evidentiary rules (ibid.: 737).

In Rehnquist's dicta is the claim that the Court should grant less respect for *stare decisis* and precedent in civil rights cases such as death penalty cases than should be given in cases involving economic claims. Legislatures should be given far more leeway to change rules of criminal procedure or adopt other types changes in civil rights than they should when altering property or economic arrangements.[12]

Further evidence to substantiate the claim of a rethinking of *Carolene Products* jurisprudence appears in the numerous expressive freedom, religion, and criminal due process cases. This evidence will be discussed in more detail in subsequent chapters. In all of these cases, Scalia demonstrates generally less willingness to support individual rights claims against majoritarian wishes, except in cases where he thinks the legislative process has malfunctioned. Yet, as we will argue in chapters two through four, Scalia is selective about those instances in which he thinks the political process has malfunctioned; often he limits his use of judicial review to policy areas where he appears to disagree with the majoritarian outcome. In these cases, Scalia employs judicial power in a manner consistent with the assumptions of *Carolene Products* footnote number four, except to support discrete and insular groups or values not traditionally linked with the assumptions of the *Carolene Products* era jurisprudence. Yet in many areas where for the last fifty years the Court had second-guessed the political process, Scalia now seems willing to defer.

As a discussion of Scalia's death penalty cases in chapter eight will indicate, he is willing to give broad deference to legislative determinations to execute convicted criminals. A good example of his attitude towards the

death penalty is found in *Stanford v. United States* (1989). In upholding
the imposition of the death penalty for individuals who committed crimes
at the age of sixteen or seventeen, Scalia looks for a consensus among the
different states and legislatures that the imposition of the death penalty for
individuals this age is cruel *and* unusual. In finding that many states do
allow for the execution of people this age (ibid.: 2977–9), Scalia refuses to
strike down these executions as a violation of the cruel and unusual clause
of the Eighth Amendment and instead defers to legislative judgments of
the different states to determine whether such executions should be permitted. The significance of *Stanford* is that in a question invoking a Bill of
Rights claim, Scalia is content to defer to the desires expressed by the political process and majoritarian wishes, and not to act to protect a discrete
and insular minority, i.e., a prisoner, from the political process. This is a
departure from the logic of *Carolene Products* jurisprudence.

A final piece of evidence about Scalia's approach to the assumptions of
Carolene Products jurisprudence is that the justice has never cited footnote
number four of *United States v. Carolene Products* to support a civil rights
claim and, as noted in earlier in this chapter, he has apparently gone out of
his way to avoid referring to it (Schultz 1992: 1255–65). One very clear
indication that Scalia is prepared to give legislatures greater leeway to legislate in the areas of civil rights can be found in *Employment Division v. Smith*
(1990), in which Scalia appears to repudiate the logic of *Carolene Products*
in rejecting a First Amendment religious claim while upholding the denial
of unemployment benefits to a Native American who used peyote in a traditional Indian religious ceremony.

> Values that are protected against governmental interference through enshrine-
> ment in the Bill of Rights are not thereby banished from the political process
> . . . It may fairly be said that leaving accommodation to the political process
> will place at a relative disadvantage those religious practices that are not widely
> engaged in; but that unavoidable consequence of democratic government
> must be preferred . . . (ibid.: 1606).

What becomes clear in *Smith* is that Scalia is prepared to defer more to
the political process on civil rights claims than is typical of the *Carolene
Products* ara, while cases such as *Dolan, Lucas,* and *Nollan* suggest that
he is similarly prepared to defer less deference to legislatures to regulate
economics and property than is typical of the *Carolene Products* era.

What we have then is a rethinking of the relative level of analysis that
Scalia is willing to give to economic and civil rights. His economic and civil
rights decisions neither seem to accept fully the logic of the *Carolene Prod-*

ucts era, nor do they seem fully prepared to move back to the substantive due process logic of the *Lochner* era. In fact, as noted earlier, Scalia has stated that he does not think that the Court should or can go back to that jurisprudence. What seems to be emerging is something different. It is a move toward a post-*Carolene Products* jurisprudence where some type of rethinking of the property and civil rights dichotomy is proposed. Such a rethinking is premised upon breaking with the use of different levels of analysis presently used to review the legislative process, depending upon whether economic or civil rights claims are at issue. What appears to be occurring after *Dolan* is a move towards using some type of intermediate level of analysis for all types of rights based claims.

The reasons for this apparent move towards a post-*Carolene Products* jurisprudence may be based in part on Scalia's ideology or a particular political philosophy (Siegel and Spaeth 1993), his increased skepticism towards the capacity of legislatures to deliberate without being affected unduly by pressure politics (Schultz 1992: 1265–71; Farber and Frickey 1991: 47–55); upon Scalia's understanding of the intent of the framers, or on all of the above reasons mutually reinforcing one another to produce the essential values and assumptions that define Scalia's jurisprudence. Whatever the reason, such a move towards a rethinking of property and civil rights claims represents a profound change for the Court, with Scalia leading the way. Subsequent chapters will develop the implications of these claims more fully.

Notes

1. See Ackerman (1991) for a discussion of the different eras or constitutional moments in American history that roughly parallel or include the distinctions made between the *Lochner* and *Carolene Products* eras in this chapter.
2. See Paul (1988); Epstein (1985); Pollot (1993); and Coyle (1993) as examples of those scholarly works calling for a rethinking of the current levels of protection that the Court and the Constitution give to property rights.
3. See Schultz (1995); Freitag (1994); Levitt (1993); and Bosselman (1993), for essays that address various aspects of Scalia's views on property and land use regulations.
4. See Fisher (1993: 1394), where the author argues that Scalia departs from the intent of the framers in *Lucas* to address the issue of regulatory takings.
5. See *Muglar v. Kansas* (1887), and *Miller v. Schoene* (1928) for elaboration of the public nuisance or noxious use exception.
6. See Epstein (1993), whose criticism of Scalia's approach in *Lucas* helps clarify the regulation versus takings distinction.

7. Stevens, on pages 324 and 329, contends that the majority does not really derive its standard of analysis from state precedent, but from resurrecting substantive due process claims.

8. See Gillman (1993) and Ely (1992) for discussions of the role of the Supreme Court in articulating constitutional protections for property rights claims.

9. See Siegan (1988); Hovenkamp (1988: 394–98); and Maltz (1987: 225–6) as support for Field's claim that the protection of economic rights was an important goal of the Radical Republicans in framing the Fourteenth Amendment.

10. Hovenkamp (1988) offers a good review of the Court's economic and legal philosophy from the Civil War to the New Deal, which parallels claims made here.

11. Provine (1980) offers a discussion of how a justice's self-perception of his or her role and the role of the Court influence the type of cases that the Court selects, as well as how those cases are decided. In part, Scalia's redefinition of the Court's attitude towards property and personal rights cases indicates a rethinking of a personal judicial, and institutional role for the Supreme Court.

12. Parenthetically, such a claim also seems to depart from the long-established precedent in *Calder v. Bull* (1798) in which Justice Chase argued that the Constitution gave legislatures less flexability to change criminal laws than civil laws. Rehnquist's dicta seems to reverse this claim and give greater flexability to the courts to alter criminal laws as opposed to civil laws dealing with property and contracts.

Chapter 2

Constitutional Interpretation and the Political Process

A cardinal tenet of American representative democracy is that Congress and state legislatures have the primary responsibility for making law and policy. Critics of the Warren Court contended that its judicial activism failed to respect and defer to majoritarian bodies. Instead, the justices sought to make their own policy and act in a countermajoritarian fashion (Bickel 1986); (Bork 1990); (Meese 19). As a result, the Court was viewed by some conservatives as wrongly substituting its own policy preferences for those of Congress and state legislatures (Rabin 1989); (Horowitz 1977). Presidents Nixon and Reagan both pledged to rein in the federal courts and to appoint judges and justices who would simply interpret and not make the law. Consequently, these would be judges who would be unwilling to preempt the legislative process by engaging in judicial activism.

Antonin Scalia, along with Court of Appeals Judges Robert Bork, Richard Posner, Frank Easterbrook, and Supreme Court Justice Sandra O'Connor, among others, was one of those Reagan appointees selected to carry out the President's pledge to change the direction of the federal judiciary. Since Scalia's 1982 appointment to the federal court of appeals, and his 1986 elevation to the Supreme Court, numerous scholars and news analysts have attempted to ascertain the impact he has had on transforming constitutional doctrine and the Supreme Court. The development of this scholarship was unusual because Scalia had been on the federal bench less than ten years and on the Supreme Court for barely five when he already attracted more attention than other most other justices. Justices such as Byron White, Harry Blackmun, and John Paul Stevens had been on the Court much longer and presumably should have attracted greater attention. This unusual attention, no doubt, was prompted in part by the belief that

Scalia would be one of the major architects of a more conservative Reagan-Rehnquist Court one that would roll back any remaining Warren Court precedents that had not been washed away during the Burger years.

Scalia's elevation to the Supreme Court placed him in the middle of many controversies such as abortion and the death penalty. Since he joined the Court, Scalia has also been at the center of other disputes, including less publicized issues such as executive authority, separation of powers, the role of the political process versus the judiciary in protecting individual rights, and the merits and legitimacy of using different interpretive strategies to read the Constitution. While each of these issues may appear discrete, they are not. These policy, process, and interpretative controversies invoke questions regarding the particular political philosophy that Scalia brings to the Court and how that philosophy influences his constitutional adjudication.

This chapter explores Scalia's impact on the Court by concentrating on his views toward judicial review and the legislative-political process. By looking beyond Scalia's opinions and scholarly writings and their implications, this chapter assesses the uniqueness of Scalia's political philosophy. By political philosophy, we mean his views on the basic institutions and processes of American government and politics, including the allocation of power among the major national institutions, the regulation of elections, and the staffing of federal positions through political appointments. By looking at Scalia's political philosophy we can assess his attitudes toward the role of the federal courts in American society, how much deference he gives the legislative process, and how he thinks the judiciary should interpret decisions and laws produced by Congress. This assessment will allow us to appraise both the accuracy of critics in their evaluation of Scalia's impact and in whether if, in fact, the justice has transformed the Supreme Court in the direction promised by Reagan.

This chapter is divided into several substantive sections. The first examines Scalia's views on constitutional adjudication and his use of the framers, the *Federalist Papers,* and other extratextual historical materials to clarify the meaning of the Constitution. This discussion will show how Scalia's political philosophy is informed, at least in part, by his understanding of the intent of the framers of the Constitution. Since Scalia's constitutional interpretative method often invokes the framers, understanding the political values he ascribes to them will help clarify the substantive political and ideological values that inform Scalia's constitutional jurisprudence and, hence, his view of how the American political process is organized and should operate.

The second section of this chapter will examine the justice's conception of the role of the federal courts in American society. Specifically, the discussion will examine his approach to the logic of judicial action suggested by footnote four of *Carolene Products* (1938), as well as how his approach to this case influences his views on interpretation and the governmental process. Third, we will examine his view of legislatures (especially Congress) and the Presidency. A fourth topic will be his views on patronage, political parties, and spoils. The fifth section will be devoted to his views on campaign finance reform. Examination of these last three subjects illuminates Scalia's views of the interaction between the governmental and political processes.

The final section is a preliminary assessment of Scalia's political philosophy. It offers some conclusions and ideas that will be explored more fully in subsequent chapters. Overall, the main argument of this chapter is that the existing Scalia scholarship has, in many respects, failed to provide an accurate description of the his political philosophy. We will contend that Scalia's various scholarly writings and judicial opinions reveal a political philosophy that endorses a specific conception of the political process that is mediated by his interpretative method and views on what the framers intended. In effect, Scalia invokes the framers to support many of his positions, but such invocation otherwise hides a political ideology sympathetic to classical Manchester Liberalism. Such an ideology, as originally articulated in nineteenth-century England, emphasized limited government, faith in the marketplace, commitment to legalism, materialism, property rights, and enforcement of majoritarian morality as essential to the creation of free society (Dolbeare 1969: 16–18, 22–23). Ironically, Scalia can only promote his view of the process by extensive use of federal judicial power.

In addition, Scalia's jurisprudence endorses a strong executive and a weak Congress, because such a political alignment favors his political agenda (Stock 1990: 161, 192), and because it reflects his understanding of the framers' fear of legislative power. Thus, contrary to the existing Scalia scholarship which contrasts Scalia's interpretive methods and his political views, we see the two elements as reinforcing one another. Moreover, contrary to claims by other analysts who see Scalia's opnions as guided by a consistently applied interpretive strategy and a vision of judicial restraint, Scalia's ideology generates an inconsistently applied interpretive method that results in a mercurial attitude towards legislative power and the political process (D.A. Strauss 1991: 1699, 1716); (Tushnet 1991: 1717, 1740). This suggests that Scalia's commitment to judicial restraint and his deference to the legislative process as selective at best, indicating perhaps that ideology rather than judicial neutrality governs his decisions. Despite this rejection of judicial restraint, Scalia has still been faithful to Reagan in using the bench to articulate many important conservative political values.

Constitutional Interpretation and Intent of the Framers

During the Reagan presidency, serious debates arose concerning the correct interpretive techniques to use when reading the Constitution. These debates were precipitated by continued frustration manifested by then-Attorney General Meese and other conservatives in reaction to a Supreme Court that, despite numerous judicial appointments by Republican presidents, had failed to support their agenda when it came to issues such as abortion, crime, and federalism. The conservatives believed that the Court was continuing to substitute its policy views for those of Congress, the Presidency, and the majority of the American people. To limit the Court's ability to impose its vision and hence to act in a what Bickel first described as a countermajoritarian fashion (Bickel 1986), the remedial mechanism advocated rested on limiting justices' judicial discretion to read into the Constitution their own political and policy values.

Concerns about judicial discretion and judicial restraint began with the writing of the United States Constitution. Yet Warren Court decisions such *Brown v. the Board of Education* (1954), *Miranda v. Arizona* (1966), and *Mapp v. Ohio* (1961), as well as *Roe v. Wade* (1973) under the Burger Court, prompted critics to argue that the Court was acting in a countermajoritarian fashion and reading into the Constitution rights, such as privacy, that simply did not exist. The proposed solution to this putatively inappropriate judicial behavior was the development of neutral or general principles to guide and limit judicial discretion and policy making (Wechsler 1959); (Bickel 1986); (Bork 1971); (Bork 1990).

One approach intended to limit judicial discretion and activism was to argue that the only proper way to interpret the Constitution was to read it in accordance with the intent of its framers. For example, in a 1971 essay Robert Bork argued for the creation of a theory of constitutional law to address the problem of defining the legitimacy of the Supreme Court's power of judicial review in American society. According to Bork, a theory would prevent the court's role from changing with changing personnel. Bork argued that judicial review did not fit readily in a democratic society. By that, he states,

> Madisonian democracy is committed to majoritarianism, but there is also a counter-majoritarian premise that some areas majorities should not control. The majority should not decide on minority rights (Bork 1971: 3).

Recent works on constitutional theory state that the courts protect politically vulnerable minority interests through judicial review and the power to interpret the Constitution (Ely 1980; Guinier 1994). Following Bickel's reasoning, Bork says that the Court can only be countermajoritarian when its decisions are constrained, defined, and legitimized by judicial review. Hence, the Court's legitimacy must rest on judicial review where its decisions are made according to neutral principles. To make neutrally principled decisions, principles must not only be applied but also defined and derived. If the Court makes it own principles, it is substituting its values for those of Congress. Giving the Court self-selection of principles seems to give the judiciary great latitude to determine values that will govern its decisions. Therefore, to limit judicial activism and to prevent the values from changing with shifting personnel, the Court must not be allowed to choose the fundamental values that will govern its decisions.

In part, Bork's method of limiting interpretive freedom requires that when the constitutional text is clear, the justices should stick to the text and the intent of the framers. The only legitimate way to change the Constitution is through the amendment process, not through judicial construction (Bork 1990: 143). If the text is not clear, the Court should defer to the legislature or majority for the articulation of the values to guide the decision. This means that the judiciary must either let the majority construct or determine fundamental values that will be applied, or let the majority or the legislature decide the issue. In short, Bork states that the ". . . court cannot, however, avoid being a naked power organ merely by practicing the neutral application of legal principle. The Court can act as a legal rather than a political institution only if it is neutral as well in the way it derives and defines the principles it applies" (Bork 1990: 146).

Attorney General Meese pursued this line of argument, addressing his concerns towards the proper role of the Supreme Court in our constitutional system (Meese 1985). Meese contended that the founders' views represented the proper role of the Court. For Meese, the Court's job is twofold: First, to act as an independent body to maintain limited government and check factions; and second, to help people obey laws through the assertion of moral force. By fulfilling these proper functions, the Court contributes to checks and balances and the moral foundations of our constitutional system. However, justices are not platonic guardians; they have become a political body, one that has recently erred in its approach to the Bill of Rights by disregarding the founder's intent on federalism, criminal law, and freedom of religion.

Overall, Meese suggested that the Court is confused about the Bill of Rights, which was created to limit the national government. In applying it to the states, the justices have made a political or policy choice. The Court's application of the Bill of Rights in recent judicial decisions shows that the

Court is engaged in ad hoc decision making rather than coherent jurisprudence. As a result the Court could drift back to the Warren Court excesses and thus hurt prospects for a limited and energetic government. Ultimately, this would upset the basic checks and balances the Founders designed. To control this drift and ad hoc decision making, Meese advocated what he called a "jurisprudence of original intention." This jurisprudence consists of defensible principles that are not tainted by ideological predilection. These principles would ensure that the Constitution represents the consent of the governed rather than rule by unelected justices. Using the intent of the Founders would guarantee that we have a "real" independent Constitution, not simply a document meaning whatever the justices say it means. For Meese, a jurisprudence of original intent is the only reliable way to anchor meanings and ensure that judicial discretion is limited.

Consistent with the views expressed by Bork and Meese, Scalia advocated this interpretative strategy for discerning the Constitution's meaning. In his scholarly writings, speeches, and judicial opinions, Scalia has advocated what he calls "originalism" in reading the Constitution. He has also appealed to the constitutional framers, the *Federalist Papers*, and other historical sources to help him identify the original intent of the Constitution. This appeal to original intent appears to have shaped Scalia thinking on how our political system should operate and which institutions should make which decisions. Appeals to the framers may also legitimize policy views of Scalia's that are part of his political philosophy.

In a law review article, Scalia provided a qualified defense of originalism as a guide to interpretations of the Constitution (Scalia 1989b). First, Scalia outlined what he considers to be the principal defects of nonoriginalism. The first is that nonoriginalism is incompatible with the very principle that legitimizes judicial review; the text of the Constitution says nothing that allows the courts to inquire into the validity of federal statutes (Scalia 1989b: 854). For Scalia, the theoretical underpinnings that make the courts the principal expositors of social values are weak. Legislatures seem more appropriate expositors of social values and of determinations concerning whether a statute is compatible with the Constitution (ibid: 854). In effect, the first defect of nonoriginalism is that it fails to provide a good constitutional argument for the current role of the judiciary in American society.

A second defect is that no version of it offers the same consistency and predictability of interpretation as does originalism (ibid.: 855). For example, Scalia asks, whose values should be considered if the Constitution is read in terms of contemporary values? Often, such a reading would simply reflect the values of the judge or justice. A third defect of nonoriginalism lies in the apparent illusory benefit that this interpretative approach allows for an expansion of rights beyond the original Constitution and that some versions of nonoriginalism are able to keep the Constitution up to date to reflect current values (ibid.: 855–6). However, Scalia argues that if the meaning of the Constitution can change, why could not the changes reflect a shrinkage in rights? Additionally, such an approach suggests that the Constitution's meaning would fluctuate with the composition of the Court. Hence, the idea of the Constitution as anchoring rights and defining the structure of the government would be undermined.

Given these problems with nonoriginalism, Scalia defends a qualified form of originalism. Scalia notes some difficulty in ascertaining historical intent, suggesting that this may be a task better suited to historians than lawyers (ibid.: 856–7). However, such historical problems are not insurmountable, and Scalia uses Chief Justice's Taft's analysis in *Meyers v. United States* (1926) to show how we can understand executive appointment power through a study of early American history. A second possible defect Scalia notes in originalism resides in always and strictly following the intent of the framers about issues, such as the meaning of the Cruel and Unusual Punishment clause of the Eighth Amendment. Here, Scalia argues that while flogging may have been a permissible punishment for the framers, he did not think that this punishment should be sustained by the judiciary today (ibid.: 861). In sum, Scalia claims that he is a faint-hearted originalist in that he believes that the historical intent of the framers should be followed as much as possible. If the Constitution needs its values updated, elections and the political process are supposed to address the issue (ibid.: 862).

In his other writings and judicial opinions, Scalia demonstrates his commitment to originalism by often appealing to the Founders and historical intent to buttress his reading of specific Constitutional passages. Through this information, we can discern much about Scalia's political values and views on the proper organization of the political system. For example, Scalia views the *Federalist Papers* as an important authority on the meaning of the Constitution. Scalia refers to the *Federalist Papers* in two of his articles (Scalia 1983; Scalia 1989) and in at least fifteen of his own opinions on subject matters ranging from separation of powers, *Morrison v. Olson* (1988); interest group politics, *Norman v. Reed* (1992); state sovereignty and sovereign immunity, *Tafflin v. Levitt* (1990); and judicial power, *Planned Parenthood v. Casey* (1992).[1] In these opinions he cites *Federalist* 7, 10, 47, 48, 49, 51, 70, 78, 81, and 82, using *Federalist* 47 through 49 the most often, especially to support the importance of separation of powers to the framers. Scalia also invokes *Federalist* 78, especially to support his belief that the Court should stay away from certain policy issues, such as abortion. In addition to the *Federalist Papers*, Scalia has also invoked Farrand's *Records of the Constitutional Convention*,[2] Blackstone's *Commentaries*,[3] Joseph Story's *Commentaries*,[4] and assorted other speeches or comments by or about the framers of the Constitution, including references to George Mason, Henry Lee, Patrick Henry, John Dickinson, and Gouverneur Morris.

How have these sources been used to clarify constitutional intent and what image of the political system emerges from them? Scalia has invoked and quoted *Federalist* 47 through 49, along with reference to Montesquieu (who is credited with first articulating the concept of separation of powers), to defend his views on separation of powers. Scalia has cited Montesquieu in *Synar v. United States* (1986), to support the contention that the Constitution mandates a strict separation of powers among the different branches of government and that delegations of power from one branch to another must be strictly limited. In *Young v. ex rel Vuitton et fils S.A.* (1984), *Mistretta v. United States* (1989), *Morrison v. Olson* (1988), *Synar v. United States* (1986), and in an article on standing (Scalia 1983), Scalia appeals to *Federalist* 47 through 51 to defend his opinions opposing: judicial appointment of prosecutors in criminal cases; the authority of the U.S. Sentencing Commission; the special prosecutor law; and the Gramm-Rudman-Hollings Law. Scalia, in quoting Madison from *Federalist* 47 on the importance of separation of powers, notes that the framers said that "no political truth is certainly of greater intrinsic value, or is stamped with the authority of more enlightened patrons of liberty" (Scalia 1983: 881).

In *Norman v. Reed* (1992), Scalia cites *Federalist* 10 to indicate that the framers feared that political factionalism threatened the integrity of the legislative process. The picture of the legislative process that emerges here, and that similarly reemerges in other cases discussed later in this chapter as well as in chapters two and three, is that legislatures are dangerous and powerful political institutions, capable of abusing political power, threatening the presidency, and being captured by powerful interests (Scalia 1976: 686, 688). For example, Scalia quotes from *Federalist* 48:

It is not infrequently a question of real nicety in legislative bodies, whether the operation of a particular measure will, or will not, extend beyond the legislative sphere. On the other side, the executive power being restrained within a narrow compass and being more simple in nature, and the judiciary being described by landmarks still less uncertain, projects of usurpation by either of these departments would immediately betray and defray themselves (Scalia 1983: 882).

On this point Scalia again quotes from the *Federalist* to indicate that the purpose of the president was to protect the president from "encroachments of the popular branch" and to "enable him [the president] to defend himself" (Scalia 1976: 688). Thus, Scalia's apparent belief that the framers feared legislative power seems to buttress his commitment to separation of powers and limits on delegation as ways to prevent abuses of legislative authority. It may also reflect, as will be discussed in chapter two, Scalia's general skepticaism towards the use of legislative history, legislative politics, and deference to administrative interpretations of the law when the plain meaning of statutes are unclear.

While Scalia depicts the framers as fearful of legislative power, this does not necessarily mean that he wishes to augment the authority of the other two national institutions of government. On the one hand, because the framer's feared the legislature as a threat to the presidency (Scalia 1979: 20), this has led Scalia to use judicial power to defend the power of the presidency from Congress. Scalia did not believe that the framers feared executive power since its power was sharply limited in scope. Yet Scalia also invokes original intent to defend broad presidential prerogative power to protect the executive branch from Congress and to defend broad presidential authority (Scalia 1989: 859). However, Scalia's fear of executive power has not translated into the belief that the judiciary should necessarily usurp or assume more political authority.

Scalia approvingly notes how *Federalist* describes the judiciary as a natural aristocracy (Scalia 1987: 35–6). Elsewhere, Scalia argues in *Tyler Pipe Industry v. Washington Department of Revenues* (1987), that the framers had a narrow conception of what "case and controversy" meant, thus justifying a narrowing of the range of eligible disputes that could be brought before the Court. Scalia also has argued that the framers' principle of separation of powers mandates that standing should be limited in to order to prevent an expansion of judicial power (Scalia 1983: 881). In *Young v. ex rel Vuitton* (1987), Scalia invokes the framers, *Federalist* 78, and their commitment to separation of powers to support his claims that the judiciary may not expand its power to appoint prosecutors in certain types of cases. In *Freytag v. C.I.R.* (1991), *Federalist* 78 is invoked to clarify the duties and tenure of Article I judges in contrast to those of Article III judges. Scalia notes that the framers indicated that all judges should hold their offices during good behavior. Finally, *Federalist* 78 is cited in *Planned Parenthood v. Casey* (1992) to rail against the creation of an "imperial judiciary," the Court's involvement in the abortion issue, and to invoke the framers to support his contention that *Roe v. Wade* should be overturned, and that legislatures should be entrusted to make policy in this area. In fact, as noted above, Scalia's reading of the Constitution and his appeal to the framers' intent commit him to a position that makes Congress and legislatures primarily responsible for making policy and updating the Constitution to reflect current social values. It is not the job of the judiciary to read a right to privacy into the Constitution. Instead, Congress and the states must create and protect such a right, if they choose to do so.

Despite his fear of legislatures, Scalia still entrusts them with the responsibility to make policy and he does not support giving the judiciary increased authority to make policy and protect rights. As discussion later will show, throughout Scalia's writings and opinions this almost schizophrenic view toward legislative power repeats itself. On the one hand Scalia is willing to place faith in the political process to legislate on religion, abortion, and the death penalty, while at the same time he fears legislative power issues such as affirmative action, and property rights protection, and he opposes the use of legislative history to interpret statutes. Scalia's invocation of the framers' intent appears to support contrasting contentions on legislative power, depending on the policy area involved.

Separation of powers, as far as limiting institutional authority, appears to be the chief institutional or structural means Scalia invokes to protect individual liberty, instead of generally appealing to the judiciary and the Bill of Rights to defend individuals. This model of government relies on structural processes and legislative authority to protect individual rights. In many ways, this view overlooks the need for a Bill of Rights in the same way that the Federalists overlooked or ignored the needs for a Bill of Rights in 1787 in their debates with the anti-Federalists. Yet when the Bill of Rights is adjudicated, the intent of the framers has been invoked both to support and limit rights. In Scalia's 1989 essay, "Originalism," framers' intent means that the accused must be permitted to face his accuser directly in open court (Scalia 1989b: 863). This mandate of the Confrontation Clause was reflected in *Coy v. Iowa* (1988), in which Scalia argued against a screen to shield child witnesses from the accused in sexual abuse cases. Although claiming to be a faint-hearted originalist in that he finds some punishments in violation of the Cruel and Unusual clause of the Eighth Amendment, Scalia has invoked the framers or original historical intent in *Harmelin v. Michigan* (1991) and *Thompson v. Oklahoma* (1988) to uphold mandatory life-without-parole sentences for illegal drug possession and the death penalty for youths under sixteen. In both cases he invoked deference to the values of the framers, not those of contemporary society, to justify interpretations of the Bill of Rights.

To complete Scalia's view of the political system, he has invoked the *Federalist Papers* and the framers in *Tafflin v. Levitt* (1990), *Welch v. Texas*

Dept of Highways and Public Transportation (1987), and *U.S. v. Stanley* (1987) to defend state governments and state sovereign immunity. However, in *Tyler Pipe Industry v. Washington Department of Revenues* (1987), the framers are invoked to indicate how they supported free trade and broad authority of the federal government to prevent states from interfering in interstate commerce. These references seems both to support federalism, especially if these cases are read in terms of Scalia's opinions that defer to states legislating on the death penalty and abortion, and limit parochial state behavior if it interferes with economic free trade.

The picture that emerges from Scalia's reading of the framers is a view that makes separation of powers the chief means to protect individual liberty. As is argued next, this model of American politics that the post-1937 assumptions that the judiciary is the main institution charged with the protection of individual rights through aggressive enforcement of the Bill of Rights. Scalia's constitutional views mandate that legislative and judicial power be limited, but it is unclear how much executive authority and state power is circumscribed under Scalia's reading of the original intent of the framers. In addition, Scalia's reading of the Constitution suggests a mercurial attitude towards legislative power; in some policy areas he is willing to defer, while perhaps in others he is not. No clear rule seems to indicate when he believes the political process adequately protects rights. As will be argued later, his views seem to be guided by his own political ideology and policy preferences. Hence, while Scalia claims to defer to the intent of the framers to clarify the meaning of the Constitution, his own admission in "Originalism"—that ascertaining the historical intent is often difficult— suggests that perhaps ideological factors influence how Scalia reads what the framers meant or what he claims the framers meant. As many critics have noted (Dworkin 1986; Brest 1980), the Constitution is an open text and ascertaining intent is problematic, thus permitting individual bias and beliefs to influence interpretations.

Judicial Power, Judicial Review, and Discrete and Insular Minorities

Other scholars who have examined Scalia's position on the constitutional role and duties of the judiciary in American society have concentrated on his views towards standing and separation of powers (Brisbin 1990: 6–8). For example, Brisbin and Smith claim that Scalia is acting as an institutional guardian of the Supreme Court, that he wishes to preserve the Court as an elite institution, and that this goal may be secured by limiting access to the Court and by keeping the judiciary out of issues that ought to be resolved by the political institutions of the government (ibid.: 7–9,10–11, 25–26). Evidence to support these claims is found both in numerous decisions Scalia wrote on the court of appeals and on the Supreme Court, as well as in scholarly works of Scalia before joining the Court.

In a 1979 essay, then-University of Chicago Law Professor Scalia argued that "Congress is . . . the first line of constitutional defense, and the courts —even the activist modern courts—merely a backdrop" (Scalia 1979: 20). According to Scalia,

> Congress has an authority and indeed a responsibility to interpret the Constitution that are not less solemn and binding than the similar authority and responsibility of the Supreme Court . . . Moreover, congressional interpretations are of enormous importance—of greater importance, ultimately, than those of the Supreme Court (ibid.: 20).

While Congress is the primary institution maintaining constitutional integrity, it does not have carte blanche authority to check executive authority or regulatory power though the use of legislative vetoes. What Scalia argues in this essay is that the legislative veto is a form of "legislation in reverse" (ibid.: 22), that legislative vetoes are clearly contrary to the intent of the framers, and, more importantly, are a violation of Article I, section 7, clause 3 of the Constitution. A legislative veto is an usurpation of the executive authority invested in the President, and if the legislative veto is left unchecked, it will alter the constitutional balance between Congress and the presidency and ultimately undermine democratic government (ibid.: 24–25).

This article raises several points important to understanding Scalia's political philosophy. First there is Scalia's desire to protect executive power, along with his general deference to Congress, to make policy and interpret the Constitution. Growing out of his notion of separation of powers, there is a sense of institutional identity and function for each of the three major branches of the government. His respect for congressional constitutional interpretation reveals his willingness to make the judiciary less of a prominent and activist guardian of the Constitution than it has been in the past. His defense of separation of powers suggests that even the judiciary has clearly delineated powers that can neither be encroached upon by other branches nor extended by the courts.

Scalia's vision of the judiciary is articulated in more detail in a 1983 article written while he was on the federal court of appeals (Scalia 1983). In this article, Judge Scalia claimed that the doctrine of standing is a "crucial and inseparable element" of the concept of separation of powers (ibid.: 881). Failure to respect the notion of standing will result in the "overjudicialization of the process of self-governance" (ibid.: 881), and in giving greater respect to general claims of the citizenry than a single plaintiff with a particularized injury (ibid.: 882).

Scalia claims that the Founders' conception of standing was developed to limits judicial power (ibid.: 882). In chronicling the evolution of the doctrine of standing, he notes how it expanded well beyond the original conception of the Founders such that now the standing requirement is almost no limit upon the ability of claimants to bring cases to court (ibid.: 891–893). The result of this expansion has been to require the courts to "address issues that were previously considered beyond their ken" (ibid.: 892).

Scalia argues that it is inappropriate for the Court to be involved in matters such as majoritarian policy-making because that is not the function that the judiciary was designed to assume in our society (ibid.: 896). Scalia also suggests that even if they did assume this policy-making function, "there is no reason to believe they will be any good at it." Instead, the concept of standing was "meant to assure that the courts can do their work well" (ibid.: 891), and that work is to "restrict the courts to their traditional undemocratic role of protecting individuals and minorities against the impositions of the majority, and [this] excludes them from the even more undemocratic role of prescribing how the other two branches should function in order to serve the interests of the majority itself" (ibid.: 894).

Scalia's claim in this essay is that the concept of standing must be returned to the original understanding of the term (ibid.: 897–898). Only by drawing a narrow definition of standing that respects particularized "concrete" injury (ibid.: 895) to an individual, which separates her from the rest of citizenry, can the courts assume their traditional role of "protecting minority rather than majority interests" (ibid.: 895). The judiciary's main tasks, consistent with the logic of Founders, is to protect the constitutional rights of minorities against the tyranny of the majority. Yet his claim that it is the role of the courts to protect minorities against majoritarian excess does not necessarily appear inconsistent with the role the judiciary has assumed since 1938.

In *United States v. Carolene Products* (1938), the Court hinted at a new role for the judiciary in the wake of the triumph of the New Deal and the repudiation of the Court's "first" New Deal decisions (Ackerman 1985: 714–715). In that decision the Court noted its willingness to defer to Congress regarding economic regulation, but in footnote four of Justice Stone's opinion, he hinted that a different standard of scrutiny might apply in other cases.

As noted in chapter one, the Court's interpretation of footnote number four of *Carolene Products* was directed in support of intervention to protect African-Americans and women, among others, who either lacked adequate political representation or who were the targets of prejudice and discrimination. Thus, at least on its face, the logic of *Carolene Products* footnote number four and Scalia's comments that the primary function of the courts is to protect minorities against majorities appear consistent and compatible. Scalia seemingly accepts the basic role of the courts as defined by this footnote.

However, analysis of Scalia's affirmative action decisions, scholarly writings, and use of this footnote in his own decisions suggests disagreement with the role of the judiciary implied by *Carolene Products*. First, a Westian Law review of all of Scalia's D.C. Court of Appeals decisions during his tenure as judge indicates no citations or use of *Carolene Products* as a source citation. During Scalia's tenure as justice on the Supreme Court through the 1993 term, there were only a handful of references to *Carolene Products*.[5] Among those citations, although none came from Scalia, we still find an interesting pattern.

In *Nollan v. California Coastal Commission* (1987), Scalia was in the majority opinion, and the dissenters cited *Carolene Products* (and not footnote four) in reference to economic regulation and eminent domain takings (*Nollan* 1987: f.n.1, 694.) In two cases, *Baker v. South Carolina* (1987) and *New York Club v. New York City* (1987), the majority cited *Carolene Products* in reference to special scrutiny to be given to participants closed off from the political process (*Baker* 1987: 513) or placed in a suspect classification. (*New York* 1987: 17). Scalia wrote concurrences with the majority opinion in both cases, but he specifically dissented from those sections of the majority opinion of both *Baker* and *New York Club* where *Carolene Products* is cited. In *United States v. Munoz-Flores* (1990), Scalia concurred with the majority opinion, but *Carolene Products* was cited by Stevens and O'Connor in a separate concurrence with the majority. In *Richmond v. Croson* (1989), O'Connor writes the majority opinion that overturned Richmond's thirty percent set aside minority business enterprise (MBE) program. She cited *Carolene Products* footnote four and John Hart Ely's *Democracy and Distrust* to uphold the proposition that powerless minorities (here, whites) deserve special protection. (*Croson* 1989: 722). Scalia concurred with the majority, but wrote his own separate opinion. Only in *Airline Pilots v. O'Neill* (1991) did Scalia specifically join an opinion in which *Carolene Products* was cited. In this case, Stevens's opinion for the Court cited *Carolene Products* and several other cases to support the proposition that "legislatures, however, are subject to some judicial review of the rationality of their actions" (*Airline Pilots* 1991: 1134).

Overall, Scalia does not use *Carolene Products* as precedent or authority for a specific pattern of judicial review. As *Baker* and *New York Club* indicate, he seems to go out of his way to reject the *Carolene* premises. However, Scalia's failure to cite this case may not be an indication that he is hostile to minority rights or that he rejects the logic of footnote four. As Bruce Ackerman (Ackerman 1985) and Neil Komesar (Komesar 1984) have pointed out, the logic and definition of judicial role underlying *Carolene Products* is incomplete and in need of revision. Among other things, the footnote fails to clarify what constitutes political malfunctions or which minorities are discrete and insular (ibid.: 411, 415, 424–425); (Ackerman 1985). Scalia's opinions perhaps reflect not so much a complete rejection of *Carolene Products*, but perhaps a rethinking of it and an attempt to give it a new meaning. There is good evidence for this proposition, and it carries with it significant implications for Scalia's view of the political process.

Let us return to *Croson*. In that case numerous passages indicate that the majority examined the openness of the legislative process in Richmond, Virginia. For example, the majority discussed the legislative history of the MBE program, and the majority inquired into the reasons given for the MBE program and decision-making process that produced that policy. They suggested that the deliberative process was not open and representative but closed to nonminorities (*Croson*, 712–716 [O'Connor]). Additionally, the majority claimed that the Richmond political process failed to show how the thirty percent set aside was reasonable or that the program was not simply the product of the "shifting preferences" of group and racial politics in the city. Overall, the majority stressed that their decision declaring the city's MBE program unconstitutional was significantly motivated by their concern with the way the decision was made (ibid.: 720–724).

Justice Scalia, in his concurrence, was direct in his views and stated that this program looked to be no more than the product of pressure politics (*Croson* 1989: 736- 738). Several of Scalia's decisions have noted that legislatures are often not acting in the deliberative fashion they are supposed to and, instead, are either adversely influenced by interest groups or pressure politics. This view of the legislative process has influenced Scalia's approach to statutory interpretation that questions legislative intent. Scalia, in referring to the *Federalist Papers* and the problems of factions influencing a legislative process, suggested that the Court had a role in inquiring into the structure or fairness of the legislative process to prevent it from damaging the rights or interests of weak or unrepresented groups (*Croson* 1989: 737). After discussing Madison's views on the danger of factions and the tyranny of the majority in politics, Scalia stated, in reference to the politics of the Richmond MBE program: "The prophesy of these words came to fruition in Richmond in the enactment of a set-aside clearly and directly beneficial to the dominant political group, which happens also to be the dominant racial group" (Croson 1989: 824).

The majority, as noted above, even referred to Carolene Products and reaffirmed its role in protecting discrete and insular minorities. Here, the Court noted the black majority on the Richmond City Council and suggested that it had illegitimately worked to the disadvantage of a white minority that clearly needed some judicial protection. In sum, a conservative Rehnquist Court, of which Scalia was a part, demonstrated that it too was concerned with the integrity of the political decision-making process and with preventing any groups from exerting undue influence upon it. The point here is that Scalia was not hostile to what he saw was a discrete and insular minority (the white minority) being persecuted by a majority. His claim in Croson, then, was to invoke some type of strict scrutiny to keep the political process from closing out a weak minority.

Scalia's Croson opinion suggests not necessarily a hostility to Carolene Products, but rather a rejection of an application that has sustained affirmative action and preferential action for blacks. For example, in his scholarly writings, Scalia has stated that he is "opposed to racial affirmative action for reasons of both principle and practicality" (Scalia 1979: 156). In his dissent in Johnson v. Transportation Agency (1986), Scalia rejected the gender-based affirmative action program of Santa Clara County and argued that the hiring of a woman whose written employment-test score was less than that of a white male (Johnson) resulted in discrimination against Johnson (ibid.: 662). In fact, Scalia goes on to say, much as he did in Croson, that affirmative action plans are simply the product of politics and not proper constitutional or social policy (ibid.: 676–677).

A final but important point on how Scalia appears to interpret the Carolene Products precedent is found in three cases where some revised form of footnote four logic is employed (although not cited by him). First, in Nollan v. California Coastal Commission (1986), Scalia wrote the majority opinion that struck down a California zoning/environmental law compelling a property owner to give the public a right-of-way across his property to the beach and ocean. The majority considered this right-of-away an uncompensated takings. But more importantly, Scalia indicated that this law infringed upon individual ownership rights, and the strict scrutiny employed in this instance was necessary to prevent legislatures and the political process from singling out specific individuals to contribute to the public good. Thus, property rights appear to deserve special protection against legislative action.

A second appeal to Carolene-like logic is found in his dissent in Austin v.

Michigan Chamber of Commerce (1990). Here he argued against a Michigan law that placed some restrictions on the ability of some corporations to disperse money out of corporate treasury funds for political purposes. According to Scalia, the requirement that money spent for political purposes must be segregated from other corporate funds eliminates the voice of powerful associations and impoverishes public debate (ibid.: 1416). While no evidence supports Scalia's claim that placing limits upon the voice of these powerful associations would do what Scalia claims, i.e., "impoverishing public debate," look at who he is protecting—a wealthy and well-financed organization—against the majority. In many ways, in this case as well as in *Croson v. Richmond*, the logic of footnote four of *Carolene Products* is invoked to protect wealthy corporations and white constituencies, neither of which can, within easy reach of imagination (or traditional interpretations of *Carolene Products*), be considered "discrete and insular minorities" (per paragraph three) or closed off from the political process (per paragraph two). In both instances, Scalia is unwilling to defer to the electorally accountable branches to make policy and therefore the courts must intervene.

Yet Scalia has no difficulty deferring to the political process in cases such as *Employment Division v. Smith* (1990), where he appears to repudiate the logic of *Carolene Products* when it comes to protecting a Native American man from majoritarian excess:

> Values that are protected against governmental interference through enshrinement in the Bill of Rights are not thereby banished from the political process . . . It may fairly be said that leaving accommodation to the political process will place at a relative disadvantage those religious practices that are not widely engaged in; but that unavoidable consequence of democratic government must be preferred . . . (ibid.: 1606).

While Scalia is willing to defer to the political process to protect Native Americans, he is not willing to do so for corporations, and he appears to be quite content to raise white males, property rights, and corporations to the status of a discrete and insular groups or to second-guess legislatures in order to protect his favored minorities.

Scalia has not abandoned *Carolene Products* and the logic of correcting political malfunctions; rather it appears that his definition of when the system malfunctions is triggered more by different interests, substantive (political) values, or policy preferences than those interests, values, or preferences that had motivated the Warren Court. Thus, as Neil Komesar correctly pointed out, *Carolene Products* is not completely process-oriented and value-neutral; substantive values determine when the logic is invoked and whom to protect (Komesar 1984: 411). Scalia's jurisprudence is not completely driven by method, as George Kannar and others claim (Kannar 1990: 1298–1299), but is guided perhaps by his substantive political values, which determine how and when Scalia will employ judicial review and scrutiny over the legislative process.

Party Politics, Patronage, and Administrative Organization

In 1990 the Supreme Court held in *Rutan v. Republican Party of Illinois* that the State of Illinois could not consider political affiliation when hiring, transferring, or promoting individuals because such a consideration violated the First Amendment rights of individuals applying for government employment. Justice Brennan wrote the opinion for the majority while Scalia wrote the dissenting opinion, joined by Rehnquist, Kennedy, and O'Connor. *Rutan* was not an aberration or an isolated judicial attack on spoils, but rather represented a continuation and extension of a series of patronage decisions over the last twenty years in which the Court has attempted to limit the ability of governmental units to employ the spoils system in the staffing of the bureaucracy.[6] Scalia's dissent in *Rutan* is interesting, as it reveals his sense of the relation among party politics, elections, and administrative organizations.

Rutan was a 5–4 decision, and it revealed the most intense debate on the Court surrounding judicial assault upon patronage and spoils since Powell's dissent in *Branti v. Finkel* (1979). In the majority was Brennan writing the decision, joined by Marshall, White, and Blackmun, with Stevens writing a separate concurring opinion. In dissent was the "Reagan" Court of Rehnquist, Scalia, O'Connor, and Kennedy.

The case grew out of a challenge to the Illinois governor's use of party affiliation when hiring, rehiring, transferring, and promoting individuals. Rutan challenged this patronage practice and the majority opinion on the Court struck down the practice, as an unconstitutional infringement of the First Amendment rights of these individuals. Significantly, Brennan cited his decisions in *Elrod v. Burns* (1976) and *Branti v. Finkel* (1979) and extended those rulings that had applied to patronage dismissals to also include patronage hirings, transfers, promotions, and recalls after layoffs. Brennan argued that the government interests in patronage were not vital enough to justify the limitation of the First Amendment rights of these workers.

The majority used this decision in a debate with the dissenters from this

case and *Branti* to justify the importance of limiting patronage in government. As in *Elrod*, Brennan argued that preservation of both the democratic
process and party organization is not furthered by patronage (*Rutan* 1979:
2737). Moreover, because civil service rules have already limited the number of patronage positions available, the linkage between parties and patronage is now weak. Thus, " . . . parties have already survived the substantial decline of patronage employment practices in this century" (ibid.:
2737).

In dissent, Scalia launched a ferocious attack on the majority's antipa-
tronage position by arguing that although the merit principle is clearly the
"most favored" way to organize governments, it is neither the only way to
do it, nor does it enjoy exclusive constitutional protection (ibid.: 2747).
Referring to George Plunkitt in his discussion of patronage, Scalia described
spoils as part of the American administrative/political tradition, but he
backed off from claiming that it is of "landmark status: or one of our accepted political traditions" (ibid.: 2748).

Scalia's dissent is founded upon two basic claims. First, he rejected the
idea that the merit principle is the only constitutional way to organize the
bureaucracy. Thus, he deferred to legislative wisdom in making this choice.
Elected officials and not the courts should decide how to staff the bureaucracy. Second, Scalia also defended patronage as having a rational basis,
because it supports strong parties, party government, and popular government. Clearly the second claim will be linked to his first and more important constitutional claim.

The primary constitutional line of attack that Scalia used in his dissent
was that the strict-scrutiny standard used by the majority in this case (as
well as in *Elrod* and *Branti*) to protect the rights of federal employees is
inappropriate and ought to be rejected in favor of a balancing of interests
test (*Rutan* 1990: 2749, 2752). There are two parts to this claim for a new
standard. First, Scalia argued that the restrictions on the speech of government employees had been held to be different from the restrictions that
could be placed on the general citizenry (ibid.: 2749). Second, if the government does have more latitude to act with regard to its own employees, then
the Court needs only to ask is if there is a rational-basis for its regulations
(ibid.: 2749). Scalia argues, then, that so long as the government can show
a rational basis or a reasonable governmental purpose, and that this purpose
outweighs the "coercive" effects on the employee, then the Court should
defer to the legislature (ibid.: 2752). In Scalia's words, "the whole point of
my dissent is that the desirability of patronage is a policy question to be
decided by the people's representatives" (ibid.: 2752).

The second part of Scalia's dissent showed how patronage does serve an important governmental interest. Arguing in favor of patronage as one way to staff bureaucracies, Scalia stated that ". . . the Court simply refuses to acknowledge the link between patronage and party discipline, and between that and party success" (ibid.: 2753). Scalia cited numerous works in political science and public administration that discussed parties' importance to American government and how strong parties provide challengers with the resources needed to take on an incumbent. Crucial to the formation of a strong party is reward of patronage, which will entice and reward workers (ibid.: 2753–2758). Among other points, Scalia indicated how parties, supported by patronage, will foster two-party competition, the integration of excluded groups, and build alliances (ibid.: 2753–2758). All of these functions are important to democracy and can be aided by patronage.

Scalia made two important points. First, he placed the justification for patronage upon the same or similar legal footing as the Hatch Act decisions of *United Public Workers v. Mitchell* (1947), and *U.S. Civil Service Commission v. Postal Workers* (1973), both of which upheld restrictions upon the partisan political activity of federal employees. The second point was his forceful argument for patronage that parallels the pre civil service reform and Jacksonian defenses of spoils. In effect, Scalia joined Rehnquist and Powell from earlier patronage cases (as well as Rehnquist, Kennedy, and O'Connor in the *Rutan* dissent) in rejecting much of the language of neutral competence and administration reform that had been used to seek the eradication of spoils.

Overall, Scalia's dissent offered a political vision that endorsed one of the most brazen types of partisan pressure politics and political activity, i.e., patronage (Kannar 1991: 1860). In determining how to organize an administrative agency, a legislative body should determine if party affiliation is an appropriate qualification for employment. Not only does the *Rutan* dissent endorse a respect for legislative deliberations that Scalia otherwise questions, but it also supports a free-wheeling laissez-faire "To a victor belongs the spoils" vision of political activity. Political activity, party maintenance, and electoral behavior should not be restricted or encumbered even by the First Amendment rights of government employees.[7]

The Paradoxes of Campaign Finance Reform

The last area of politics that this chapter explores is the issue of campaign finance reform. Since his elevation to the Supreme Court, Scalia has had the opportunity to rule on two cases involving the political spending by nonprofit corporations. In both cases, he argued on First Amendment grounds in favor of striking down applicable campaign finance restrictions.

In the first case, *Federal Election Commission v. Massachusetts Citizens for Life* (MCFL) (1986), the Supreme Court was asked to rule on the application of a Federal Election Campaign Act (FECA) provision that "prohibits corporations from using treasury funds to make expenditures 'in connection with' any federal election and requires that any expenditure for such purpose be financed by voluntary contributions to a separate segregated fund." MCFL was a nonprofit, nonstock corporation that supported pro-life issues through a variety of activities that included an infrequently published newsletter. In question was whether § 441b of FECA applied to an MCFL newsletter published prior to an election primary, which urged Massachusetts citizens to vote for pro-life candidates even though the publication did not refer to any specific candidates (ibid.: 620,623). The Court held that this newsletter was a violation of § 441b. But this provision, as applied to MCFL, was unconstitutional because it excessively burdened the organization's First Amendment rights.

In reaching these conclusions, the Court first asked whether requiring corporations to set up segregated funds for political expenditures was a sufficiently compelling state interest to justify incidental limits upon corporate free speech rights (ibid.: 627). It answered yes, and the Court indicated that

> [w]e have described that rationale in recent opinions as the need to restrict "the influence of political war chests funnelled through the corporate form," *NCPAC*, 470 U.S. at 501, 105 S.Ct. at 1470; to "eliminate the effect of aggregated wealth on federal elections," *Pipefitters*, 407 U.S., at 416, 92 S. Ct., at 2264; to curb the political influence of "those who exercise control over large aggregations of capital," *Automobile Workers*, 352 U.S., at 585, 77 S. Ct., at 538; and to regulate the "substantial aggregations of wealth amassed by the special advantages which go with the corporation form of organization," *National Right to Work Committee*, 459 U.S., at 207, 103 S.Ct., at 559 (ibid.: 627).

The Court, with Scalia in the majority, held that preventing the "corrosive influence of concentrated corporate wealth" (ibid.: 627) was a sufficiently compelling state interest to require separate segregated political funds to ensure that resources acquired in the economic marketplace would not give an unfair advantage in the political marketplace (ibid.: 627). Segregated funds as prescribed by § 441b would ensure that the political ideas expressed by the corporation indicate the voluntary political support for the ideas articulated, rather than the ability of a company to amass wealth through its economic actions (ibid.: 627–628).

The Court noted that the justifications for § 441b restrictions do "not uniformly apply to all corporations" (ibid.: 631). Some corporations, such as the MCFL, "have features more akin to voluntary political associations than business firms, and therefore should not have to bear burdens on independent spending solely because of their incorporated status" (ibid.: 631). Groups such as MCFL—formed for ideological purposes, lacking shareholders, and not acting as a conduit for a business or a union—are really political associations and not corporations (ibid.: 631). The special accounting procedures and requirements that compliance with § 441b would entail are "more extensive than [they] would be if it (MCFL) were not incorporated" (ibid.: 626). Because this segregated fund requirement is overly broad in its application to the MCFL, its application in this case is unconstitutional.

Scalia's joining of the majority opinion in *MCFL* stands in curious contrast to *Austin v. Michigan Chamber of Commerce* (1990), in which he dissented from a majority holding that upheld a similar segregated fund requirement in Michigan. The six-person majority held that corporations, even some nonprofit ones such as the Michigan Chamber of Commerce, which received its money from business members of the local chambers of commerce, could constitutionally be prohibited from using direct corporate-treasury funds for independent expenditures to support or oppose candidates for office. Following upon arguments made in *MCFL* and *Buckley v. Valeo* (1976), the Court ruled that campaign finance laws may, to some extent, regulate the conditions that affected the marketplace of ideas to ensure that this marketplace functions fairly and efficiently. Specifically, the majority gave greater weight to an expanded definition of corruption than was referred to by the Court in *Buckley* and *MCFL*. Instead of viewing corruption as merely a narrow, individual, quid pro quo exchange between a candidate and a lobbyist or interest group, the majority expressed concern over "a different type of corruption in the political arena: the corrosive and distorting effects of immense aggregations of wealth that are accumulated with the help of the corporate form and that have little or no correlation to the public's support for the corporation's political ideas" (*Austin* 1990: 1397). Therefore, the State of Michigan may constitutionally regulate corporate political activity more strictly than many expected the Court to allow. Corporate treasury spending to support or oppose candidates running for office, even by some nonprofit corporations like the Chamber, may be prohibited.

Unlike the MCFL, the Michigan Chamber of Commerce was not

deemed by the majority to be an ideological and voluntary political association and thus exempt from Michigan's requirements to segregate political funds. Surprisingly, Scalia dissented and held that the Michigan law interfered with the First Amendment rights of the Chamber, which he presumably considered a voluntary political association (ibid. 1416).

Three claims are important to Scalia's dissent and response to the majority holding. First, he maintains that the majority's opinion is a departure from previous Court campaign finance cases. Second, he regarded the holding as a clear case of censorship because it is not a narrowly tailored limitation upon the political expression of a speaker, i.e., a corporation. Third and perhaps most important, even "if the law were narrowly tailored to serve its goal, . . . that goal is not compelling" (ibid.: 1414). Overall, Scalia claimed that the holding is inconsistent with the First Amendment both by way of its original intent and by way of recent rulings on this Amendment.

To support these claims, Scalia argued against the majority's position that legislatures can regulate corporate speech because "[s]tate law grants [corporations] special advantages" that allow them to amass wealth (ibid.: 1408). Citing *Pickering v. the Board of Education* (1968) and *Speiser v. Randall* (1958) Scalia reminds the majority that the "[s]tate cannot exact as the price of those special advantages the forfeiture of First Amendment rights" (*Austin* 1990: 1408). The only way speech can be limited is to secure a compelling state need. In this case, the majority's contention that large corporate treasuries and corporate spending threated public discourse is not narrowly tailored enough to justify limits upon their ability to speak (ibid.: 1409, 1413). It is not drawn narrowly enough because the law excludes the "war chests" (ibid.: 1413) of certain individuals whose wealth may similarly pose the potential of corruption, and whom the Court has already held cannot be prohibited from making independent expenditures to express their political views, while also including within the ban many corporations that may not be wealthy and are subject to the Michigan law (ibid.: 1413).

Scalia also indicated that the Michigan Chamber of Commerce is more like a voluntary political association as described by the majority in *MCFL*, and by Alexis de Tocqueville in *Democracy in America* (ibid.: 1415–1416). However if the three criteria in *MCFL* used to distinguish corporations from voluntary associations are applied, (i.e., voluntary associations are formed for ideological purposes, lack shareholders, and do not act as conduits for a business or a union), then it is debatable whether the Chamber met any of these requirements very well or at all. Unfortunately, Scalia gave no argument to show how the *MCFL* rules apply to the Chamber of Commerce in *Austin*. Suppressing these voluntary associations, according to Scalia, is destructive:

To eliminate voluntary associations—not only including powerful ones, but *especially* (Scalia's emphasis) including powerful ones—from the public debate is either to augment the always dominant power of government or to impoverish public debate (ibid.: 1416).

To burden the Chamber with a segregated political fund requirement would be analogous to encumbering the MCFL with such a fund requirement. Such a requirement would place an excessive burden upon the free speech rights of the Chamber and thus would be unconstitutional in this case.

Moreover, Scalia contended, even if the law correctly distinguished between voluntary associations and corporations, and " . . . if the law were narrowly tailored to achieve its goal . . . that goal is not compelling" (ibid.: 1413). According to Scalia, the "potential danger" (ibid.: 1414) of corporate wealth is not enough to justify the Michigan law that established the narrow tailoring necessary to support the state's objective of restrictions upon corporate political speech. In breaking with the holding dicta that he joined in with the majority in *MCFL*, Scalia questioned whether state interests could ever be sufficiently compelling to place a limit upon a corporation's First Amendment rights. Scalia's contention is that the Michigan law is directed at corporations qua corporations, the wealth that they have amassed, and the presumed potential for corruption such wealth has in our society (ibid.: 1415). Such legislation, for Scalia, is clearly a form of censorship directed at the agent of a specific type of speech, and it is inconsistent with the First Amendment, the intent of Madison and Jefferson, as well as the observations of de Tocqueville on society's need for free speech and voluntary associations in society.

Scalia also argues that the majority's special corporate exception for the regulation of political speech is inconsistent with previous rulings such as *FCC v. League of Women Voters of California* (1984), which struck down bans on political editorializing by noncommercial broadcasting systems. In his view, the majority holding also misuses *FEC v. National Right to Work Committee* (1982), and jumps from the assertion in that case that " . . . we accept Congress' judgment that the special characteristics of the corporate structure create a potential for . . . influence that demands regulation to the overbroad and not narrowly tailored limitation upon all corporate speech" (*Austin* 1990: 1413).

Scalia sees *Austin* as a departure from *Buckley v. Valeo* (1976), a case that struck down direct contributions to candidates, but left in place independent expenditures such as those the Michigan law aimed to prohibit. Scalia contended that whereas *Buckley* sought to eliminate direct quid pro quo corruption where money is given to a candidate with the understanding of reciprocity, the Michigan law instead addressed the "New Corruption" problem whereby the speech of one unpopular participant is reduced in order to "enhance the relative force of others" (ibid.: 1411). Reducing speech by one participant will have the net effect of reducing the total amount of speech in society, and will limit the amount of free expression, diversity of thought, and exchange of ideas in society (ibid.: 1411). Thus, this law is a form of censorship.

Overall, Scalia's dissent in *Austin* amounts to the claim that the Michigan law as applied to the Chamber of Commerce is unconstitutional either because it burdens a voluntary political association, or because the law aims at suppressing corporation speech to eliminate corruption.

When Scalia's views in *MCFL* and *Austin* are examined together, we find he makes two points. First, he seems to be rejecting the goal of corporate campaign finance reform he endorsed in *MCFL*. In *Austin* he declared the regulation to be a form of censorship. Second, he also seems to be moving towards equating corporations with Tocqueville's notion of voluntary political associations. In doing so, he either provides an analysis of Tocqueville to show the parallels between the two entities or relies upon legal arguments to show why the rules formulated in *MCFL* to distinguish associations from corporations need to be amended, applied differently, or rejected.

If we accept the logic of Scalia's thought in *Austin*, elections represent the expression of the political ideas and corporations are an important expression of political ideas. Thus, to regulate corporate spending in elections would be to suppress important First Amendment rights of free expression and that would result in censorship and in a damage to the electoral process.[8]

Conclusion: Scalia's Political Philosophy

Analysis of Antonin Scalia's scholarly writings and judicial opinions on constitutional interpretation, the framers, and various aspects of the political process tells us much about the about the values that inform his political philosophy.

First, Scalia employs am interpretive strategy premised upon the intent of the framers, yet it is a method that is not ideologically neutral. It is influenced by a political philosophy that has distinct views on how the political process ought to operate. Second, Scalia's political philosophy or vision, along with his approach to judicial review, suggests that he is rethinking of the *Carolene Products* logic, at least in selected policy areas. This issue will be addressed in more detail in the following chapters, yet it is sufficient to say for now that Scalia has been unwilling to defer to legislative bodies in the area of affirmative action and the protection of white males, property rights, and campaign finance reform as it affects corporations. However, he seems content to defer in the areas of abortion, tort liability for the press, the death penalty, religious practices of minorities, and political patronage, among other policy areas. Although Scalia is apparently no longer willing to defer to legislatures in the areas traditionally covered by footnote four of *Carolene Products*, he does appear to be willing to second-guess in new areas. Scalia's own writings, as well as his appeals to the framers and the *Federalist Papers*, suggest that he is often suspicious of legislative integrity, and perhaps that suspicion might explain this facially erratic pattern of legislative deference. Yet no clear rule or criterion in his decisions or writings has emerged to tell readers when judicial review is needed because the legislative process has malfunctioned. All that Scalia has given us are policy areas where he will or will not defer. Contrary to his claims and those of his critics, Scalia does not demonstrate a consistently applied attitude towards the legislative process that could be characterized as judicial restraint or as consistent with some type of neutral originalism.

Scalia's opinions in limiting campaign finance and patronage reform, as well as his views on party politics and governmental organization, demonstrate a sympathy for what is traditionally more characteristic of the Jacksonian era than of the recent twentieth century reform movement. It is also a sympathy for a survival of the fittest, a free political market of democratic competition where all ideas and tactics are permitted. Overall, Scalia's views in these policy areas describe a judicial role in the political process that is different than the role the Court has previously adopted from *Carolene Products*. By that, we mean that while Scalia's view appears to apply the formal logic of footnote four, the substantive application of the note is applied to individuals or policy areas that depart from the traditional application of the case. In some way, as noted above, this view is a throwback to an era of greater reliance upon separation of powers and legislative autonomy to protect rights, except in those cases where he believes that the political process has malfunctioned.

Second, while Scalia may often invoke the framers' authority, it is not clear that he uses the framers consistently. Instead, his appeal to the framers may serve to legitimize decisions that he has already made on the basis of other values. Scalia's jurisprudence reflects a preference for policies that have been labeled as Manchester Liberalism. This version of liberalism is more supportive of property rights than civil rights, of the marketplace than the government, and of the enforcement of majoritarian morality than respecting individual ethical choices when those choices are at odds with majoritarian preferences. Scalia's jurisprudence tends to be more supportive of the goals of classical Liberal thought than of those goals supported by the twentieth century New Deal welfare state.

Third, this chapter questions previous scholarship on Scalia that argues that his jurisprudence is primarily methodologically driven, and that his methodology is consistently applied. Instead we are left with a view of Scalia's political process that reveals an inconsistent deference to legislative decision-making, if we assume that his jurisprudence is methodologically driven. If we assume that Scalia's jurisprudence is at least partially results-oriented, and that his willingness to defer (or not defer) to other branches is controlled by his political philosophy and policy preferences towards specific issues, then his writings and decisions reveal a profound commitment to use judicial power to serve specific goals of concern to President Reagan and other political conservatives.

Notes

1. Other cases where the *Federalist Papers* are invoked to clarify historical or constitutional intent are: *Young v. ex rel Vuitton et fils S.A.* (1984: 2143, 2146), citing *Federalist 78; Tyler Pipe Industry v. Washington Department of Revenues* (1987: 2828, 2829), citing *Federalist 7; Freytag v. C.I.R.* (1991: 795–96), citing *Federalist 78; Blatchvord v. Native Village of Noatak* (1991: 694), citing *Federalist 81; Norman v. Reed* (1992: 750), citing *Federalist 10; Tafflin v. Levitt* (1990: 801), citing *Federalist 82; Planned Parenthood v. Casey* (1992), citing *Federalist 78; Morrison v. Olson* (1988: 2622–5, 2634, 2638, 2647), citing *Federalist 47, 49, 51, 70, 73, and 81; Richmond v. Croson* (1989: 737), citing *Federalist 10; Synar v. United States,* (D.D.C. 1986: 1402), citing *Federalist 48.*

2. *Honig v. Doe* (1988: 613); *Sun Oil Company v. Wortman* (1988: 2122); *Morgan v. United States* (D.C.Cir 1986: 447); *Tyler Pipe Industry v. Washington Department of Revenues* (1987: 2828, 2829); and *Morrison v. Olson* (1988: 2623, 2634, 2635).

3. Blackstone is cited in one article (Scalia 1989–90) and in at least four cases, i.e., *Harmelin v. Michigan* (1991: 853); *Michael H. v. Gerald D.* (1989: 2343); *Thompson v. Oklahoma* (1988: 2714); and *U.S. v. Williams* (1992: 367).

4. *Burnham v. Superior Court* (1990: 2111) and *Richmond v. Croson* (1989) cite Story's views on clarification of the founding.

5. Those six cases are *Nollan v. California Coastal Commission* (1986); *South Carolina v. Baker* (1987); *New York State Club v. City of New York* (1987); *Richmond v. Croson* (1989); *United States v. Munoz-Flores* (1990); and *Airline Pilots v. O'Neill* (1991).

6. *Elrod v. Burns* (1976) and *Branti v. Finkel* (1979), had previously placed limits upon the use of patronage in the staffing of bureaucracies.

7. Scalia's dissent in *Tashjijan v. Republican Party of Connecticut* (Scalia dissenting); (1986: 559) where he upholds a Connecticut law that places restrictions upon who may vote in a Republican Party primary appears to be a counterexample where he does not support a "wideopen, no holds barred" form of political activity and organization.

8. Scalia's claims here anticipate and parallel his decisions granting broad constitutional protection for corporate free speech claims, suggesting that he finds corporations important political agents worthy of significant political protection. This support for corporate speech and political activity, as will be discussed in chapters six and seven, comes at the expense of his narrowing of similar types of rights for individuals.

Chapter 3

Statutory Interpretation and Legislative Politics

Antonin Scalia's approach to statutory interpretation has generated controversy since he was first appointed to the federal court of appeals. This controversy has continued and grown since his elevation to the Supreme Court. Specifically, Scalia's attack on the use of legislative history to interpret and guide judicial readings of statutes has set off a significant debate on the Court, in Congress, and in the press. Efforts to overturn several controversial Supreme Court civil rights decisions in the 1991 Civil Rights Act highlight this controversy, as Congress sought to ensure that the legislation was read the way Congress intended it to be understood (Pear 1991; Note 1992).

This chapter explores Justice Scalia's views on the legislative process and his interpretive methodology that questions legislative deference and the use of legislative intent to guide the reading of statutes. Recent scholarship has mainly focused on Scalia's interpretive method (Slawson 1992; Note 1994). By contrast, this chapter will expand the scholarly focus and examine his views toward the legislative process and decision-making, including the approach and methodology he has used in interpreting legislative pronouncements. The chapter will first assess recent scholarship that describes Scalia's interpretive jurisprudence. The goal is to improve understanding of the controversy surrounding Scalia's treatment of legislatures and statutory interpretation. The second section will explore Scalia's view of the legislative process and intent, indicating how both elements shape his construction of Congress's laws.

Contrary to the conclusions of other scholars, we will argue that although Scalia premises many of his interpretative claims in terms of valid and generally well-accepted legal claims or tools of statutory construction, he employs an inconsistently applied interpretive method that adopts an inconsistent approach towards legislative power and the political process (Strauss 1991: 1716; Tushnet 1991: 1740). This inconsistent attitude towards statutory interpretation and using legislative intent results from Scalia's often-distrustful view of legislative power, (Brisbin 1992: 129) and that distrust is often a consequence of his political preferences. Such an inconsistency and use of policy preferences, it will be argued, is troublesome especially in light of Scalia's own assertions that the courts should generally recognize the power of legislatures to make policy and that the " . . . only checks on the arbitrariness of federal judges are the insistence upon consistency and the application of the teachings of the mother of consistency logic" (Scalia 1989–90: 588). This inconsistency is also troubling in light of his well-publicized claims about how statutes should be read.

Assessing Scalia's Impact and Performance: The Status of Current Scholarship

At the end of Scalia's initial terms on the Court, one set of scholarly analyses examined his interpretive method and the sources of his disagreement with other conservative members of the Court. George Kannar sought to understand Scalia's approach to reading the Constitution (Kannar 1990). Kannar locates Scalia's rejection of appeal to author's or founders' intent in the justice's pre-Vatican II Catholicism and his father's professorial background in Romance literature; he contends that they are key to Scalia's insistence on reading statutes and the Constitution in terms of the plain meaning that the words convey (Kannar 1990: 1299, 1316). Dan Farber and Phillip Frickey, on the other hand, explain his interpretive approach as a function of the justice's general distrust of legislative politics and his questioning of the judiciary's ability to ascertain legislative intent from the committee reports and comments of particular legislators (Farber and Frickey 1991: 89–95). They also agree with other studies that Scalia's methodology is important to his approach to the law (ibid.: 89–91).

Arthur Stock notes Scalia's unwillingness to defer to legislative intent and other extra-textual evidence when interpreting congressional statutes (Stock 1990: 160–61), yet Stock indicates that Scalia is willing in cases such as *White v. Illinois* (1992: 744) to defer to extra-textual evidence such as the *Federalist Papers* when interpreting the Constitution (Stock 1990: 180). Stock argues that this interpretive strategy is "inconsistent" and is meant to limit legislative power in order to benefit executive and judicial power (Stock 1990: 160–161, 190–191).

Jean Morgan Meaux, Richard Nagareda, and Jay Schlosser see Scalia's interpretive strategies, including his skepticism towards legislative intent and history, as important to his jurisprudence in the areas of executive and administrative authority (Meaux 1987: 227), the First Amendment (Nagareda 1987: 722), and church/state issues (Schlosser 1988: 387). Finally, Daniel Reisman contends that the justice's interpretive method is not strictly a textual approach but appeals to extratextual values, including a belief in a strong executive government (Reisman 1988: 50). Scalia's jurisprudence and appeal to a neutral methodology actually mask his commitment to executive power and his depreciation of congressional authority (Reisman 1988: 92–93; Strauss 1991: 1716).

During the same time period, another related line of scholarship concentrated on Scalia's definition of the Court's role in American society, his attitude toward the other major branches of government, and his views on substantive doctrinal issues such as the First Amendment. Gary Hengstler reviews Scalia's 1987 speech that endorses limiting the Court's appellate workload by creating special tribunals to handle routine issues such as social security disability and freedom of information disputes (Hengstler 1987). Chris Smith argues that the justice's "strong views on separation of powers and the institution of the Supreme Court place him at odds with his colleagues (Smith 1990: 785). Moreover, Smith claims that Scalia's commitment to separation of powers has given him the role as "stalwart guardian of American government institutions" (ibid.: 809) Richard Brisbin reaches a similar conclusion in his numerous writings on the justice (Brisbin 1990: 105), and he indicates that Scalia's deference to Congress and the Presidency as the primary policy-making institutions is important to the justice's conception of American politics. (Brisbin 1990: 5–6; Brisbin 1992). All these authors agree that the Scalia's willingness to limit standing and deny access to the federal courts are attempts to preserve the federal judiciary— especially the Supreme Court—as an elite institution in American politics (Smith 1990: 794–795; Brisbin 1990: 6–9; Meaux 1987: 246).

Overall, Scalia is characterized as a brilliant and opinionated justice. He is regarded as favoring a strict and aggressively enforced conception of separation of powers and limited access to the courts, and some deferring to Congress and more to the President. These themes, taken together, characterize Scalia as a justice who favors limiting judicial power and deferring to the other branches of government. Moreover, this scholarship, while noting his conservative political views, mostly downplays, if not ignores, his ideology as controlling his interpretive jurisprudence. Emphasis is placed instead upon his legal pragmatism, his democratic vision of American society, and most importantly, his neutral interpretive methodology as being crucial to the decisions he reaches.

Does Scalia consistently and neutrally apply his interpretive methodology? Is ideology as unimportant as the existing scholarship seems to suggest? We contend that the answer is no, and argue that the Scalia scholarship has missed the ways in which the justice's ideology and approach to statutory interpretation often reinforce one another.

Scalia and the Legislative Process

An initial reading of Scalia's writings would suggest that he views the Court's relationship to Congress and other legislative bodies as one gives general deference to the latter's policy-making discretion. In a 1979 essay, then University of Chicago Law Professor Scalia argued that "Congress is . . . the first line of constitutional defense, and the courts—even the activist modern courts—merely a backdrop" (Scalia 1979a: 20). According to Scalia,

> Congress has an authority and indeed a responsibility to interpret the Constitution that is not less solemn and binding than the similar authority and responsibility of the Supreme Court . . . Moreover, congressional interpretations are of enormous importance—of greater importance, ultimately, than those of the Supreme Court (ibid.: 20).

Although Congress is the primary institution that maintains constitutional integrity, it does not have carte blanche authority to check executive might or regulatory power through the use of legislative vetoes (ibid.: 19). Instead, what Scalia argues in this essay is that the legislative veto is a form of "legislation in reverse" (ibid.: 22), that legislative vetoes are clearly contrary to the intent of the framers, and, more importantly, that they are a violation of Article I, section 7, clause 3 of the Constitution (the Presentment Clause). Specifically, a legislative veto is a usurpation of the executive authority invested in the President, and if the legislative veto is left unchecked, it will alter the constitutional balance between Congress and the presidency. Thus, he argues, it will ultimately undermine democratic government (ibid.: 24–25).

This essay reveals several issues that are important to understanding Scalia's interpretive strategy. First, is Scalia's concern with protection of executive power, along with his general deference to Congress to make policy and interpret the Constitution in response to majority demands. Thus, he provides a sense of institutional identity and function for each of the three major branches of the government. His respect for Congress's constitutional interpretation reveals his willingness to make the judiciary less of a prominent and activist guardian of the Constitution than it was in the recent past. His vision of separation of powers indicates that even the judiciary has clearly delineated powers that can neither be encroached upon by other branches nor extended by the courts themselves. Hence, Justice Scalia invokes the principle of separation of powers to defer to legislative and executive power and to remove the judiciary from consideration of political policy questions. The reason for limiting the judiciary's role is to allow the other branches to assume their responsibilities as policymakers.

Scalia's scholarly writings and decisions provide clear evidence that he respects the legislative process as the primary institution with policy-making authority. For example, in an article entitled "The Doctrine of Standing as an Essential Element in the Separation of Powers," Scalia asserts that the judiciary should keep out of those "affairs better left to the other branches" (Scalia 1983: 891). In another article, entitled "Originalism: The Lesser Evil," Scalia describes the basic decision-making process in a democracy:

> A democratic society does not, by and large, need constitutional guarantees to insure that its laws will reflect "current values." Elections take care of that quite well (Scalia 1989b: 862).

Elsewhere in the same, essay Scalia states that "... the legislature would seem a much more appropriate expositor of social values" than the judiciary (Id.: 854). Thus, Scalia appears to have a vision of the political process that endorses judicial deference to legislative policy-making.

As noted in chapter one and consistent with his apparent support for legislative deference, numerous examples of policy issues testify to the associate justice's willingness to let the legislative process act unimpeded by judicial scrutiny. In his scholarly writings, Scalia states that "how much to spend for welfare programs is almost invariably a prudential [choice]" and this choice should not be excluded from the deliberations in the "governmental process" (Scalia 1985: 126). Moreover, in *Liberty Lobby Inc. v. Anderson* (D.C. Cir. 1984), Scalia argued that "... legislatures rather than courts should determine whether damages in libel suits against the press should be limited." Furthermore, in *Stanford v. Kentucky* (1989), Scalia wrote the majority opinion upholding the imposition of the death penalty for sixteen and seventeen-year-olds. In this case Scalia emphasized that he so decided because the imposition of the death penalty for individuals this age was not cruel and *unusual* since a "majority of the States that permit capital punishment authorize it for crimes committed at age 16 or above." (Ibid.:

2976) Thus, deference to the wisdom of state legislatures is important to upholding a death penalty policy.

In another example, *Rutan v. Republican Party of Illinois* (1990), Scalia contended that the use of spoils is not a violation of employees' or potential employees' First Amendment rights, and that the merit system is not the only way to staff the government. In Scalia's words, "the whole point of my dissent is that the desirability of patronage is a policy question to be decided by the people's representatives." (ibid.: 2752) Thus, when to use party affiliation for hiring purposes is a legislative question.

In the context of religious freedom issues, in *Smith v. Employment Division of Oregon* (1990), the justice indicated that many values found in the Bill of Rights, such as those protections offered to the practices of religious minorities, are not banished from consideration in the political process:

> Values that are protected against governmental interference through enshrinement in the Bill of Rights are not thereby banished from the political process . . . It may fairly be said that leaving accommodation to the political process will place at a relative disadvantage those religious practices that are not widely engaged in; but that unavoidable consequence of democratic government must be preferred . . . (ibid: 1606).

Therefore, and in opposition to the role of the judiciary suggested by footnote number four in *United States v. Carolene Products* (1938), legislatures may deliberate policy matters that affect personal religious practices of discrete and insular groups without the federal courts intervening to protect those groups.

In *Norman v. Reed* (1992), a 1991 term case, Scalia dissented from the majority opinion that struck down an Illinois statute that required new third-party candidates to secure 25,000 signatures and meet other procedural hurdles not required of candidates of established parties. Here the majority argued that the purpose of the statute was to deny unpopular or minority-party candidates access to the statewide ballot and thus challenge the political power of more established parties (ibid.: 708). Scalia instead would give significant deference to the "State of Illinois's arrangement of its elections" to prevent the "dangers of factionalism" (ibid.: 709, 711) that might threaten Cook County or Illinois should numerous political parties form.

Finally, as early as 1978, Scalia argued that in regards to abortion, the Court "had 'no business' deciding an issue which had been determined through the democratic process" (Meaux 1987: 228). Not surprisingly, in *Webster v. Reproductive Health Services* (1989), in which a majority upheld several state restrictions upon the right to obtain an elective abortion, Justice Scalia contended that *Roe v. Wade* (1973) should be overruled, and that the Court should defer to other branches to make policy in this area:

> The outcome of today's case will doubtless be heralded as a triumph of judicial statesmanship. It is not that, unless it is statesmanlike needlessly to prolong this Court's self-awarded sovereignty over a field where it has little proper business since the answers to most of the cruel questions posed are political and not juridical—a sovereignty which therefore quite properly, but to the great damage of the Court, makes it the object of the sort of organized public pressure that political institutions in a democracy ought to receive (ibid.: 3064).

From Scalia's perspective, welfare spending, press liability, the death penalty, the practices of religious minorities, political patronage, regulation of third parties, and abortion are instances in which the political process should be allowed to operate freely and unobstructed by judicial scrutiny.

Despite Scalia's apparent respect for legislative discretion in these cases, his view of legislative politics is that they are not always worthy of respect and deference. As Bernard Schwartz contends, the justice views legislative policy decisions as nothing more than pressure politics (Schwartz 1990: 244). This view underlies Scalia's belief that attempts to ascertain intent of legislatures when reading statutes are unwise and often it is better to defer to the executive or administrative organizations when looking for statutory meaning.

Chevron and Legislative Skepticism

The legal justification for many of Scalia's claims on statutory interpretation, as well as his skepticism towards legislative politics can be located in his frequent appeals to *Chevron, U.S.A., Inc. v. National Resources Defense Council* (1984). According to Scalia, the *Chevron* precedent offers a consistent approach that the judiciary ought to apply when seeking the meaning of federal statutes (Scalia 1989a: 517). Quoting Justice Stevens, Scalia proposes a two-step process in seeking this understanding:

> First, always, is the question [of] whether Congress has directly spoken to the precise question at issue. If the intent of Congress is clear, that is the end of the matter; for the court, as well as the agency, must give effect to the unambiguously expressed intent of Congress . . .

. . . If, however, the court determines that Congress has not directly addressed the precise question at issue, the court does not simply impose its own construction on the statute, as would be necessary in the absence of an administrative interpretation. Rather, if the statute is silent or ambiguous with respect to the specific issue, the question for the court is whether the agency's answer is based on a permissible construction of the statute (Scalia 1989a: 511–12).

Prior to his appointment to the Court, Justice Stephen Breyer, in a 1986 article on *Chevron*, argued that there were two ways to read this decision. One approach, which he labelled the more complex reading, suggests that a "range of relevant factors," perhaps even the statute's legislative history, may be considered when seeking to determine if Congress delegated interpretative power to administrative agencies. However, there is also a simpler approach to reading *Chevron*, which Breyer associated with the Court of Appeals for the District of Columbia Circuit where Scalia sat as judge:

Yet the language may also be read as embodying a considerably simpler approach, namely, first decide whether the statute is "silent or ambiguous with respect to the specific issue" and, if so, accept the agency's interpretation if (in light of statutory purposes) it is "reasonable" (Breyer 1986: 373).

Scalia has adopted what Breyer has characterized as the simpler reading of *Chevron*. What *Chevron* means to Scalia is that if the plain meaning of a statute is not clear, reasonable executive determinations of the statute ought to be applied and preferred over alternative interpretations. For example, in both *I.N.S. v. Cardoza Fonseca* (1987) and *Sullivan v. Everhart* (1990), among other decisions, Scalia cites *Chevron* to support his claims that the plain meaning advanced by Congress in its statutory language should guide judicial interpretations unless the law is ambiguous, then deference to administrative agencies should prevail—if such administrative interpretations exist.

Scalia argues that the virtue of *Chevron* does not lie in its respect for separation of powers (Scalia 1989a: 515–516). According to Scalia, prior to *Chevron*, the court engaged in resolving ambiguity by assuming one of two things:

(1) Congress intended a particular result, but was not clear about it, or (2) Congress had no particular intent on the subject, but meant to leave its resolution to an agency . . . *Chevron*, however, if it is to be believed, replaced this statute-by-statute evaluation (which was assuredly a font of uncertainty and litigation) with an across-the-board presumption that, in the case of ambiguity, agency discretion is meant (Scalia 1989a: 516).

Thus, contrary to claims that Scalia's desire for bright line rules for interpretation underpin his support for this doctrine (Brisbin 1992), other factors seem to motivate his support for *Chevron*.

While Scalia acknowledges that the *Chevron* rule is not perfect, it is for him an improvement over previous judicial practices that sought to understand legislative intent on a case-by-case basis. Scalia makes a blanket and perhaps not-unfounded claim that statutory ambiguity was intended to give agencies some discretion to interpret the law. However, it is equally possible that statutory ambiguity or silence is not necessarily intended, yet results from political compromises, unforeseen situations, or the inability to resolve policy issues (Breyer 1986: 376). Alternatively, as Scalia notes, a statute's level of clarity or ambiguity may be disputed, raising questions about how definitive the *Chevron* rule is in resolving statutory meaning (Scalia 1979a: 520–21). Given these options, Scalia chooses the first, contending that the search for intent is often a futile process, and the courts should adopt the rule that Congress intended for an administrative agency to make the interpretative choice.

> And to tell the truth, the quest for the "genuine" legislative intent is probably a wild-goose chase anyway. In the vast majority of cases I expect that Congress neither (1) intended a single result, nor (2) meant to confer discretion upon the agency, but rather (3) didn't think about the matter at all (Scalia 1989a: 517).

Scalia's skepticism towards legislative intent here is echoed and enhanced in other opinions in which he describes the legislative process as corrupted by interest group politics or lacking the deliberative qualities it should possess. In short, given that the legislative process is tainted, a search for intent is futile.

Good examples of this skepticism are evidenced in cases concerning affirmative action. In *Johnson v. Transportation Agency* (1986), Scalia describes the origin of preferential treatment programs as residing in pressure politics.

> It is unlikely that today's result will be displeasing to politically elected officials, to whom it provides the means of quickly accommodating the demands of organized groups to achieve concrete, numerical improvement in the economic status of particular constituencies (ibid.: 677).

In *Richmond v. Croson* (1989), Scalia sees the thirty percent MBE set-aside program as the product of the type of factional politics that Madison in *Federalist* 10 sought to prevent (ibid.: 736–737). Scalia declares, echoing

Madison, that "an acute awareness of the heightened danger of oppression from political factions in small, rather than large, political units dates to the very beginning of our national history" (ibid.: 737). Faction- based politics are clearly the source of affirmative action programs, and they can damage the integrity of the legislative-deliberative process.[1]

Additionally, in his dissent in *Austin v. Michigan Chamber of Commerce* (1990), Scalia attacks a Michigan law aimed at requiring business corporations that wish to make political contributions and spend money for political purposes to set up special segregated funds for these purposes. Scalia depicts this law as the product of the type of pressure politics and unchecked public opinion that Jefferson, Madison, and de Tocqueville would have opposed and wanted to contain (ibid.: 1415–16). Here, Scalia attacks the majority opinion for supporting legislation aimed at rooting out the "New Corruption" (ibid.: 1415), and he also attacks the Michigan law aimed at corporate campaign contributions as representing no more than a form of public censorship of an unpopular speaker (ibid.: 1415–16).

Besides affirmative action and campaign finance reform, the justice second-guesses the legislative process in other areas. In *Nollan v. California Coastal Commission* (1987), he seemed to suggest that property deserved some type of special protection against legislative excess.[2] Elsewhere are general indications that Scalia is suspicious of the integrity of legislative political decisions, because they are often compromised by interest group politics. In other, scattered, opinions Scalia suggests that policy decisions often are either the product of pressure politics or the preferences of legislative staff members, with neither of these sources containing discernible legislative deliberation or rationality.

In sum, Scalia's affinity for the *Chevron* doctrine lies in his skepticism toward the politics that has undermined Congress and the legislative process and in his preference for an efficient means to address statutory silence or ambiguity. Given what he views as the fragmented nature of policy-making, searching for a unified intent is impossible, especially if that search involves an appeal to legislative history, including recourse to committee reports, statements of representatives, etc. Hence, Scalia has articulated other approaches to clarifying the meaning of statutes.

In *Green v. Bock Laundry Machine Co.* (1989), Scalia clarifies his views on how to understand statutes and approach intent:

> The meaning of terms on the statute-books ought to be determined, not on the basis of which meaning can be shown to have been understood by a larger handful of the members of Congress; but rather on the basis of which meaning is (1) most in accord with context and ordinary usage, and most likely to have

been understood by the *whole* Congress which voted on the words of the statute (not to mention the citizens subject to it), and (2) most compatible with the surrounding body of law into which the provision must be integrated—a compatibility which, by a benign fiction, we assume Congress always had in mind. I would not permit any of the historical and legislative materials discussed by the Court, or all of it combined, to lead me to a result different from the one these factors suggest (ibid.: 1994).

In other cases, Scalia develops additional claims against the use of legislative history. For example, in *Hirschey v. F.E.R.C.* (D.C. Cir. 1985), Scalia disagrees with the majority opinion's attempt to use legislative intent to ascertain the meaning of a statute:

I frankly doubt that it is ever reasonable to assume that the details, as opposed to the broad outlines of purpose, set forth in a committee report come to the attention of, much less are approved by, the house which enacts the committee's bill. And I think it is time for the courts to become concerned about the fact that routine deference to the details of committee reports, and the predictable expansion in that detail which routine deference has produced, are converting a system of judicial construction into a system of committee-staff prescription (ibid.: 7–8).

In *Green v. Bock Laundry Machine Co.*, Scalia reiterates this theme:

I am frankly not sure that, despite its lengthy discussion of the ideological evolution and legislative history, the Court's reasons for both aspects of its decision are much different from mine. I respectfully decline to join that discussion, however, because it is natural for the bar to believe that the judicial importance of such material matches its prominence in our opinions—thus producing a legal culture in which, when counsel arguing before us assert that "Congress has said" something, they now mean, by "Congress," a committee report. (ibid.: 1995)

In addition, in *Wisconsin Public Intervenor v. Mortier* (1991), Scalia questions the value of committee reports in clarifying whether the Federal Insecticide, Fungicide, and Rodenticide Act (FIFRA) was meant to supersede state regulation of pesticides (ibid.: 2488–89). Here, he argues that committee reports are not only unclear on this issue, but are not even relevant because they do "not necessarily say anything about what Congress as a whole thought" (ibid:, 2489). In Scalia's opinion, reading legislative history is a recent phenomena representing a " 'weird endeavor' " that is no more than a " 'psychoanalysis of Congress' " (ibid.: 2490). Moreover, in *Conroy v. Aniskoff* (1993), he states that the greatest defect of legislative history is its illegitimacy. We are governed by laws, not by the intentions of legislators . . . But not the least of the defects of legislative history is its indeterminacy. If one were to search for an interpretive technique that, *on the whole*, was more likely to confuse than to clarify, one could hardly find a more promising candidate than legislative history (ibid.: 238).

In *Thunder Basin Coal v. Reich* (1994), Scalia issues a concurrence that attacks the majority's use of legislative history, contending that the use of legislative history is an "illusion" if asserted as an "important factor" to reading statutes (ibid.: 45). Overall, it is clear that Scalia finds the search for statutory intent to be as illegitimate as his search for constitutional intent is legitimate.

Interpretive Politics and the Limits of *Chevron*

Since Scalia spurns the search for legislative intent or history to clarify the meaning of statutes, he prefers to use other interpretive techniques to clarify meaning. Consistent with his reading of *Chevron*, the plain meaning of the text is his preferred way to read a statute. In *United States v. Granderson* (1994), Scalia states that it "is best, as usual, to apply the statute as written, and to let Congress make the needed repairs" (ibid.: 629). In *Chicago v. Environmental Defense Fund* (1994), and *United States v. Alvarez-Sanchez* (1994), as well as elsewhere, Scalia claims that the plain meaning of the text clarifies the meaning of a law.

However, in cases where the plain meaning of the text does not resolve the issue, Scalia will often combine the plain-meaning rule with other techniques, such as using dictionary meanings of terms (Karkkainen 1994: 440; Note 1994: 1439). In fact, while all the justices, at least during the 1992 term, for example, used the dictionary occasionally to help them clarify words, Scalia uses the dictionary in a greater percentage of his opinions than do the other justices (Note 1994: 1438–1440). As early as his tenure on the Court of Appeals, Scalia resorted to the use of dictionaries and the dictionary meaning of terms to clarify language. In *Block v. Meese* (D.C. Cir. 1986), a movie distributor was challenging a State Department classification of two Canadian films critical of Reagan environmental policies as political propaganda pursuant to the Foreign Agents Registration Act of 1938. In part, what was at issue was the Reagan Administration's interpretation and statutory definition of "political propaganda," as it applied to these documentaries. The distributor claimed that the labelling of the films by the government constituted a form of government disapproval of these films and, thus, constituted a violation of the distributor's First Amendment free speech rights. Scalia rejected these claims. To support his arguments, Scalia relied upon dictionary definitions of propaganda found in *Webster's Ninth New Collegiate Dictionary*, published in 1983, and *The Random House College Dictionary*, published in 1982. Scalia noted that while the ordinary usage of propaganda connoted disapproval, a broader meaning of the term also includes " 'ideas, facts, or allegations spread deliberately to further one's cause or to damage an opposing cause.' "³ Utilizing this broader meaning of the word, Scalia argued

> [I]t seems to us that in labelling something "propaganda" the government is not expressing its own disapproval but is merely identifying an objective category of speech of which the public generally disapproves (ibid.: 1312).

In *Crandon v. United States* (1990: 171–72), Scalia employs *Webster's Second New International Dictionary* to clarify the meaning of salary and compensation in a statute. His interpretation results in the narrowing of the meaning of the statute, permitting private employers to give cash payments to former workers who join the government (Karkkainen 1994: 440). In *Smith v. United States* (1993: 156–57), Scalia also employs *Webster's New International Dictionary*, published in 1939, to examine the meaning of terms in a statute. Finally, in *Chisom v. Roemer* (1991: 2372), and *Bray v. Alexandria Women's Health Clinic* (1993), Scalia cites *Webster's Second New International Dictionary*, published in 1950, to review the meaning of terms found in a 1964 and 1871 statute, respectively.⁴ In these last cases, Scalia's dictionary usage narrows civil rights protections, while in *Smith*, the use of dictionary definitions defeats the application of a crime statute meant to address firearms. Overall, as some critics have noted, Scalia's dictionary use seems inconsistent; he often follows no clear logic when seeking to match a particular statute or term to a specific edition of a dictionary (Note 1994: 1448). As a result, the dictionary he selects may miss the particular or special use of a term that a statute invokes and that ordinary dictionary meanings miss; or that Scalia's approach may assume incorrectly that Congress intended a specific dictionary meaning for a term; or the dictionary edition that Scalia uses captures inadequately the meaning of a term in a statute, especially if the dictionary and the statute are from different years (Note 1994: 1442, 1448–49). Dictionary usage to supplement the plain meaning rule is fraught with inconsistencies, not the least of which is that a dictionary often offers several different definitions and usages for a word. This lack of one single, precise meaning for a term, as well as the choice of what dictionary to use when, as well as the decision to decide to even use a dictionary, gives Scalia significant discretion to clarify meaning in a way that matches his agenda.

A final technique that Scalia uses to assist clarifying the plain meaning of a statute is the "expressed meaning" or "clear statement" rule (Karkkainen 1994: 450). Under the clear statement rule, questions of ambiguity are resolved against some putative goals of the legislature unless the legislative statute in question clearly states that the goal or purpose was intended. In *United States v. Nordic Village, Inc.* (1992: 187), Scalia argues that committee reports may not be used to clarify the intent of laws and that waivers "of the Government's sovereign immunity, to be effective, must be 'unequivocally expressed.' " As a result, the government could not be sued to recover financial transfers in a bankruptcy proceeding. Similarly, in adjudicating the retroactivity of the 1991 Civil Rights Act to cases pending on appeal when the Act became law, Scalia's concurring opinion in *Landgraf v. USI Film Products* (1994: 266) mandated that a "clear statement" was necessary by Congress to indicate that they wished the act to apply retroactively. In the absence of a clear statement, the applicability of the act was narrowed.

Similar appeals to some version of a clear statement rule and rejection of the use of legislative history are offered in *United States v. R.L.C.* (1992: 594), *Kaiser Aluminum & Chemical Corporation v. Bonjorno* (1990: 841), and *Holmes v. Securities Investor Protection Corporation* (1992: 1327–28). In all of these cases, Scalia's use of the clear statement rule narrowed the scope of legislation.

Finally, in *E.E.O.C. v. Arabian American Oil Company* (1991: 1236–37), at issue was whether 1964 Civil Rights Act, Title VII employment discrimination provisions applied to a U.S. citizen working for an American company overseas. Scalia, while first citing then rejecting the *Chevron* principle that demands deference to administrative agencies, argues that absent a clear statement by Congress, U.S. statutes have no extraterritorial application. The result here is to prevent the extension of a civil rights protections.

Facially, Scalia's rules governing statutory interpretation might be summarized thus: the plain meaning of the text should govern a reading of a law. If a plain meaning is not discernible, one should follow the *Chevron* rule and defer to an administrative interpretation, if one exists, unless either a clear statement or a dictionary definition of words in a statute helps resolve the ambiguity. At no point is one permitted to consult legislative history or intent, including any assessment of committee reports, etc. However, this entire lattice for statutory construction is open to discretion, allowing ample room for policy and personal preferences to enter. First, as noted by Stephen Breyer, the import of what *Chevron* means is open to interpretation. Second, once *Chevron* rules have been invoked, Scalia himself acknowledges questions about how clear the language must be to be considered unambiguous, and this obviously gives the justice some room to apply discretionary criteria, such as when to invoke dictionaries, interpretation of administrative agencies, or other extratextual evidence to assist him. No clear mechanical or interpretive rule seems to back Scalia's employment of his methodology and, despite claims that he wants clear rules to govern interpretation (Brisbin 1992), what seems to be true is that Scalia's construction of statutes is influenced both by his policy preferences and by his ambivalent attitude towards Congress and legislative politics.

Scalia's opinions contain many examples of how he employs his interpretive techniques and rules of construction to favor policy outcomes he supports despite his general plea that Congress is the primary institution responsible for policy-making and that the courts ought to defer to legislatures. In *Rust v. Sullivan* (1991), Scalia joined Rehnquist's majority decision that upheld a regulation of the Secretary of Health and Human Services barring abortion counseling in federally funded Title X clinics. The Court claimed that the Secretary's regulations were made pursuant to 42 U.S.C. § § 300- 300a-6, which at 300a-4 1008 stated that "none of the funds appropriated under this subchapter shall be used in programming where abortion is a method of family planning."

In this case, Scalia was unwilling defer to Congress when it came to the political question of abortion counseling. Instead, Scalia was willing to second-guess Congress when there was no evidence presented that the legislation was the product of pressure politics. Additionally, while Scalia usually dissents from appeals to legislative history, here he was willing to join a decision that assumed or reconstructed a legislative history or intent when both were noted by the majority to be ambiguous (ibid.: 1767–1768). Scalia refused to follow his usual methodological rules or the usual canons of judicial interpretation and legislative deference that would assume that Congress was not seeking a constitutional challenge when it wrote this act.[5] Instead, Scalia acted in a contrary fashion in order to reach a constitutional issue on a policy that he felt strongly about. Similarly, in *Posters 'N' Things Ltd. v. United States* (1994: 555), and in an article addressing administrative rule-making (Scalia 1977: 39), Scalia cited legislative history to support his arguments.

Elsewhere, Scalia has again expressed skepticism towards ascertaining legislative intent, except when it seems to support a particular holding he endorses (Scalia 1982: 21). For example, in *Sable Communications v. F.C.C.* (1989), Scalia wrote a concurring opinion that relied in part on the use of legislative history to uphold the banning of "dial-a-porn" services over telephones (ibid.: 2840). In *Jett v. Dallas Independent School District* (1989), Scalia appeals to legislative intent in a concurring opinion (ibid.: 2730–31), holding that an individual who is allegedly victimized by a municipal employee's discrimination may not hold the municipality responsible for the discrimination. Here, Scalia uses legislative intent to indicate that Congress did not intend 42 U.S.C.A §§ 1981 and 1983 to apply to municipalities for employee violations of other employee rights. Moreover, in *Chisom v. Roemer* (1991), Scalia dissents from the majority opinion upholding the application of Section 2 of the 1965 Voting Rights Act, as amended. In his dissent, Scalia uses the legislative history of the act to show why Congress did not intend to apply the act to state judicial elections (ibid.: 2369).

Overall, Scalia's ambivalence towards the legislative decision-making process has led the justice to assert that it is not possible to ascertain a comprehensive legislative history. Consequently, this has moved the justice toward alternative means for interpreting statutes based on the plain English meaning of the words employed (Farber and Frickey 1991: 89–90).

Yet, despite claims by some observers that Scalia defers to Congress out of respect for it as the primary policy-making body representing majority factions (Brisbin 1992), many of his own opinions do not support these claims. Rather in them he repeatedly demonstrates an apparently contradictory commitment to deference to legislatures and a deep distrust for their politics. His distrust is the product of his belief that: (1) local legislatures and perhaps Congress are often captured by factions and interest group politics; or (2) legislative content and votes are not the product of rational deliberation by elected representatives, but are the product of staff or committee work. Hence, while some of Scalia's own scholarly writings advocate legislative deference and respect (ibid.: 5–7; Nagareda 1987), the justice's opinions also often reject an appeal to legislative intent as an unreliable means to interpret statutes. Overall, we are left with a record that shows Scalia's view of legislative politics as a process threatened by the evils of faction and interest that Madison feared and discussed in *Federalist* 10 and 51. We are also left with an interpretive strategy that seems to narrow the scope of legislative authority, except in cases where he seems to support the particular outcomes of the legislation.

Conclusion: Explaining Scalia's Interpretive Bias

Scalia's methods of statutory interpretation, including rejection of legislative history and the appeal to *Chevron* and the plain meaning of the text have found little support on the Supreme Court, with the notable exception of Justice Thomas.[6] Given Justice Breyer's criticism of Scalia's reading of *Chevron* and Breyer's reliance on legislative history in his lower court opinions (Gellhorn 1994: 20), Scalia and Breyer are likely to have numerous disagreements regarding the canons of statutory interpretation. Breyer's presence on the Court should provide David Souter additional support to combat Scalia's approach to interpretation.

Examination of Antonin Scalia's scholarly writings and judicial opinions suggests that Congress often loses (Stock 1990); critics are wrong, however, in asserting that Congress always loses. At times the justice seems willing to depart from some of his preferred rules of statutory construction. In general, he appears unwilling to defer to legislative bodies in questions of affirmative action and the protection of white males, property rights, campaign finance reform as it affects corporations, and in the authorization of abortion counseling in federally funded clinics. He seems content to defer in the areas of abortion regulation, tort liability for the press, the death penalty, practices of religious minorities, and political patronage. Scalia's own writings indicate that he is often suspicious of legislative integrity, and that suspicion or his interpretive methodology might explain this facially erratic pattern of legislative deference. Yet no clear rule or criterion in his decisions or writings has emerged to tell readers when judicial review is needed because the legislative process has malfunctioned. No discernible rule seems to exist to explain how clear language must be in order to be considered unambiguous, when or how a dictionary should be used, or what traditions or presumptions require a clear statement rule to be provided before tradition will be trumped by a statute.

While Scalia has provided a variety of legal precedents and rules that appear to construct a neutral statutory methodology, the employment of that methodology does not appear to be neutral. Scalia's record demonstrates use of a methodology that is policy-orientated, with legislative deference selectively employed, based on the policy areas in which the justice is willing to defer. Contrary to his claims and those of his scholarly observers, the justice does not utilize a consistently applied attitude and approach toward the legislative process or toward the use of legislative intent.

Is it imperative for Scalia or the judiciary in general to be consistent? While Scalia has indicated that legislatures "are subject to democratic checks upon their lawmaking," (Scalia 1989–90), and by implication, are not subject to the test of consistency, the "only checks on the arbitrariness of federal judges are the insistence upon consistency" and the application "to each case a system of abstract and entirely fictional categories . . . which are designed, if logically applied, to produce 'fair' or textually faithful re-

sults" (ibid.: 588–89). Scalia appears to agree with a long line of legal scholarship that the hallmark of judicial decision-making and the chief check
upon such abuses is the consistent application of neutral and general principles of law to particular cases (Wechsler 1959). Yet the Associate justice has
also echoed the well-known aphorism of Emerson's that "a foolish consistency is the hobgoblin of little minds" (Scalia 1989–90: 586). In some cases
a "sacrifice of consistency" is permitted if such consistency would produce
a result that is "simply wrong" (ibid.: 589).

The question is: how does Scalia know when the legislative process is or
is not tainted or "simply wrong results" would be produced by the application of consistency, justifying a departure from consistency? When is pressure politics really pressure politics and not simply the reasonable mobilization of coalitions, interests, or minorities to produce a majority (Van Horn
1989)? How does Scalia distinguish between good majority-building in legislatures that respond to the will of the electorate from catering to special
interests? No consistent rule or category is provided by the justice, despite
Scalia's claim that such categories are necessary to check the judiciary. This
absence of a rule, along with Scalia's erratic pattern of deference and second-guessing of legislatures leaves us with many questions about the consistency, methodology, and aims of his statutory construction, unless we assume that the justice's interpretive methodology is not neutral and instead
is guided by some substantive values that would tell him when deference is
demanded or not.

One possible set of values that may guide his interpretation of legislation
is his sympathy for executive over legislative power. As noted above, many
authors have recognized Scalia's support for strong executive power. The
separation of powers cases, *Mistretta v. United States* (1989), *Morrison v.
Olson* (1988), and *Synar v. United States* (1986), are instances in which
Scalia favored executive power and discretion over legislative control and
discretion. A dismissal of legislative history and a preference for a textualist
approach to reading statutes limits the deference one gives to Congress
and, thus, implicitly favors presidential or executive authority by giving the
latter more leeway to interpret statutes. Hence, one could explain many of
his decisions or departures from legislative deference by postulating that,
when congressional-legislative power comes into conflict with presidential-
executive power, Scalia will apply his methodology to favor the latter.
While this rule may explain many of the cases noted in this chapter, it can
not account for decisions where questions of conflict between congressional
and presidential power are not at issue. The issue of affirmative action, for
example, is not readily explained by this approach. In addition, cases such
as *Sable Communications v. F.C.C.* (1989), where the justice was willing to

defer to Congress and to the use of legislative intent, also make this claim difficult.

Another way to explain his decisions is to look at the policy areas where Scalia favors deference versus those where he does not. Such scrutiny might reveal a pattern of decisions or a political philosophy that guides his interpretive strategy. Given his willingness to defer to legislatures in the areas of the death penalty, religious expression, and tort liability for the press, and his unwillingness to defer in the areas of property rights, campaign finance reform as it affects corporations, and affirmative action as it affects white males, Scalia appears to endorse a specific conception of the political process that endorses an ideology sympathetic to classical Manchester Liberalism. Such an ideology, as originally articulated in nineteenth century England, emphasized limited government, faith in the marketplace, commitment to legalism, materialism, property rights, and enforcement of majoritarian morality as essential to the creation of free society (Dolbeare 1969: 16–24). It is possible (and not surprising) that either Scalia's (or any justice's or judge's) own political values influence how he uses his interpretive methodology, or his interpretive methodology is not neutral (Baum 1992: 144–58; Gadamer 1986: 289–305). The methodology may instead be governed by other values that indicate when he is willing to defer to congressional-legislative power. These values may include a rethinking of what the logic of the *Carolene Products* decision means (Ackerman 1985).

In light of the patterns evident in Scalia's judicial behavior, it is somewhat surprising that most of the scholarship on Scalia's rules of statutory construction has ignored the influence of his ideology on his decision-making and approach to the law. Scalia's claim that he uses a consistent methodology and his use of a methodology has in some cases improperly created the perception that he pursues neutral, principled decision-making.

Thus, whether it be Scalia's support of presidential power or his political values, scholars have been inaccurate in concluding that Scalia's jurisprudence is primarily methodologically driven, that his methodology is consistently applied, and that the values motivating his use of judicial review are significantly majoritarian. On the other hand, as many legal theorists have told us, there is an "open texture" to language and the law (Hart 1961: 120–132). This means that words have no finite and definitive meaning and that meanings are significantly determined by use and context. Moreover, the duty of congressional lawmakers is to make general policy statements, not write bills of attainder. General policy prescriptions are necessary so that the judiciary can engage in the process of interpretation that asks if a particular set of facts fits under a law. The point here is that many legal theorists have argued that mechanical jurisprudence, or simple application of the law to some facts, is impossible (Hart 1961; Dworkin 1978; Dworkin 1986), thus leaving room for a justice like Scalia to use some discretion to determine the meaning of laws and how they apply to concrete situations. In sum, Scalia, more than other justices states an aspiration for consistent principles and methodologies, but his interpretive strategies do not reflect this aspiration. In identifiable instances, Scalia manifests inconsistency that is produced by political or policy choices about how particular rules will be applied or invoked.

In assessing Justice Scalia, we actually see an interpretive strategy being used in conjunction with *Carolene Products* type claims to mask or reinforce his own political philosophy. If we assume that his jurisprudence is methodologically driven, or driven by some vision of separation of powers or American political institutionalism, Scalia's jurisprudence reveals an inconsistent use of legislative history and deference to legislative decision-making. If we assume that Scalia's jurisprudence is either consciously or unconsciously result-oriented and that willingness to use legislative intent or to defer to other branches is controlled by his political philosophy and policy preferences towards specific issues, then his writings and decisions reveal a profound commitment to the use of judicial power to serve specific policy goals he supports.

Such a hypothesis should not come as a surprise. In an address to a conference on federalism, Scalia cautioned conservatives to "keep in mind that the federal government is not bad but good. The trick is to use it wisely" (Scalia 1982a: 22). Clearly, Scalia's decisions seem to bear this caution in mind and reveal an attempt to use federal judicial power shrewdly to create a political process that nourishes policy preferences that the justice supports.

Notes

1. Compare this discussion about factions and the political process to similar views in his dissent in *Norman v. Reed* (1992: 711).

2. See "Economic Affairs as Human Affairs" (Scalia 1987) where he makes similar comments about the importance of private property to individual freedom.

3. Ibid., 1311, quoting *Webster's Ninth New Collegiate*.

4. Other cases where Scalia employs a dictionary to help interpret the plain meaning of a statute include *Hartford Fire Insurance Company v. California* (1993: 2901); *Austin v. United States* (1993: 2813); and *Deal v. United States* (1993: 1996).

5. See Blackmun's dissent in *Rust* (1991: 1778–1780) for development of this criticism.

6. For example, see *United States v. Alvarez-Sanchez* (1994: 327), where Thomas appears to adopt the plain meaning rule for interpreting statutes.

Chapter 4

The Institutions of American Government

In establishing their reputations on the Supreme Court, individual justices can become closely associated with specific legal theories or types of decisions. Justice William O. Douglas is remembered as a great civil libertarian because of his consistent support for individuals' rights. Justice Felix Frankfurter is recognized as "the Court's foremost advocate of judicial self-restraint in recent times" (Wasby 1988: 286). During the Rehnquist Court era, Chief Justice William Rehnquist established himself as "the Court's leading conservative" (Grossman and Wells 1988: 85), and Justices William Brennan and Thurgood Marshall were the "most liberal justices" on economic and civil liberties issues (Goldman 1987: 161). Among the other members of the Rehnquist Court, Justice Antonin Scalia attracted special notice from scholars and commentators for developing a distinctive role and reputation very quickly during his earliest terms on the high court. Scalia's approach to constitutional interpretation gave him a unique vision of the proper structure and distribution of authority for the American governmental system. As this chapter will discuss, Scalia's role as the defender of this vision not only isolated him from his colleagues in important cases but also produced contradictions in the consequences of his opinions.

Scalia's Uniqueness

Although Scalia is usually described as "very conservative" (Witt 1986: 149), his distinctiveness does not rest upon political conservatism. Justice Scalia is frequently labeled as "[a]n ideological conservative" (Grossman and Wells 1988: 85), he has nevertheless warned other conservatives against reflexively condemning the federal government. In a speech to the Federalist Society about political conservatives' penchant for criticizing the federal government, Scalia said, "I urge you, then—as Hamilton would have urged you—to keep in mind that the federal government is not bad but good. The trick is to use it wisely" (Scalia 1982a: 22). Moreover, Scalia's notable deviations from the Supreme Court's conservative bloc in selected civil liberties cases preclude him from sharing Chief Justice Rehnquist's and Justice Thomas's distinctive consistency in deciding cases as political conservatives. For example, Scalia joined the liberal justices in recognizing flag burning as a form of constitutionally protected political speech (*Texas v. Johnson* 1989), and he opposed mandatory drug testing for U.S. Customs Service employees (*National Treasury Employees Union v. Von Raab* 1989).

Scalia's uniqueness stems from his notable role as the Court's most consistent, forceful advocate of constitutional interpretation according to the original meaning intended by the framers. He does not use this approach exclusively or consistently, but he relies on this basis for interpretation more than other justices on the Court. Scalia's approach differs from that of Edwin Meese, the Reagan administration's visible and controversial defender of interpretation by original intent (Meese 1986), because Scalia recognizes that the theory has weaknesses and because he claimed that he would not always apply it, especially in regard to the Eighth Amendment. According to Scalia, originalism is "not without its warts. Its greatest defect, in my view, is the difficulty of applying it correctly" (Scalia 1989a: 856). Scalia also observed, "Having made that endorsement [of originalism], I hasten to confess that in a crunch I may prove a faint-hearted originalist. I cannot imagine myself, any more than any other federal judge, upholding a statute that imposes the punishment of flogging" (ibid.: 866). Scalia's textualist orientation reinforced his differences with Meese, the true believer in original intent, because Scalia believes in following the original *meaning* of the framers' words rather than engaging in a potentially fruitless search for the framers' precise intentions (Kannar 1990: 1307). Thus, to Scalia, as he said in his confirmation hearings, "[I]f somebody should discover the secret intent of the framers was quite different from what the words connote, it would not make any difference" (ibid.).

Usually, Scalia's textualist originalism leads him to agree with the opinions and outcomes supported by the Court's political conservatives. After all, some of his colleagues are willing to dabble in originalism when it advances their preferred outcomes and the application of original intent frequently produces narrower definitions of individuals' rights than those produced by the Warren and Burger Courts (Smith 1989b). For example, despite rejecting original intent as the guiding principle for constitutional interpretation (Marcotte 1987), Rehnquist has used originalism to justify his criticisms of the Supreme Court's decisions mandating strict separation of church and state. In a case in which the Court majority rejected the Alabama legislature's effort to bring sponsored prayer back into the public schools, Rehnquist wrote that "It would come as a shock to those who drafted the Bill of Rights . . . to learn that the Constitution, as construed by the majority [on the Supreme Court] prohibits the Alabama Legislature from 'endorsing' prayer" (*Wallace v. Jaffree* 1985: 113). Unlike his conservative colleagues, however, Scalia's adherence to textualism and originalism can lead him to support liberal case outcomes in some cases. In a case concerning the Confrontation Clause, Scalia lashed out at his conservative colleagues for ignoring the Constitution's text and intended meaning when issuing a policy-oriented decision to permit children who are victims of sex crimes to provide testimony through closed-circuit, one-way television broadcasts (*Maryland v. Craig* 1990). According to Scalia:

> Seldom has this Court failed so conspicuously to sustain a categorical guarantee of the Constitution against the tide of prevailing current opinion. The Sixth Amendment provides, with unmistakable clarity, that "[i]n all criminal prosecutions, the accused shall enjoy the right . . . to be confronted with the witnesses against him." (ibid.: 3171)

Scalia's interpretive approach also leads him to deviate from his usual conservative allies in other kinds of cases, including those concerning separation of powers and other issues regarding the institutions of American government.

All of the justices undoubtedly believe that their decisions preserve rather than threaten the constitutional governing system. Justices other than Scalia frequently base their opinions upon the maintenance of appropriate roles and authority for institutions of government. Examples are common in which other justices, both liberal and conservative, evince concern about maintaining the structure and authority of the country's governing institutions. Liberal Justice Brennan argued that the Supreme Court should not intrude upon congressional statutory authority to define the scope of habeas corpus:

> It is Congress and not this Court who is " 'responsible for defining the scope of the writ [of habeas corpus].' " . . . Yet the majority, whose Members often pride themselves on their reluctance to play an "activist" judicial role by infringing upon legislative prerogatives, does not hesitate today to dismantle Congress' extension of federal habeas to state prisoners. (*Butler v. McKellar* 1989: 1226–1227)

In the case of a conservative, Justice Anthony Kennedy criticized the Court majority for permitting a district judge to force a school district to increase taxes in order to fund a remedial school desegregation plan (*Missouri v. Jenkins* 1990: 1667): "Today's casual embrace of taxation imposed by the unelected, life-tenured federal judiciary disregards fundamental precepts for the democratic control of public institutions." By contrast, Scalia is unique in the tone and substance of his defense of governmental institutions. He may share the foregoing sentiments expressed by his colleagues, but he applies them more strictly and in different situations. As subsequent sections of this chapter will discuss, Scalia's strong views on separation of powers and the integrity of the judicial branch place him at odds with his colleagues on the Court. Moreover, Scalia's strident opinions continually warn his colleagues that they will cause serious harm to the governing system and the country if they do not heed him.

Because constitutional principles serve as a kind of civil religion for Americans, many commentators have used "the analogy of the Constitution to a sacred text [and] the Supreme Court to a holy institution" (Levinson 1988: 17). In applying the analogy to Justice Scalia's role on the Court, he can be viewed as a kind of "prophet." Religious literature refers to prophets "crying in the wilderness" as solitary voices instructing and warning the world about eternal truths (e.g., Matthew 3:3: "The voice of one crying in the wilderness, Prepare ye the way of the Lord, make his paths straight"; Isaiah 40: 3: "The voice of him that crieth in the wilderness, Prepare ye the way of the Lord, make straight in the desert a highway for our God"). Because of the dire warnings that he issues, Scalia's chosen approach for protecting governmental institutions has cast him in the role of the Supreme Court's "Prophet of Doom." However, as Scalia vigorously advances his views on the preservation of governmental institutions, he actually contributes to the very harms that he claims to find so disturbing. Because of his own actions, Scalia's warnings to the Court may inadvertently become self-fulfilling "prophecies."

Separation of Powers

In no area of law is Justice Scalia more deserving of the reputation as the Court's "Prophet of Doom" than in separation-of-powers jurisprudence. He is the solitary voice warning the other eight justices about the harms of blurring the boundaries between the branches of government. Even before he became a Supreme Court justice, Scalia had earned a reputation as an active advocate for the maintenance of clear lines of authority between

Congress and the Executive. In the mid-1970s, Scalia was the Assistant Attorney General in the Ford Administration who testified before Congress in opposition to the "legislative veto" (Craig 1988: 53–56). The legislative veto is the practice of Congress in which "[t]he president or some executive branch agency is granted authority to act in a given policy or administrative area, but with the stipulation that the subsequent resolution of one or both houses of Congress may overturn the executive action" (Ladd 1987: A33). In the characterization of Barbara Hinkson Craig, "Assistant Attorney General Scalia was a willing knight well prepared to ride into battle. . . . [The] feisty constitutional expert had no doubts in his own mind about the legislative veto's unconstitutionality, and no hesitancy in speaking his mind to anyone who would listen" (Craig 1988: 53). This description of Scalia's behavior early in his career could be applied with equal accuracy to Scalia's confidence in and assertiveness about his viewpoints as a Supreme Court justice.

As a law professor, Scalia wrote a law review article (Scalia 1979a), described by legal scholar James G. Wilson (1986a: 1200) as "one of his most influential," criticizing the legislative veto as a usurpation of executive power by Congress. Scalia subsequently authored the amicus brief opposing the constitutionality of the legislative veto that was submitted to the Supreme Court by the American Bar Association in *Immigration and Naturalization Service v. Chadha* (1983), the case in which the Supreme Court ultimately struck down the legislative device (Craig 1988: 185). The *Chadha* case concerned a provision of the Immigration and Nationality Act that authorized either house of Congress to invalidate, by resolution, the decisions of executive branch officials to allow particular deportable aliens to remain in the United States. Scalia was the driving force behind the ABA's amicus brief:

> Scalia had to mount a considerable effort to get the Bar Association to file a brief, and to file one that would accomplish his purpose—which was to present a strong argument for the Court's ruling as broadly as possible. It was fortunate for him that he first did not need to obtain a vote of approval from the House of Delegates. . . . If Scalia had to get a vote of approval from the entire membership, his goal might very well have been thwarted. (ibid.: 1985)

According to Barbara Hinkson Craig, his "talents as a skilled negotiator were put to their full test as he worked with [another attorney] who was more than a little resistant to attacking the veto as broadly as Scalia wished" (ibid.: 186).

Subsequently, as a judge on the U.S. Court of Appeals for the District of Columbia Circuit, Scalia wrote an article in which he emphasized the importance of separation of powers within the American governing system by emphasizing James Madison's well-known statements (Scalia 1983). According to Scalia:

> The federal prescription on the subject [of separation of powers] is not as wordy [as the Massachusetts Constitution]. . . . One should not think, however, that the principle was any less important to the federal framers. Madison said of it, in Federalist No. 47, that "no political truth is certainly of greater intrinsic value, or is stamped with the authority of more enlightened patrons of liberty." (ibid.: 881)

While serving as an appellate judge, Scalia sat on the three-judge district court panel that determined in *Synar v. United States* (D.D.C. 1986) that the Gramm-Rudman-Hollings Act for automatically cutting and balancing the federal budget was an unconstitutional infringement upon executive power. The Gramm-Rudman-Hollings Act provided for mandatory budget cuts whenever Congress and the President failed to meet a statutory schedule for reducing the federal deficit. The budget-cutting process within the act involved the preparation of a "sequestration order" by the comptroller general that mandated the required cuts. Scalia is widely rumored to have authored the unsigned, per curiam opinion that was subsequently affirmed by the Supreme Court's 1986 decision in *Bowsher v. Synar* (Wilson 1986a: 1201). Thus, as an assistant attorney general, law professor, and federal judge, Scalia played an important role in two historic separation-of-powers cases, *Chadha* and *Bowsher*. In both instances, the Supreme Court decided the cases in accordance with Scalia's restrictive views. In assessing his legal career, Justice Scalia commented that "[i]f there is anyone who, over the years, has had a greater interest in the subject of separation of powers, he does not come readily to mind" (Scalia 1988).

In *Chadha* and *Bowsher*, the majority of justices on the Supreme Court applied rigid, formalistic conceptions of separation-of-powers principles in order to strike down Congressional actions that infringed upon executive power. Chief Justice Burger wrote for the Court in *Chadha*:

> The Constitution sought to divide the delegated powers of the new Federal Government into three defined categories, Legislative, Executive, and Judicial, to assure, as nearly as possible, that each Branch of government would confine itself to its assigned responsibility. The hydraulic pressure inherent within each of the separate Branches to exceed the outer limits of its power, even to accomplish desirable objectives, must be resisted. (1983: 951)

In *Bowsher*, Burger's majority opinion reiterated the same themes about the importance of keeping the branches of government separate and preserving executive power (1986: 3192): "Congress in effect has retained control over the execution of the Act and has intruded into the executive function. The Constitution does not permit such an intrusion."

In two subsequent cases, *Morrison v. Olson* (1988) and *Mistretta v. United States* (1989), the entire Supreme Court, except for Justice Scalia, applied a more flexible conception of the appropriate distribution of functions and authority within the governing system. According to Louis Fisher (1990: 236), "[t]he Rehnquist Court appear[ed] to be moving back to a pragmatic reading of the separation [of powers] doctrine."

In *Morrison v. Olson*, a case that Scalia subsequently labeled as "perhaps the most significant separation[-]of[-]powers case in many years" (Scalia 1988), the Supreme Court considered a challenge to the constitutionality of the Ethics in Government Act, a statute that governed the selection and authority of independent counsels who investigate wrongdoing by officials in the executive branch. The statute was challenged on separation-of-powers grounds because the independent counsels were appointed by a special panel of judges, rather than by the President, and because executive branch officials have limited ability to remove the counsels "only for good cause, physical disability, mental incapacity, or any other condition that substantially impairs the performance of such independent counsel's duties," despite the fact that the investigation and prosecution of federal crimes are normally under the control of the President. In a 7-to-1 decision, which was argued prior to Justice Kennedy's confirmation and that had Scalia as the lone dissenter, the Supreme Court endorsed the constitutionality of the independent counsel law.

The majority opinion, written by Chief Justice Rehnquist, took a flexible, pragmatic approach to separation of powers by declaring that "we have never held that the Constitution requires that the three branches of Government 'operate with absolute independence' " (*Morrison v. Olson* 1988: 2620). Rehnquist concluded that involving the judiciary in the selection of independent counsels and limiting the executive's control over the counsels do not undermine the powers of the executive branch nor disrupt the proper balance between the branches.

Justice Scalia expressed his disagreement with the majority in the strongest possible terms. As is characteristic of Scalia's opinions, he eschewed diplomacy in explaining his opposition to the majority's views and instead forthrightly condemned his colleagues' reasoning. Justice Scalia's vigorous dissents in separation-of-powers cases are consistent with Michael Patrick King's observation that his "dedication to the doctrine of separation of powers may be his strongest present doctrinal commitment, aside from his rejection of affirmative action. Compromise of his principles on the basic structure of government under his view of the Constitution is unlikely" (1988: 67). For example, Scalia's *Morrison* dissent purported to highlight "[t]he utter incompatibility of the Court's approach with our constitutional traditions," and he condemned "the folly of the new system of standardless judicial allocation of powers we adopt today" (*Morrison v. Olson* 1988: 2628, 2631). His dissenting opinion concluded with a warning: "By its short-sighted action today, I fear the Court has permanently encumbered the Republic with an institution that will do it great harm" (ibid.: 2640).

Scalia adheres to a principled view of separation of powers in which the functions of the respective branches of government are neatly and firmly separated. According to Scalia, because prosecution is normally an executive function, investigation of criminal wrongdoing—including the appointment and removal of prosecutors—must be under the complete control of the President. He therefore viewed the independent counsel law, which was drafted and enacted by Congress, as constituting improper legislative interference with executive authority.

Unlike his colleagues on the Supreme Court, Scalia sees clearly defined separation-of-powers principles in the text of the Constitution and in the intentions of the framers. With respect to textualism, Scalia asserted, "As I described at the outset of this opinion, [the words of Article II] d[o] not mean *some of* the executive power, but *all of* the executive power [shall be vested in the President]" (ibid.: 2626). By contrast, some scholars have claimed that "the [separation-of-powers] doctrine can only be inferred from the structure of the [Constitution]" (Wilson 1986: 967–968). With respect to the Constitution's originally intended meaning, Scalia wrote "[The majority opinion] fails to explain why it is not true that—as the text of the Constitution seems to require, as the Founders seemed to expect, and as our past cases have uniformly assumed—all purely executive power must be under the control of the President" (*Morrison v. Olson* 1988: 2641).

Legal scholars agree with Scalia that the Supreme Court has failed to adhere to a consistent, clear separation-of-powers doctrine:

> Our separation of powers jurisprudence is abysmal because the Supreme Court has failed for over two hundred years of our history to develop a *law* of separation of powers. The Court has reached a collection of results in separation of powers cases—some sensible and pragmatic, others utterly asinine. But what the Court has undeniably failed to do through all of these cases is to develop a *law* of separation of powers, a body of principle and theory that is coherent and useful. (Elliot 1989: 507)

There are doubts, however, about whether the words and original intentions of the Framers dictate the rigid views espoused by Scalia. The pragmatic actions of government officials immediately after the Constitution was ratified cast doubt upon Scalia's view that the Framers intended to implement a rigid, clear principle of separation of powers. According to Gerhard Casper:

> The shaping of governmental structures began in earnest in 1789 and, of course, has not concluded to this date. Precedents were set by the President and Congress in response to complex problems as they occurred, and were influenced by earnest consideration of principles and practical considerations of state craft, but also, to be sure, by political considerations. (1989: 260)

Although the Watergate investigation illustrated the problems of permitting the President to investigate himself and his aides and, consequently, motivated Congress to enact the independent counsel law, Scalia has evinced little recognition of the practical lessons from Watergate, Iran-Contra, and other executive branch scandals. Instead, Scalia adheres to an idealized view of the American governing system in which the people, through their votes, can effectively redress wrongdoing in the executive branch. According to Scalia:

> Under our system of government, the primary check against prosecutorial abuse is a political one. The prosecutors who exercise this awesome discretion are selected and can be removed by a President, whom the people have trusted enough to elect. Moreover, when crimes are not investigated and prosecuted fairly, nonselectively, with a reasonable sense of proportion, the President pays the cost in political damage. (*Morrison v. Olson* 1988: 2638)

This view fails to recognize how the American governing system actually operates: "Justice Scalia erroneously presumes that the voters will always have access to information about presidential actions, despite the fact that executive officials can control the flow of information through their ability to (mis)classify documents as 'secret'" (Smith and Johnson 1989: 1122). This deficient practical assessment of how the government actually works extends to other implications from Scalia's approach. Richard Pierce notes that because of the growth and changes in the structure of the federal government, especially the reliance upon administrative agencies, "[i]f a majority of the Court were to accept Justice Scalia's strong version of separation of powers, the Court would confront a daunting task in restructuring the federal government" (1988: 5).

Scalia is willing to rely on some practical arguments about separation of powers. For example, Scalia argued in *Morrison* (1988: 2637–2640) that the appointment of a prosecutor to investigate a single person reduces the prosecutor's professional detachment and impartiality. However, he presents only those arguments that are consistent with the primacy of his rigid views on the clearly divided authority within the structure of American government. Peter Shane argued that Scalia's practical arguments in *Morrison* were "in fact, the most subtle and compelling" among those presented by the justices, but even this scholar ultimately concluded that Scalia's arguments "are not so weighty as to overcome the burdens of text and history in divining Congress's powers over government organization" (1989: 624–625).

In *Mistretta v. United States* (1989), the Supreme Court addressed the constitutionality of the United States Sentencing Commission, an independent body composed of three federal judges and four other presidential appointees responsible for establishing sentencing guidelines to be applied in federal criminal cases. Eight justices, in an opinion authored by Justice Harry Blackmun, endorsed the Sentencing Commission by applying a pragmatic conception of separation of powers. In determining that Congress can delegate power to other governmental entities, Justice Blackmun declared that "our jurisprudence has been driven by a practical understanding that in our increasingly complex society, replete with ever[-]changing and more technical problems, Congress simply cannot do its job absent an ability to delegate power under broad general directives" (*Mistretta v. United States* 1989: 654). The majority applied its self-declared "flexible understanding of separation of powers" (ibid.: 659) to find that "the 'practical consequences' of locating the Commission within the Judicial Branch pose no threat of undermining the integrity of the Judicial Branch or of expanding the powers of the Judiciary beyond constitutional bounds" (ibid.: 665).

Naturally, this flexible approach to separation of powers collided with Justice Scalia's strict views, so Scalia once again became a solitary dissenter warning the majority about the gravity of its error in endorsing the commission. Scalia bemoaned "the regrettable tendency of our recent separation-of-powers jurisprudence" to treat strict constitutional principles as flexible concepts and cautioned the majority that "we will live to regret it" (ibid.: 682). Scalia concluded with the dire prediction that the long-term consequences of the majority's approach to separation-of-powers jurisprudence "will be disastrous" (ibid.: 683).

Justice Scalia's long-standing devotion to separation of powers reflects the supreme importance he attributes to the issue. As Wilson (1986a: 967) observed, "Scalia endorsed James Madison's comment that the doctrine of separation of powers is more sacred than any other in the Constitution."

Why is it that Scalia issues harsh criticisms and dire warnings to his colleagues on the Court for deviating from his rigid views on separation of powers? Although it is true that Scalia's judicial opinions on the subject are primarily aimed at "enhanc[ing] executive control of administration" (Brisbin 1992: 109), a more fundamental concern motivates Scalia's interest in separation of powers. Fundamentally, Scalia sees individuals' personal rights and liberties as resting upon the preservation of clearly divided authority between the branches of government. As Justice Scalia explained in a televised panel discussion:

> The public generally, law students, and, I am sorry to say, most lawyers, regard separation-of-powers issues as dealing with a hyper-technical picky-picky portion of the Constitution. Of concern to politicians, perhaps, but of no real interest to the people. What the people care about, what affects them, is the Bill of Rights. . . . That is a *profoundly* mistaken view. . . . For the fact is, that it is the structure of government, its constitution, in the real sense of that word, that ultimately preserves or destroys freedom. The Bill of Rights is no more than ink on paper unless . . . it is addressed to a government which is so constituted that no part of it can obtain excessive power . . . (Scalia 1988)

Scalia also noted the importance of this underlying concern in his dissent in *Morrison v. Olson*: "While the separation of powers may prevent us from righting every wrong, it does so in order to ensure that we do not lose liberty" (ibid.). In Scalia's eyes, any deviations, no matter how minor or apparently inconsequential, from the strict boundaries that separate the authority and functions of the respective branches of government may eventually threaten individual liberty by placing too much power in a single branch of government.

In his public-speaking engagements, Justice Scalia likes to compare the many specific, but historically unfulfilled, individual rights guaranteed in the old constitution of the Union of Soviet Socialist Republics with the limited but effective rights contained in the American Bill of Rights. The Soviet Constitution contained specific guarantees about freedom of speech and thought, as well as rights to housing and employment. Free speech and political dissent, however, were seldom actually tolerated. Scalia makes this comparison to demonstrate that separated power within the governing structure rather than explicit constitutional guarantees actually ensures individual liberty (ibid.). Scalia also emphasizes that the original Constitution did not even contain a Bill of Rights to show that the framers felt that the structure of government provided the most important protection for individuals' rights. Thus, Scalia argues that the authors of the Constitution

acted first to design the structure of the governing system and initially presumed that they did not need a Bill of Rights because they believed that the
descriptive allocation of governmental authority would provide an adequate
basis for a stable, free society (ibid.).

Scalia recognizes that relatively few people appear to share his view that
strict separation of powers within the American governmental system is the
paramount value to be protected at all costs. He has noted that most people
do not recognize the importance of separation of powers in protecting liberty: "It is a lot easier to get a crowd to form behind a banner that reads
'Freedom of Speech or Death' than behind one that reads 'Bicameralism or
Fight.' But, in point of fact, as those Founders knew who spent four months
debating these issues, the latter goes much more to the heart of the matter"
(ibid.). Thus, it is understandable that Scalia used strong language as the
lone dissenter in the separation-of-powers cases. He apparently views himself as the sole guardian of the institutional structure of American government and, therefore, the single voice recognizing the potential threats to
individual liberty. In characterizing the foundation underlying the American democracy, Scalia has declared that "structure is destiny" (ibid.), and
the tone of his warnings to the other justices indicates that he sees the
country's future as a functioning democracy threatened by the majority's
Morrison and *Mistretta* separation-of-powers decisions.

Judicial Institutions

In his role as institutional guardian, Justice Scalia seeks to protect and preserve the judiciary as well as other governmental institutions. As in separation-of-powers cases, because his colleagues on the Court do not always
agree with his concerns about preserving the Supreme Court and the judiciary, Scalia serves as the "Prophet of Doom," issuing warnings about the
harms that will befall the judicial branch.

In his first major address to the American Bar Association after being
appointed to the Supreme Court, Justice Scalia expressed concern about
the "continuing deterioration" of the prestige of the federal courts (Taylor
1987: 1). Scalia described his aspirations as a law student to become a federal judge because the federal courts were the "forums for the big case"
(Hengstler 1987: 20). According to Scalia, the framers of the Constitution
intended the federal judiciary to be a "natural aristocracy . . . of ability
rather than wealth" (Taylor 1987: 1). In his eyes, however, the federal courts
have lost their appropriate stature because they are overloaded with too
many routine cases. From Scalia's perspective, it would not be fruitful to

address the federal courts' caseload problems by appointing new judges. In his view, an increase in the number of federal judges merely dilutes the prestige of judicial office and "aggravates the problem of [maintaining the courts' elite] image" (ibid.: 12). Scalia also opposed the proposal to create an "Intercircuit Tribunal," a high appellate court intended to assist the Supreme Court, because such a new court, according to Scalia, would "only exacerbate the systemic problems I have been discussing" (Hengstler 1987: 20). In opposing the proposed court, Scalia disagreed with Chief Justice Rehnquist, who had endorsed the proposal the previous year. Because, in Scalia's words, "I wanted to be a judge, not a case processor" (Taylor 1987: 12), he proposed the creation of specialized courts "for large categories of high-volume, relatively routine cases—Social Security disability cases, for example, and freedom-of-information actions—to be disposed of with finality before an administrative law judge, providing appeal to the courts on issues of law only if the ALJ's decision is reversed by the agency" (Hengstler 1987: 20).

Scalia's concerns about "preserv[ing] the essence of a valuable institution" (Taylor 1987: 12) are shared by many other commentators who note that the Supreme Court and other federal courts have become overburdened by a continuing flood of litigation (Chemerinsky and Kramer 1990; Robel 1990). Like Scalia, others have concluded that, in the words of Howard Ball (1987: 124), "[s]ooner or later, the justices of the Supreme Court must come to grips with the causes of the caseload increase and devise new ways to deal with this major problem." Scalia's concerns have been reflected in his case opinions. For example, Scalia referred explicitly to the risk of encouraging more litigants to file legal actions in criticizing the majority's recognition of public employees' constitutional right to be free from employment discrimination because of their political party affiliations (*Rutan v. Republican Party of Illinois* 1990). Scalia concluded that "[w]hen the courts are flooded with litigation under the most unmanageable of standards . . . brought by that most persistent and tenacious of suitors (the disappointed office-seeker) we may be moved to reconsider our intrusion into this entire field" (ibid.: 2758–59).

The difficult question, of course, is what to do about the burden upon the Supreme Court and other federal courts. Scalia's proposed remedy, namely, limiting access to the federal courts, reflects his conception of the federal judiciary as an elite institution whose resources and attention are reserved for "important" issues. His rejection of proposals to increase the number of federal judges is similarly based upon his goal of preserving an elite institution, but one can seriously question whether Scalia is accurate in characterizing 750 federal judges out of more than 650,000 lawyers in the late 1980s as really any less elite than the 300 federal judges out of only 285,000 lawyers in 1960 (Hengstler 1987: 20; Stumpf 1988: 237).

In addition to his concerns about rising caseloads and the preservation of the judiciary's elite status, Scalia has warned the other justices against involving the Supreme Court inappropriately in issues that are not suitable for judicial resolution. Scalia vigorously disagreed with all of his colleagues about the Supreme Court's actions in several important cases and resorted to dire warnings and sarcastic attacks to convey the stridency of his views about the preservation of the Court.

In the controversial case of *Webster v. Reproductive Health Services* (1989), a slim five-member majority approved Missouri's regulations restricting abortions. Scalia's scathing concurring opinion in the case condemned both his allies and opponents on the abortion issue. In a sarcastic tone, Scalia attacked the other members of the majority for failing forthrightly to overturn *Roe v. Wade* (1973):

> The outcome of today's case will doubtless be heralded as a triumph of judicial statesmanship. It is not that, unless, it is statesman-like to needlessly prolong the Court's self-awarded sovereignty over a field where it has little proper business since the answers to most cruel questions posed are political not juridical—a sovereignty which therefore quite properly, but to the great damage of the Court, makes it the object of the sort of organized public pressure that political institutions in a democracy ought to receive (*Webster* 1989: 3064).

In his self-styled prophetic role as institutional guardian, Scalia predicted "great damage to the Court" from a continuation of "another term with carts full of mail from the public, and streets full of demonstrators, urging us—their unelected and life-tenured judges who have been awarded those extraordinary, undemocratic characteristics precisely in order that we might follow the law despite the popular will—to follow the popular will" (ibid.: 3064–3065).

What precisely is the harm that Scalia sees when citizens send letters to the justices and carry signs in front of the Supreme Court? There is no doubt that Scalia, who proved to scholars from his very first term that he was "a person with strong views" and "a justice confident in his ability" (Rubin and Melone 1988: 99) would never admit, let alone agree, that public lobbying affects justices' decisions. Retired Justice Lewis Powell has confirmed that communications from the public have little effect upon the justices. According to Powell, "if you are a federal judge appointed for life, you are not likely to be influenced by people marching around the court" (Sanders 1990: 13). Powell disagrees with Scalia about the detrimental implications of such public activity: "Frequently, there are demonstrations around the court. In our democratic system, that is a plus" (ibid.). When asked during a public lecture whether the justices are affected by people demonstrating outside the Court about the abortion issue, Scalia replied, "[o]ne must hope not and I think not" (Myers 1989: C2). Thus, the harm to the Supreme Court, according to Scalia, is not that judicial decisions will be affected, but rather that the Supreme Court's *image* will be tarnished. As Scalia declared in the abortion case: "Alone sufficient to justify a broad holding is the fact that our retaining control, through *Roe*, of what I believe to be, and many of our citizens recognize to be, a political issue, continuously distorts the public perception of the role of this Court" (*Webster v. Reproductive Health Services* 1989: 3065).

The intensity of Scalia's tone and his isolation from his colleagues increased in the 1990 "right-to-die" case, *Cruzan v. Missouri*, in which the Supreme Court considered whether parents could disconnect life-support systems from their daughter who was in a persistent vegetative state after an automobile accident. In a 5-to-4 decision, in which Scalia concurred "with evident reluctance." (Greenhouse 1990a: A19), the majority prevented the parents from discontinuing life-sustaining care because there was a lack of clear evidence about what the daughter would have wanted them to do.

Eight justices, including four in the majority and the four dissenters, found that the Fourteenth Amendment's protection of "liberty" contains a constitutional right to avoid unwanted medical treatment. Justice Scalia, however, in a concurring opinion characterized by the *New York Times* as "the most bitter in tone" (ibid.: A19), warned his colleagues that they were doing great damage to the institution of the Supreme Court: "I would have preferred that we announce, clearly and promptly, that the Federal courts have no business in this field. . . . This Court need not, and has no authority to, inject itself into every field of human activity where irrationality and oppression may theoretically occur, and if it tries to do so it will destroy itself" (*Cruzan v. Missouri* 1990: 2863).

Scalia did not specify how the Supreme Court will be "destroy[ed]," but the predicted harm to the Court presumably stems from the deterioration of the Court's judicial image as a result of improper participation in political disputes. Scalia appears to be concerned about protecting the Supreme Court's "legitimacy" as a judicial institution.

The term "legitimacy" is utilized for several concepts that are applied by scholars to the judiciary (Hyde 1983). For example, in the process of deciding that statutes or executive actions are constitutional, the Supreme Court, through its endorsement, is regarded as providing "legitimacy" for the actions of other governmental actors. According to Robert Dahl (1981: 161), "[o]rdinarily the main contribution of the Court is to confer legality and constitutionality on the fundamental policies of the successful [national political] coalition [in Congress and the White House]." Alternatively, "legitimacy" may be used as an evaluative statement in regard to the propriety of the Supreme Court's making a particular decision. In this sense, legitimacy refers to the judiciary's constitutional authority to undertake specific actions (Smith 1993a: 20). Scalia's concerns about the image of the Supreme Court represent a third concept of "legitimacy" which involves the public's *beliefs* about the appropriateness of judicial actions—beliefs that can affect both the public acceptance and implementation of court decisions. Thus, Scalia seeks to maintain the Court's image as a legitimate (i.e., judicial rather than political) institution to preserve the Court's effectiveness in issuing enforceable legal decisions. As Joel Grossman and Richard Wells (1988: 11) summarized the view that Scalia apparently shares, "The legitimacy of courts rests in their fidelity to the law and its enforcement. . . . If courts do not preserve their distinctiveness from other political bodies, if they cease being 'courts,' then their claim to legitimacy—and their power—will erode."

Although recent scholarship casts doubt upon the argument that the Supreme Court's power is threatened by public opposition to unpopular judicial decisions (Lasser 1988), it is generally accepted that judicial effectiveness depends upon public acceptance of courts as legal institutions. If the public and other governmental actors do not accept judicial decisions as legally binding, then there may be widespread resistance to such decisions, accompanied by a corresponding loss of stability for society. According to Gregory Caldeira (1986: 1209), "[t]he lack of any formal connection to the electorate and its rather demonstrable vulnerability before the president and Congress mean that the United States Supreme Court must depend to an extraordinary extent on the confidence, or at least the acquiescence, of the public." Thus, the justices must take care to insure that their decisions are developed, presented, and perceived as legal rather than political pronouncements. As Justice Felix Frankfurter once wrote, "[t]he [Supreme] Court's authority—possessed of neither the purse nor the sword—ultimately rests on sustained public confidence in its moral sanction" (*Baker v. Carr* 1962: 267). Justices other than Scalia are cognizant of the fact that, in Justice Blackmun's words, "[t]he legitimacy of the Judicial Branch ultimately depends on its reputation for impartiality and nonpartisanship" (*Mistretta v. United States* 1989: 672–673), but Scalia has assumed the most extreme stance for identifying threats to the Court's image and for issuing dire predictions about the detrimental consequences of recent decisions.

Self-Fulfilling Prophecies

Justice Scalia's fundamental disagreements with his colleagues about separation of powers are motivated by Scalia's desire to preserve the structure of government in order to protect individual rights. In the separation-of-powers cases, Scalia was a lonely, vocal dissenter. Did these decisions generate the "great harm" and "disastrous" consequences for individual rights predicted by Scalia?

As a result of the Supreme Court's decisions in *Morrison* and *Mistretta*, a relatively small number of executive branch officials were investigated and prosecuted by independent counsels, and all persons convicted of federal crimes committed after November 1, 1987, have been subject to the sentencing guidelines developed by the Sentencing Commission. None of these individuals suffered any formal loss of the full panoply of constitutional rights guaranteed to criminal defendants by the Bill of Rights. If these Supreme Court decisions have, as Scalia predicted, diminished individual rights by improperly increasing the power of specific officials within the federal government, then the extent of that harm has proved impossible to measure, nor can we conclude that these decisions have broad detrimental consequences. Because it is difficult to identify a specific reduction in individual liberty that resulted from these separation-of-powers cases, Scalia's warnings and dire predictions apparently concern a generalized loss of liberty which *may* eventually emerge from the evolution of developments which *could* follow from these initial deviations from strict separation-of-powers principles. In other words, Scalia's emphasis on fidelity to an abstract theory of separation of powers leads him to fear and decry the hypothetical long-term consequences of even minor violations of that theory since he can point to no specific reduction in liberty from the Court's failure to adopt his view. In his views concerning affirmative action, Scalia has been characterized as placing "theory above history and context" (Wilson 1986a: 1172–1173). In the separation-of-powers cases, Scalia's academic approach similarly emphasizes theoretical potential harms to liberty rather than immediate, identifiable consequences for individuals' rights.

Although Scalia's predicted consequences of the Supreme Court's recent separation-of-powers jurisprudence have not come to fruition, contemporary Supreme Court decisions addressing issues other than separation of powers have significantly affected individual rights. Commentators have raised the question whether the Rehnquist Court initiated "a war on individual rights" (Epstein 1990: A14) because the scope of constitutional protections for individuals was narrowed in many case decisions (see Decker 1992; Domino 1993; Kairys 1993). As indicated by the discussion elsewhere in this book analyzing civil liberties decisions, Justice Scalia, who raised concerns about preserving individual liberty in the separation-of-powers context, has been an active participant in many recent cases limiting the scope of specific individual rights.

In actuality, Scalia's prediction about the harms to individual rights is coming true, but it is due to conscious decisions by politically conservative justices rather than separation-of-powers opinions. It might seem a bit unfair to accuse Scalia of participating in a "self-fulfilling prophecy" based upon his participation in these conservative civil liberties decisions narrowing the scope of individual rights, since Scalia apparently believes that previous Court majorities improperly expanded the scope of those rights. In a specific category of cases, Scalia's twin goals concerning separation of powers and the institution of the judiciary clearly conflict. In these decisions, which affect litigants' access to the courts, Scalia's efforts to protect the judiciary lead him to harm the very individual rights that motivate his concerns about separation of powers. Thus, in serving as institutional guardian for the courts, Scalia contributes to the fulfillment of his own dire warnings about the ultimate harms of separation-of-powers cases namely, a diminution of individual liberty.

Justice Scalia's primary complaint about the current deterioration of the institution of the judiciary focuses on the excessive caseload burdening the federal courts. To remedy this malady and simultaneously increase the federal judiciary's elite status, Scalia proposed reducing the number and kinds of cases permitted to be filed in the federal courts. Scalia emphasized this goal of limiting access to the judicial system long before he was appointed to the Supreme Court. As an appellate judge, he published an article advocating increased attention to the concept of "standing" as a means of reducing the number of cases entering the court system (Scalia 1983). In Scalia's words:

> My thesis is that the judicial doctrine of standing is a crucial and inseparable element of that principle, whose disregard will inevitably produce—as it has during the past few decades—an overjudicialization of the processes of self-governance. More specifically, I suggest that courts need to accord greater weight than they have in recent times to the traditional requirement that the plaintiff's alleged injury be a particularized one, which sets him apart from the citizenry at large. (ibid.: 881–882)

As a judge on the District of Columbia Circuit Court of Appeals, Scalia consistently utilized procedural grounds to deny access to the courts by individuals seeking to pursue constitutional claims. According to Wilson:

Judge Scalia has been particularly adept at invoking procedural defenses to constitutional claims. As noted above, he ruled against sixteen out of seventeen civil plaintiffs who claimed their constitutional rights had been violated. He decided twelve of those cases on procedural grounds, ruling primarily in favor of the plaintiff only once. (1986b: 1181)

As a justice, Scalia has written or joined several opinions that advocate restricted access to the courts for individuals seeking to assert constitutional claims. For example, in *Lorance v. AT&T Technologies* (1989), Scalia wrote the opinion for the five-member majority that prevented female employees from challenging a discriminatory seniority system. In *Duckworth v. Eagan* (1989), a decision that permits police officers to deviate from traditional *Miranda* warnings in informing suspects of their rights, Scalia joined a concurring opinion by Justice O'Connor which advocated preclusion of *Miranda* claims from federal habeas corpus actions. The net effect of this argument, if it is ever adopted by a majority on the Court, would be to prevent petitioners from gaining entry into federal court if a state appellate court already considered the *Miranda* issue. Scalia has also supported successful efforts to alter habeas corpus rules in order to block death row inmates' access to federal judicial review (e.g., *McCleskey v. Zant* 1991; *Coleman v. Thompson* 1991; *Herrera v. Collins* 1993).

By seeking to prevent or to hinder certain litigants from filing effective claims in federal courts, Scalia attempts to reduce the burden upon the federal judiciary. Outright denial of access to the federal courts, as in *Lorance*, obviously has a direct effect upon individuals' ability to gain judicial protection for their rights. Advocacy of limiting judicial access to an initial review in state courts, as in *Duckworth*, raises questions about the adequacy of state court review, especially since judges in more than thirty states are elected officials whose positions are at risk if they displease the public with controversial decisions favoring individuals' rights (Baum 1990: 101–102). Possibly the claims of powerless or despised individuals, such as political minorities and criminal defendants, receive fairer consideration by appointed federal judges whose protected tenure was designed to insulate them from public pressure. As Justice Stevens noted in one dissent, "the success rate [during federal collateral review of petitioners' claims] in capital cases ranged from [sixty percent] to [seventy percent]," thus indicating that prior direct appellate reviews in state courts did not adequately detect errors (*Murray v. Giarratano* 1989: 2779).

The refusal by Scalia and the other conservative justices to give retroactive application to Supreme Court decisions, especially in capital cases in which a constitutional rights violation was acknowledged, clearly places the preservation of the judicial system above the protection of individuals' constitutional rights. In *Butler v. McKellar* (1989), for example, Scalia joined an opinion denying retroactive application to a decision that effectively acknowledged that Butler's rights were violated when police questioned him in jail without his attorney present. Thus, Butler was barred from asking a federal court to enforce his rights and order a new trial. According to a *Washington Post* investigation, however, Butler was a mentally retarded man who confessed to a crime while unrepresented by counsel during a jailhouse interrogation and who ended up on death row despite physical evidence, which his inexperienced attorney never presented in court, indicated that he probably did not commit the rape-murder (Marcus 1990: 11–12). Thus, the Rehnquist Court's trend, supported by Scalia, of limiting access to federal courts appeared to consign an innocent man to execution despite the Supreme Court's acknowledgement that his constitutional rights were violated during police questioning.

Justice Scalia suggested utilizing specialized courts to dispose of routine cases, such as Social Security disability and Freedom of Information Act claims, in order to reduce the burden on the federal courts (Taylor 1987). Specialization can, however, create risks that individual claims do not receive adequate consideration because the review process can become excessively routinized. Social Security disability claimants, in particular, have already been victimized by political policy decisions and by bureaucratic pressures upon Administrative Law Judges (ALJ) designed to limit the recognition of valid claims. For example, the Reagan administration arbitrarily cut benefits from hundreds of thousands of disability benefit recipients and then resisted judicial orders to reinstate the beneficiaries (see Cofer 1985; Mezey 1988). Although evidence shows that the review process for Social Security disability claims in many federal courts is routinized and inadequate (Smith 1988), access to the judiciary permits review by detached judges outside of the Social Security bureaucracy. Because some federal judicial officers consciously combat the tendency toward routinized decision-making in such cases (Smith 1990: 97), the continued availability of federal judicial review provides the only possibility for gaining dispassionate considered judgments about claims that have been rejected by the executive branch. Scalia's proposed reduction in access to the federal courts would adversely affect the poor claimants who need disability payments to support their families when they are unable to work.

In sum, Justice Scalia's actions and proposals for preserving the institution of the judiciary contribute to a diminution of the protection of the very individual rights that he so stridently seeks to protect in his separation-of-powers jurisprudence.

The Institution of the Supreme Court

The dire warnings contained in Justice Scalia's opinions as the sole dissenter in separation-of-powers cases comport with Scalia's characteristically strident tone in other opinions in which he disagrees with his colleagues. Some justices appear to recognize the complexity of issues as they ponder thoughtfully the difficult questions that confront the Supreme Court. For example, in *Mistretta*, Justice Blackmun demonstrated that he recognized and was troubled by the potential problems that could develop from involving federal judges in activities outside of traditional adjudication:

> We are somewhat more troubled by petitioner's argument that the Judiciary's entanglement in the political work of the Commission undermines public confidence in the disinterestedness of the Judicial Branch. . . . Although it is a judgment that is not without difficulty, we conclude that the participation of federal judges on the Sentencing Commission does not threaten, either in fact or in appearance, the impartiality of the Judicial Branch. (*Mistretta v. United States* 1989: 672–673)

Scalia's opinions, by contrast, evince the consistent confidence and self-righteousness of a "prophet" who possesses a clear, fixed vision of how cases should be decided. As he advocates this clear vision, Scalia's strident tone and concomitant penchant for attacking and condemning colleagues with whom he disagrees may ultimately undermine his goal of preserving the institutional image of the Supreme Court.

Because the justices must work together in deciding cases, the Supreme Court's decision-making process requires collegiality. The justices must maintain good relationships with each other in order to discuss opinions and form stable majorities to resolve the pressing issues presented to the high court:

> [T]here is . . . a critical group element to the Court's decision making. Part of the decisional process occurs in the group settings of oral argument and the Court's conferences. Further, justices have incentives to interact and work together on decisions outside of conference. The shared goal of seeking majority approval for an opinion in each case often requires interaction. The desire to obtain as much consensus as possible gives justices further reason to work together to reach agreement on outcomes and opinions. (Baum 1989: 149)

Contrary as it is to the conduct and manner that foster the Court's decision-making processes, Justice Scalia's forceful behavior may affect his relationships with other justices and thereby disrupt the collegial working environment on the Supreme Court.

The pessimistic prophetic language used by Justice Scalia in his efforts to serve as the guardian of American governmental institutions effectively chastises his colleagues for failing to accept his vision of harms to the governing system. Scalia's declarations that his colleagues' separation-of-powers decisions are "disastrous" and "utter[ly] incompatib[le] . . . with our constitutional traditions" are matched by critical language occasionally employed by other justices in specific dissenting opinions.[1] Over time, the repetitiveness and extremism of Scalia's complaints, when coupled with his uniquely harsh condemnations of all eight of his colleagues, such as his prediction that the other eight justices will "destroy" the Supreme Court by deciding complex moral issues (*Cruzan*: 2863), can irritate and alienate the other justices.

Greater risks arise from Scalia's characteristically strident tone when he applies his criticisms to individual colleagues rather than to the Supreme Court as a whole. In the controversial abortion case, *Webster v. Reproductive Health Services*, Scalia not only attacked his allies in the majority for their faint-hearted failure to overturn *Roe v. Wade*, he specifically declared that Justice O'Connor's concurring opinion "cannot be taken seriously" (*Webster* 1989: 3064). In *Holland v. Illinois* (1990), a decision rejecting a claim of racial discrimination in jury selection, Justice Scalia sarcastically attacked Justice Marshall for discussing discrimination issues: "Justice Marshall's dissent rolls out the ultimate weapon, the accusation of insensitivity to racial discrimination—which will lose its intimidating effect if it continues to be fired so randomly" (*Holland* 1990: 810). His accusation that Justice Marshall exaggerates the risks of discrimination and has done so in other cases is one of the most pointed personal attacks to appear in recent Supreme Court opinions.

One of Justice Scalia's foremost goals is to protect the institution of the judiciary, especially the Supreme Court. However, by employing strident language and personal attacks in his judicial opinions, Scalia may harm interpersonal relationships within the Court. As Lawrence Baum (1989: 156) notes, cordial relationships among the justices provide significant benefits for the Court's decision-making capabilities:

> Personal relations [among the justices] also can affect the decisional process. A Court in which conflicts are kept under control will be able to maximize consensus in decisions, because members work easily with each other and are relatively willing to compromise. Such a Court also may function more efficiently, because good interpersonal relations speed the process of reaching decisions and resolving internal problems.

Despite the creation of rituals designed to maintain cordial relations, such as each justice shaking hands with all of the other justices prior to conferences, personal conflicts between justices can develop. The sharp language in Justice Scalia's opinions has contributed to one commentator's characterization of the current Supreme Court era as the "season of snarling justices" because "[o]pinions of the last two years contain some of the most vituperative attacks on other justices in [C]ourt history" (Taylor 1990: A11).

Scalia's aggressive behavior during oral arguments may exacerbate any frictions caused by his caustic opinions. Justice Blackmun revealed in an interview that:

[Justice Scalia] is and always will be the professor at work. . . . He asks far too many questions, and he takes over the whole argument of the counsel, he will argue with counsel. . . . Even [Justice O'Connor], who asks a lot of questions, a couple of times gets exasperated when [Scalia] interrupts her line of inquiry and goes off on his own. She throws her pencil down and [says,] "umh, umh." (Taylor 1988: B6)

Chief Justice Rehnquist has had to interrupt questioning from the bench in order to prevent Scalia from monopolizing the entire time-period allotted for oral argument. According to David O'Brien (1990: 274), "During one of Scalia's lengthy questioning of an attorney, Rehnquist finally interrupted to tell the attorney, 'You have fifteen minutes remaining. I hope when you're given the opportunity to do so, you'll address some of your remarks to the question on which the Court voted to grant certiorari.'" On another occasion, "Chief Justice William Rehnquist was so exasperated by Scalia's rudeness during oral argument of a death penalty case . . . that he scolded the justice in public. . . . [A] scowling Rehnquist leaned over and shook his finger at Scalia while gesturing with his other hand at Kennedy [to continue questioning the attorneys]" ("Rude Robes" 1992: 5). O'Brien (1990: 274), who is personally acquainted with justices on the Rehnquist Court, acknowledges that "some justices . . . find [Scalia's outspokenness to be] irritating."

Justices are reluctant to reveal the inner workings of the Supreme Court, let alone publicly reveal any interpersonal problems, so Scalia's precise impact upon collegiality will never be known. It appears that Scalia's aggressiveness, sarcasm, and stridency have diminished his ability to persuade other justices to join in his opinions (Smith 1993b). Because the justices are human beings whose emotions and attitudes affect their decisions, Scalia's provocative tone creates risks that he will offend, alienate, and generate visible conflicts with his colleagues and thereby undermine one of his most valued objectives, namely the protection of the institution and image of the Supreme Court.

Justice Scalia's concerns about preserving the institution of the Supreme Court emphasize the protection of the Court's image and legitimacy in the eyes of the public. The strident tone of his opinions, however, may directly undermine this goal. When Scalia writes such things as "[t]his Court need not, and has no authority to, inject itself into every field of human activity where irrationality and oppression may theoretically occur, and if it tries to do so it will destroy itself" (*Cruzan v. Missouri* 1990: 2863), his warning to the other justices directly calls into question the legitimacy of the Supreme Court's decisions on moral issues such as the "right to die" and abortion. By forthrightly and combatively attacking the legitimacy of Supreme Court actions, Scalia himself fans the very flames that he fears might destroy the Supreme Court's image as a neutral legal institution. Scalia's strident tone and personal attacks on other justices, regardless of his opinions' substantive content, may, through their extreme style, undercut the justices' image as thoughtful, wise decision-makers. As Stuart Taylor, the long-time correspondent at the Supreme Court for the *New York Times*, observed (1990: A11):

> [T]here is a serious cost to public brawling on the bench: The more the justices question each other's basic common sense and good faith, the more they may deplete the reservoir of popular good will that is so essential to their singular role in American life. They might eventually find their rulings dismissed as the work of unelected, unprincipled politicians.
>
> That would be a shame, because public respect for the [C]ourt—based partly on ignorance and partly on myth—is fundamentally well-placed. The justices' constitutional interpretations owe more to political ideologies than they pretend. But far more than the Congress, far more than any recent president, justices reach decisions by searching their consciences, carefully sifting facts and law, trying to do right as they see the right. . . . Inflammatory, personal attacks diminish [the Court's integrity].

Conclusion

Justice Scalia has developed a clear, if not widely recognized, role in the Supreme Court as the self-anointed guardian of American governmental institutions. His opinions in separation-of-powers cases and his evident interest in protecting the institution of the judiciary reflect his penchant for defending government institutions in accordance with his rigid views about the dictates of the Constitution's text and original meaning. The tone and substance of his opinions serve to undermine the very goals that he claims to hold so dear. His judicial decisions on civil rights and liberties and his efforts to limit access to the court system effectively diminish the protection of individual liberty, the very goal that underlies his separation-of-powers jurisprudence. The strident tone of his opinions may tarnish both the collegiality and legitimacy of the Supreme Court and thereby undercut his efforts to preserve the Court as an elite, revered institution. Thus, his behavior and tone lead him to fulfill unwittingly the dire prophecies about threats to governmental institutions that he so loudly trumpets in his ominous warnings to the other justices.

Notes

1. For example, after the Supreme Court's conservative bloc altered a long-standing precedent affecting employment discrimination litigation, Justice Blackmun attacked the majority with the chilling comment that "[o]ne wonders whether the majority still believes that race discrimination—or, more accurately, race discrimination against nonwhites—is a problem in our society, or even remembers that it ever was." *Wards Cove Packing Co. v. Atonio*, 109 S. Ct. 2115, 2136 (1989) (Blackmun, J., dissenting).

Chapter 5

Freedom of Religion

The First Amendment's protections for freedom of religion provide the quintessential context for the fulfillment of the Supreme Court's image as the institutional protector of political minorities. The constitutional protection of free exercise of religion and prohibition against an establishment of religion are intended to prevent a tyranny of the majority from crushing the religious freedom of small and large minority sects within American society. Because religious freedom rights are the very first rights enunciated in the First Amendment to the Constitution, a widespread presumption exists that these rights embody values of the highest importance to the authors of the Bill of Rights (Schultz 1994a). Although the Supreme Court did not actively apply and protect these rights for most of American history, since the mid-twentieth century the justices have regularly invalidated governmental practices and statutes that, according to their interpretations of the First Amendment, collided with the constitutional protection for religious freedom (Abraham 1988). American history has amply demonstrated the risks to minority religions if majoritarian tyranny is left unchecked. Mormons, Jehovah's Witnesses, and other members of minority sects have been ostracized, punished, and even physically attacked for their practices and beliefs when the government—and the courts—have followed majoritarian preferences instead of protecting religious rights (e.g., Irons 1988).

Justice Scalia's opinions in cases concerning freedom of religion illustrate his interpretive approach and, moreover, what we have labeled his post-*Carolene Products* jurisprudence. Scalia has not only been outspoken in his advocacy of doctrinal change with respect to religious freedom, he has actually led the Court in a new direction with respect to free-exercise jurisprudence. As this chapter will demonstrate, Scalia's approach to religious freedom is one that defers to political majorities at the expense of minority religious interests. Rather than closely scrutinizing governmental actions

105

that implicate religious freedom, as most justices have done since the 1940s in accordance with Justice Stone's footnote four from *Carolene Products*, Scalia has advocated deference to governmental and majoritarian interests as a means to redefine First Amendment jurisprudence and judicial policies.

The Supreme Court Context

By the time of Scalia's appointment to the Supreme Court in 1986, the high court had interpreted the First Amendment's religion clauses expansively to limit governmental policies and programs that affected religion. With respect to the Free Exercise Clause, the Court had applied close scrutiny to government policies that collided with religious sects' practices. In *Sherbert v. Verner* (1963), for example, the Warren Court invalidated South Carolina's denial of unemployment compensation benefits to a Seventh-Day Adventist. The state claimed that she could find a job if she would be willing to work on Saturdays, but the Court declared that the state could not have policies that coerce people to work on their Sabbath if that clashed with their religion's practices and beliefs. The concern for minority religious practices continued during the Burger Court era. In *Wisconsin v. Yoder* (1972), the Court rejected Wisconsin's rational arguments about why children should be required to attend school until they reach the age of sixteen. The Court declared that Wisconsin needed compelling, rather than merely rational, reasons for clashing with Amish families' beliefs and practices concerning the necessity of removing their children from school at an earlier age in order for the youngsters to work and live within a closely knit religious community.

In several decisions, the Court determined that the government's interests were so strong that they outweighed asserted Free Exercise claims. For example, in *Lyng v. Northwest Indian Cemetery Protective Association* (1988), Scalia joined an O'Connor opinion that supported the construction of a logging road in a national forest despite the road's admittedly devastating effects on a location that was sacred to Native Americans. The Court also deferred to the military in permitting the Air Force to bar a Jewish officer from wearing a yarmulke with his uniform (*Goldman v. Weinberger* 1986). However, free exercise decisions generally conveyed the impression that the Court stood ready to scrutinize and invalidate statutes and governmental programs that infringed upon religious minorities practices. According to Michael McConnell (1990: 1109), "free exercise doctrine in the courts was stable, the noisy pressure groups from the ACLU to the religious right were in basic agreement, and most academic commentators were content to work out the implications of the doctrine rather than to challenge it at its roots."

With respect to the Establishment clause, the Court had ignited significant political controversies in several cases. For example, the Court outlawed sponsored prayer in public schools in *Engel v. Vitale* (1962) and limited public financial assistance for religious education in *Lemon v. Kurtzman* (1971). These decisions, among others, generated a significant political backlash against the Supreme Court in the form of a steady flow of proposed constitutional amendments and statutes intended to restore religion's place, and especially Christianity's, in public institutions (Murley 1988). The *Lemon* case was especially important because it established a test for Establishment Clause violations that the Court applied in all but a few cases through the early 1990s. The *Lemon* test, in most instances, scrutinizes governmental policies so closely that it is difficult for them to survive judicial review if there is a claim that they violate the separation of church and state. The test requires that governmental policy or statute pass all components of a three-prong test: 1) the policy must have a secular purpose; 2) the policy must neither hinder nor advance any religion; and 3) the policy must not create an excessive entanglement of government and religion. The third prong, in particular, is so ambiguous and flexible that justices could apply it in a protective manner to prevent even well-intentioned forms of government contact with or support for religion.

Although the *Lemon* test provided the basis for a strong "separationist" rather than "neutral" or "accommodationist" approach to Establishment Clause decisions (Abraham 1988: 333–346), the Court did not always apply *Lemon* in a consistently separationist fashion. For example, in *Marsh v. Chambers* (1983), a majority of justices failed to apply the *Lemon* test at all in order to avoid invalidating the presentation of prayers by clergy at the start of sessions within governmental legislative bodies. In *Mueller v. Allen* (1983), a relaxed application of the *Lemon* test in the hands of Justice William Rehnquist, a critic of the test's existence, enabled Minnesota to benefit parochial schools through a tuition tax-credit program. Although the *Lemon* test was applied with separationist rigor in most other Establishment clause cases, the inconsistency of the test's application in the early 1980s indicated that Scalia was joining a group of justices who were not united in their views on the First Amendment.

Several of Scalia's colleagues on the Rehnquist Court evinced less concern than their predecessors for the need for First Amendment protection of religious minorities. Chief Justice Rehnquist, for example, was questioned by a law clerk about the appropriateness of sponsoring a "Christmas party" at the Supreme Court. He blithely responded that he had had a Jewish law clerk once, and that clerk had not objected to the idea of such a party (O'Connor 1988). Because one member of a religious minority did not object to government sponsorship of a majoritarian religious holiday in a public building, the Supreme Court of the United States no less, then, in Rehnquist's mind, the event was unobjectionable with respect to the principles underlying the Establishment clause. This anecdote illustrates the relative insensitivity to the Establishment clause concerns that apparently contributes to Rehnquist's accommodationist perspective in many decisions.

Other justices also showed signs of insensitivity. Justice Sandra Day O'Connor ignited an embarrassing controversy by complying with a request from the Arizona Republican Party to supply a letter supporting the proposition that the United States is a Christian nation (Smith and Fry 1991). Justice Anthony Kennedy, who was appointed to the Court shortly after Scalia's arrival, wrote an opinion indicating that he believed the Christian majority was being victimized by judicial discrimination if it was not allowed to have its way in using public buildings for religious holiday displays. According to Kennedy:

> I am quite certain that ["the reasonable person"] will take away a salient message from our holding in these cases: the Supreme Court has concluded that the First Amendment creates classes of religions based on the relative numbers of their adherents. Those religions enjoying the largest following must be consigned to the status of least favored faiths so as to avoid any possible risk of offending members of minority religions. (*County of Allegheny v. A.C.L.U.* 1989: 677)

While Justice Kennedy is under no obligation to adopt a separationist perspective in his interpretation of the Establishment Clause, the views expressed in his opinion manifest an inability even to recognize the benefits of a government-neutrality approach in which all religions are, in effect, equally affected by prohibitions on governmental sponsorship of religious activities (Smith 1992). The understanding of and support for the protection of minority religions, which had motivated many of the Court's First Amendment decisions during the Warren and Burger Court eras, was diminishing during the Rehnquist Court era. Thus, Scalia found himself in a decision-making environment in which his advocacy of new approaches could attract support from some of his colleagues. Obviously, whenever he managed to gain the support of four other colleagues, he had the power to actually reshape constitutional doctrines in accordance with his own values and interpretive approaches.

Free Exercise

In his first terms on the Court, Scalia did not emerge as an advocate of change in the Supreme Court's free-exercise jurisprudence. He supported an individual's claim for unemployment compensation when religious beliefs prevented the person from working on Sundays (*Frazee v. Illinois* 1989), indicating that he apparently recognized religious rights as overriding some governmental policies. In several cases, however, he joined conservative justices in striking a balance in favor of the government's interests in clashes with asserted free-exercise rights. In *O'Lone v. Shabazz* (1987), for example, the majority supported a prison administration's refusal to accommodate Muslim prisoners' desire to move between assignment areas in the institution in order to attend religious services. The decision was not surprising because of a tradition of judicial deference to correctional policies based on institutional needs for security and order, as opposed to closer judicial scrutiny of policies less intimately connected to security, such as access to a prison law library (*Bounds v. Smith* 1977).

The most notable aspect of Scalia's behavior in his first free-exercise cases was the absence of any discernible effort to reshape the Court's legal doctrines in accordance with his views. Studies of individual terms on the Rehnquist Court indicate that Scalia typically is one of most assertive justices in expressing his views through written opinions. Although Scalia is often assigned fewer majority opinions than other justices, perhaps because his strident and sarcastic style makes him less attractive than others as the spokesperson for the Court (Smith 1993b), he exceeds the Court average for concurring opinions. His authorship of dissenting opinions is less numerically notable because of the conservative dominance on the Court during his career. His authorship of frequent concurring opinions is a clear indication of his desire to assert his viewpoints in shaping current and future jurisprudence. Generally, Scalia is not satisfied merely to see his preferred case outcomes endorsed by the Court.

In his freshman term, his seventeen concurring opinions exceeded the Court average of eight (Rubin and Melone 1988: 99). During his second term, his sixteen concurring opinions topped the Court average of ten, and the following terms his twenty-four concurring opinions doubled the average of twelve (Melone 1990: 8–9). The pattern continued in later terms. In the 1990 term, Scalia's eighteen concurring opinions far exceeded the Court average of five and, in fact, was three times more than the next most prolific concurring justices (Johnson and Smith 1992: 241). Scalia's fifteen concurring opinions and fourteen dissenting opinions exceeded the Court averages of eight and ten, respectively, in the 1991 term (Smith and Johnson 1993: 177). In the 1993 term, Scalia's nineteen concurring opinions more than doubled the Court average of nine (Smith, Baugh, Hensley, and Johnson 1994: 78). Despite this overall pattern of assertiveness, one that is evident as well in other chapters' discussions of Scalia's opinions, Scalia did not assert his views on free-exercise issues. He joined the other conservative justices in sometimes supporting and sometimes opposing individuals' claims of right, but he did not enunciate his own vision.

When Scalia finally asserted himself through opinion authorship in a free-exercise case, he rocked the legal community with his majority opinion in *Employment Division of Oregon v. Smith* (1990). In *Smith*, two Native American employees of a drug-rehabilitation clinic were fired when they ingested peyote for sacramental purposes at a Native American church ceremony. They applied for unemployment compensation but were turned down because they were regarded as having been fired for intentional misconduct. The claimants asserted that they had merely exercised their First Amendment right to practice their religion and that the state's action in denying them unemployment compensation infringed their right to free exercise of religion. In a five-to-four decision, the Supreme Court rejected their claim and supported the state's denial of benefits. The opinion written by Scalia did not merely deny the First Amendment claims of the Native American men; it also sought to rewrite, in a single opinion, the First Amendment jurisprudence on free exercise.

Scalia's majority opinion has been the object of scathing criticism from scholars (McConnell 1990; Young 1992). His reasoning and interpretive methodology appear to be so result oriented that they contradict Scalia's image as a principled decision-maker. Scalia's transformation of the Court's posture on free-exercise rights provides one of the clearest examples of his post-*Carolene Products* jurisprudence of subordinating the protection of constitutional rights to the preservation of preferences and choices of the political majority.

In his *Smith* opinion, Scalia pays scant attention to the text or history of the Free Exercise Clause. Although as other chapters of the book have discussed, Scalia's advocacy of fidelity to the text and original meaning of the Constitution is well known, no such emphasis was applied in his majority opinion. Instead, Scalia emphasized and quoted at length the Court's opinion in *Minersville School District Board of Education v. Gobitis* (1940) in which the Court endorsed the expulsion from school of Jehovah's Witness children who refused, on religious grounds, to salute the American flag. Scalia quoted Justice Felix Frankfurter's statement in *Gobitis* (1940: 594) that "[c]onscientious scruples have not, in the course of the long struggle for religious toleration, relieved the individual from obedience to a general law not aimed at the promotion or restriction of religious beliefs." This conclusion became the central justification for Scalia's support for the denial of unemployment benefits to the Native Americans in the peyote case. As McConnell (1990: 1124) notes, however, *Gobitis* had long since ceased to be a valid precedent: "[Scalia] neglected to mention that, three years after *Gobitis*, [the Court] overruled the case in one of the most celebrated of all opinions under the Bill of Rights [i.e., *West Virginia State Board of Education v. Barnette* (1943)]. Relying on *Gobitis* without mentioning *Barnette* is like relying on *Plessy v. Ferguson* [1896] without mentioning *Brown v. Board of Education* [1954]."

The other cases cited by Scalia to support his central premise consist of one case asserting the discredited notion that beliefs but not conduct are protected by the Free Exercise Clause (*Reynolds v. United States* 1879). Scalia himself contradicted that assertion in the beginning of the *Smith* opinion by stating that "the 'exercise of religion' often involves not only belief and profession but the performance of (or abstention from) physical acts" (*Employment Division of Oregon v. Smith* 1990: 1599). Scalia also cited Justice Stevens's concurring opinion in *United States v. Lee* (1982). In sum, Scalia had no viable Supreme Court precedents to cite in support of his decision. According to McConnell (1990: 1125), "the primary affirmative precedent marshalled by [Scalia] to support [his] decision consists *entirely* of overruled and minority positions." The contrived basis of decision-making appears especially weak in light of Scalia's decision to overlook the text and history of the statute in favor of reliance on precedent. Since the precedents relied upon provide so little valid support for his conclusions, his opinion reeks of political expediency.

Scalia's fundamental goal appeared to be the elimination of strict judicial scrutiny of laws of general applicability that impinge on minority religions' free exercise of their practices and beliefs. This attack on strict scrutiny is consistent, as we shall see, with Scalia's attacks on many other areas involving fundamental rights and Bill of Rights claims. By eliminating close judicial oversight, majoritarian political preferences embodied in legislation could trump any claims of religious right by minority sects. In order to achieve his objective, Scalia had to rewrite constitutional history by declaring that previous Supreme Court cases that appeared to reject laws of general applicability were actually "hybrid" cases that involved rights other than free-exercise rights alone. By choosing this means to advance his preferred outcome, Scalia forced himself to make disingenuous mischaracterizations of existing precedents.

For example, Scalia characterized *Wisconsin v. Yoder* (1972) as a case addressing the right of parents to direct the education of their children, rather than the right to free exercise of religion alone. However, "the opinion in *Yoder* expressly stated that parents do *not* have the right to violate compulsory education laws for nonreligious reasons" (McConnell 1990: 1121). Moreover, what is the constitutional basis for a parent's right to control the child's education? As a justice who has often expressed concern about fidelity to the text and history of the Constitution, Scalia's assertion of an unwritten parental right places a contrived and contradictory reliance on the kind of substantive due process or privacy rights that Scalia stridently chastises his colleagues for recognizing in other cases (see *Cruzan v. Missouri* 1990).

The conclusion of Scalia's opinion presented in clear terms his vision of free exercise rights and their subordination to political majoritarianism:

> Values that are protected against government interference through enshrinement in the Bill of Rights are not thereby banished from the political process. . . . It may fairly be said that leaving accommodation [of minority religious beliefs and practices] to the political process will place at a relative disadvantage those religious practices that are not widely engaged in; but that unavoidable consequence of democratic government must be preferred to a system in which each conscience is a law unto itself or in which judges weigh the social importance of all laws against the centrality of all religious beliefs. (*Smith*: 1606)

The jurisprudential vision advanced by this statement is one that repudiates the framers' concern with protecting religion, as well as the Supreme Court's general orientation with its roots in the *Carolene Products* footnote. Justice Stone had argued in his famous footnote that courts have a special responsibility for protecting discrete and insular minorities whose interests may be overwhelmed or ignored by majoritarian political processes. In general, Justice Stone's espoused sensitivity to judicial protection of political minorities' rights was embodied in freedom-of-religion cases. Even when the justices supported the government in such cases, they usually justified their rejection of religious freedom claims by balancing the competing interests and finding that the government's interests were substantial or compelling. By contrast, Scalia's advocacy of a post-*Carolene Products* jurisprudence in the *Smith* case is premised on an outright preference for majoritarian dominance, whether or not the majoritarian policy preference is justified by a compelling government interest. As Justice Harry Blackmun noted in his dissenting opinion in *Smith*, Oregon would have difficulty in showing that its categorical prohibition in peyote usage is essential when the federal government and twenty-three states have created exemptions for Native American use of peyote in religious ceremonies. Scalia is unconcerned about documenting the compelling nature of Oregon's interests underlying the policy. He is only concerned with establishing that free-exercise claims can be subordinated to majoritarian policy preferences. Scalia's reasoning here stands in contrast to his views on the death penalty, where the fact that many other states have permitted executions at the age of sixteen is counted as evidence to limit a Bill of Rights claim (*Stanford v. Kentucky* 1989).

Scalia will not endorse majoritarian laws that, in his words, *"by their terms impose disabilities on the basis of religion"* (*Church of the Lukumi Babalu Aye v. City of Hialeah* 1993: 2239 [emphasis in original]), but he seems determined to orient the Court toward deferring to majoritarian preferences even when their attendant policies adversely affect minority religious practices as long as the majoritarian preferences are embodied in laws of general applicability. In his only other Free Exercise Clause opinion, a concurring opinion in a unanimous decision invalidating an ordinance barring the religious sacrifice of animals, Scalia argued that the motives of legislators are irrelevant. A law could pass constitutional muster, in Scalia's eyes, even if it were explicitly intended to limit the religious practices of a single religion. Scalia believes that the judiciary should only intervene if, in fact, it detects special disabilities imposed by a law that is not one of general applicability:

> The First Amendment does not refer to the purposes for which legislators enact laws. . . . This does not put us in the business of invalidating laws by reason of the evil motives of their authors. Had the Hialeah City Council set out resolutely to suppress the practices of Santeria, but ineptly adopted ordinances that failed to do so, I do not see how those laws could be said to "prohibi[t] the free exercise" of religion. Nor, in my view, does it matter that a legislature consists entirely of the pure-hearted, if the law it enacts in fact singles out a religious practice for special burdens (*Church of the Lukumi*, 1993: 2240).

If Scalia's opinion in *Smith* had been a solo concurring or dissenting opinion, it would have provided a revealing example of Scalia's expedient use of legal rationalization, as opposed to principled methodology, as a means to advance his preferred political values. Because it is a majority opinion, it has even more importance. By persuading four justices (William Rehnquist, Byron White, John Paul Stevens, and Anthony Kennedy) to join his opinion, Scalia was able to place his jurisprudential vision into applicable constitutional doctrine with precedential value. Unfortunately for

Scalia, however, conservative Republicans and liberal Democrats in Congress joined forces in support of legislation to counteract Scalia's opinion by initiating a statutory restoration of the "compelling interest test" for free- exercise issues (Biskupic 1991). However, despite the congressional efforts to limit Scalia's impact on free-exercise cases, Scalia's post-*Carolene Products* jurisprudence has found its way into the constitutional doctrines that will, unless reversed in subsequent Supreme Court decisions, influence the ways in which judges respond to religious freedom cases.

Establishment of Religion

Justice Scalia's impact on Establishment Clause jurisprudence has been less dramatic than his impact on free-exercise rights. While Scalia has been much especially outspoken in Establishment Clause cases, he has not been able to gain majority support for his efforts to rewrite constitutional doctrine. Interestingly, while Scalia scrambled to distort precedents to support his vision of free exercise of religion, he has complete disregard for precedent when it concerns separation of church and state. Instead, Scalia prefers to use textual and historical arguments about the meaning of the First Amendment. His glaring methodological inconsistency with respect to the interpretation of the two religion clauses of the First Amendment seems to demonstrate the political motivations underlying his outcome-oriented decision-making. In both instances, he seeks to reduce judicial scrutiny of claims concerning constitutional rights and defer to majoritarian preferences at the expense of religious minorities. He simply chooses the legal rationalizations that will best support his preferred vision without apparent concern for fidelity to an interpretive methodology.

Scalia began to make known his vision of the Establishment Clause during his very first term. The Court considered a case from Louisiana in which the state legislature had mandated that public schools teach so-called "creation science" if they chose to teach the theory of evolution. In a 7-to-2 decision, the Court affirmed a lower court decision that had struck down the Louisiana law. Justice Brennan's majority opinion applied the *Lemon* test, although the Court needed to go no further than the first prong of the test concerning the motives of the legislature in enacting the statute. In this instance, the Court found that Louisiana could not identify a secular purpose underlying the statute, and that the legislation sought to restructure the state science curriculum to conform with a particular religious viewpoint. In a dissenting opinion joined by Chief Justice Rehnquist, Scalia questioned the majority's application of *Lemon*'s first prong and argued that the Court should defer to the legislature's definition of the statute and the underlying purposes of the statute:

> Whenever we are called upon to judge the constitutionality of an act of a state legislature, "we must have 'due regard to the fact that this Court is not exercising a primary judgment but is sitting in judgment upon those who have also taken the oath to observe the Constitution and who have responsibility for carrying on government' " (*Edwards v. Aguillard* 1987: 2596).

This argument comports with Scalia's regular advocacy for reducing judicial scrutiny of rights claims and placing all policies, including those affecting the definition and enforcement of individuals' constitutional rights, under the control of majoritarian political processes.

Despite Scalia's interpretive insistence against using it, he traced the legislative history of the statute to support his argument that the majority had misread the legislature's intention in applying the first prong of the test. Scalia advocated abandonment of *Lemon*'s first prong on textual and historical grounds. Within his assessment of the Court's precedential test, Scalia revealed that he takes an accommodationist approach to the Establishment Clause, which would accept government policies that advance religion:

> Given the many hazards involved in assessing the subjective intent of governmental decisionmakers, the first prong of *Lemon* is defensible, I think, only if the text of the Establishment Clause demands it. That is surely not the case. . . . It is, in short, far from an inevitable reading of the Establishment Clause that it forbids all governmental action intended to advance religion; and if not inevitable, any reading with such untoward consequences must be wrong.
>
> In the past, we have attempted to justify our embarrassing Establishment Clause jurisprudence on the ground that it "sacrifices clarity and predictability for flexibility." . . . I think it time we sacrifice some "flexibility" for "clarity and predictability." Abandoning *Lemon*'s purpose test—a test which exacerbates the tension between the Free Exercise and Establishment Clauses, has no basis in the language or history of the Amendment, and, as today's decision shows, has wonderfully flexible consequences—would be a good place to start (*Edwards v. Aguillard* 1987: 2607).

When Scalia next asserted his views in an Establishment Clause case, it became clear that he had profound disagreements with the dominant concern in Court opinions concerning the separation of church and state. Scalia began to employ the stridency and sarcasm that characterize these opinions in which his strong jurisprudential vision clashes sharply with the views of other justices. The case concerned a 6-to-3 Supreme Court decision to invalidate a Texas law that provided a tax exemption for religious publications. The opening paragraph of Scalia's dissenting opinion, joined by Chief Justice Rehnquist and Justice Kennedy, conveys the growing strength of Scalia's expressions of disagreement with the Court's Establishment Clause jurisprudence:

> As a judicial demolition project, today's decision is impressive. The machinery employed by the opinions of Justice BRENNAN and Justice BLACKMUN is no more substantial than the antinomy that accommodation of religion may be required but not permitted, and the bold but unsupportable assertion (given such realities as the text of the Declaration of Independence, the national Thanksgiving Day proclaimed by every President since Lincoln, the inscriptions on our coins, the words of our Pledge of Allegiance, the invocation with which sessions of our Court are opened and, come to think of it, the discriminatory protection for freedom of religion in the Constitution) that government may not "convey a message of endorsement of religion." With this frail equipment, the Court topples an exemption for religious publications of a sort that expressly appears in the laws of at least [fifteen] of the [forty-five] States that have sales and use taxes. . . . (*Texas Monthly Inc. v. Bullock* 1989: 907).

Scalia did not seize the occasion to renew his critique of the *Lemon* test, but he referred to his reliance on textual and historical considerations for interpreting the Establishment Clause: "I dissent because I find no basis in the text of the Constitution, the decisions of this Court, or the traditions of our people for disapproving this longstanding and widespread practice" (ibid.: 909).

In other cases, Scalia joined Court majorities to reject Establishment claims concerning such issues as religious displays on public property that mix secular and sacred symbols (*Pittsburgh v. A.C.L.U.* 1989), government grants to church organizations for youth counseling (*Bowen v. Kendrick* 1988), and meetings of religious student groups in public high schools (*Westside Community Board of Education v. Mergens* 1990). When Scalia next gave full voice to his vision of the Establishment Clause, his opinion was written at a moment in history when people anticipated that the Court would scrap the *Lemon* test in favor of an explicitly accommodationist orientation toward separation of church and state (or the lack thereof). Warren Court holdovers William Brennan and Thurgood Marshall, the Court's strongest strict separationists, had retired and been replaced by more conservative Republican appointees, David Souter and Clarence Thomas. The Court faced a case in which a parent challenged the practice of having clergy recite prayers, albeit of a nondenominational nature, at public-school graduation ceremonies. In a closely watched 5-to-4 decision, the Court banned school-sponsored prayer at graduations and apparently preserved the *Lemon* test.

In dissent, on behalf of Chief Justice Rehnquist and Justices White and Thomas, Scalia emphasized the historical basis of such prayers. In relying on history, Scalia was not merely arguing that the original meaning of the First Amendment permitted such prayers, but that historical traditions in society should define the meaning of constitutional rights. Scalia declared that the majority decision "lays waste a tradition that is as old as public-school graduation ceremonies themselves, and that is a component of an even more longstanding American tradition of nonsectarian prayer to God at public celebrations generally" (*Lee v. Weisman* 1992: 2679). Scalia explicitly advocated placing the definition and protection of constitutional rights in the hands of majoritarian political processes rather than under the control of judicial officers:

> Today's opinion shows more forcefully than volumes of argumentation why our Nation's protection, that fortress which is our Constitution, cannot possibly rest upon the changeable philosophical predilections of the Justices of this Court, but must have deep foundations in the historic practices of our people (ibid.).

Scalia stated quite clearly that nonbelievers' interests should be sacrificed in order to gain the benefits of having members of the monotheistic majority from different sects join together in generic prayers. According to Scalia, "To deprive our society of that important unifying mechanism, in order to spare the nonbeliever what seems to me the minimal inconvenience of standing or even sitting in respectful nonparticipation, is as senseless in policy as it is unsupported in law" (ibid.: 2686).

Scalia's opinion also cast contempt upon the majority's concern about the coercive impact of school-sponsored prayer upon students from minority religions or areligious families. In applying his gift for sarcasm, Scalia said, "interior decorating is a hard-rock science compared to psychology practiced by amateurs. A few citations to '[r]esearch in psychology' that have no particular bearing upon the precise issue here, . . . cannot disguise the fact that the Court has gone beyond the realm where judges know what they are doing" (ibid.: 2681).

After reviewing the historical tradition of prayer at public ceremonies, Scalia articulated his view of the limited meaning of the Establishment Clause. To Scalia, the Establishment Clause was adopted to prohibit the establishment of a national religion that people would be forced to join or provide financial support through the coercive powers of government. Scalia also was "willing to concede that our constitutional tradition . . . ruled out of order government-sponsored endorsement of religion—even when no legal coercion is present" (ibid.: 2683), although his language of concession implies that he really would limit the Clause's meaning to a ban on a national religion.

Interestingly, Justice Souter's concurring opinion engages Scalia in a debate on historical grounds. Unlike Scalia, who reviewed the history of public prayer as a traditional practice, Souter actually examined the development of the First Amendment's language and meaning as it made its way through the First Congress and into a constitutional amendment. In applying a more exacting textual and historical analysis, Souter concluded that:

> What we thus know of the Framers' experience underscores the observation of one prominent commentator, that confining the Establishment Clause to a prohibition on preferential aid "requires a premise that the Framers were extraordinarily bad drafters—that they believed one thing but adopted language that said something substantially different, and that they did so after repeatedly attending to the choice of language." . . . We must presume, since there is no conclusive evidence to the contrary, that the Framers embraced the significance of their textual judgment. Thus, on balance, history neither contradicts nor warrants reconsideration of the settled principle that the Establishment Clause forbids support for religion in general no less than support for one religion or some (ibid.: 2670).

The significance of Souter's opinion and his interpretive approach is that it helps to call into question Scalia's reputation for aspiring to apply a neutral methodology grounded in textual and historical considerations. Souter challenged Scalia on his own purported interpretive grounds, and Scalia did not rise to the challenge. Scalia's opinion focused on traditions as practiced throughout American history, while Souter addressed what is supposed to be Scalia's utmost concern, the text and original meaning of the First Amendment itself. When Scalia has claimed the "higher ground" of purportedly neutral textualism and historical analysis, other justices have helped Scalia to avoid close scrutiny by openly applying their own flexible, noninterpretivist approaches. By contrast, Scalia's reliance on text and history can appear less result-oriented. When Souter joins Scalia on the purported "higher ground," Scalia's actual approach suddenly reveals itself to be more result-oriented than some commentators had realized. It is not on the Establishment Clause issue alone that Souter's careful examinations have revealed that Scalia's grip on text and history are less firm than previously noticed:

In *Lee v. Weisman,* the school prayer case, Souter's account of the original understanding of the religion clauses was more persuasive than Scalia's. . . . Souter again beat Scalia at his own game in the Operation Rescue case. Scalia concluded that a Civil War statute did not prevent Operation Rescue from barricading abortion clinics because there was no evidence that the protesters had a "discriminatory animus" against women. Souter pointed out that the "discriminatory animus" requirement appears nowhere in the text of the law, but was invented by the Burger Court. By parsing the law that Scalia had ignored, Souter proposed an alternative way of protecting the women and punishing the protesters. (Rosen 1993: 27)

In a subsequent Establishment Clause case, Scalia launched an even more pointed attack on the *Lemon* test. A school district had denied permission for religious groups to use its facilities even though it permitted other kinds of organizations to make use of school buildings after hours. A unanimous Court invalidated the school district's practice as a violation of the right to freedom of speech in the First Amendment. Scalia seized the opportunity to advance his most vivid arguments for abandoning the *Lemon* test:

> As to the Court's invocation of the *Lemon* test: Like some ghoul in a late-night horror movie that repeatedly sits up in its grave and shuffles abroad, after being repeatedly killed and buried, *Lemon* stalks our Establishment Clause jurisprudence once again, frightening the little children and school attorneys of Center Moriches Union Free School District. Its most recent burial, only last Term, was, to be sure, not fully six-feet under: our decision in *Lee v. Weisman* conspicuously avoided using the supposed "test" but also declined the invitation to repudiate it. Over years, however, no fewer than five of the currently sitting Justices have, in their own opinions, personally driven pencils through the creature's heart. . . . (*Lamb's Chapel v. Center Moriches School District* 1993: 2149–2150).

Although Scalia exaggerated in claiming that the *Lemon* test had ever been "killed," as in eliminated, he did accurately describe several cases in which the Court had failed to apply the test. Scalia correctly noted that the Court had sometimes avoided applying the test when it appeared that the majority did not want to reach a particular result, such as the elimination of legislative prayer (*Marsh v. Chambers* 1984). Whenever the Court majority wanted to stop a government policy that arguably advanced religion, then the test was a useful tool for justifying a declaration of unconstitutionality. Scalia's forthright illustration of the flexible and inconsistent application of the *Lemon* test was apparently not sufficiently persuasive to convince a majority of justices to declare the test unusable and invalid. If the Court were to abandon the test, the justices would then be faced with the prospect of developing another basis for decision-making. Scalia has advanced an accommodationist approach that, during the Rehnquist Court era, would not have favored claimants in any Establishment Clause cases decided by the Supreme Court. It is apparent that a majority of justices do not agree with Scalia's vision as applied to all situations and therefore the survival of the *Lemon* test is understandable as the justices seek to retain some guidelines to apply in cases in which governmental policies cause them discomfort. While there is no question that the test is useful for result-oriented purposes, there is also reason to doubt that Scalia is offering a principled, as opposed to result-oriented, alternative that can garner a consensus on the Court.

In 1994, Scalia dueled directly with Souter in a case concerning New York's establishment of a special school district for a religious community so that handicapped children in the sect could benefit from public funds for their special education. In an opinion by Justice Souter, the Court found that the creation of the special school district violated the Establishment clause (*Board of Education of Kiryas Joel v. Grumet* 1994). In his dissenting opinion on behalf on Chief Justice Rehnquist and Justice Thomas, Scalia attempted to reclaim the "high ground" by asserting that "[o]nce this Court has abandoned text and history as guides, nothing prevents it from calling religious toleration the establishment of religion" (ibid.: 2506). Scalia's opinion does not join Souter in debate about the text and original meaning of the First Amendment. Instead, Scalia dissects Souter's opinion in terms of its inconsistency with some Establishment clause cases in which arguable governmental accommodation or benefit for some religious groups was permitted. Scalia's underlying emphasis is on the neutral, secular purpose that motivated the legislative action and the American tradition of accommodation of religion in some contexts.

Scalia's dissent also returns to the issue of abolishing the *Lemon* test because Justice Sandra O'Connor's concurring opinion advanced that argument. When discussing the issue of what the Court should use in place of *Lemon* for analyzing Establishment clause issues, Scalia states forthrightly, "The foremost principle I would apply is fidelity to the longstanding traditions of our people, which surely provide the diversity of treatment that Justice O'Connor seeks, but do not leave us to our own devices" (ibid.: 2515). In placing his support squarely on historical *practices* as opposed to text and original meaning, Scalia's rhetoric of principled neutrality obscures the opportunities for judicial interpretation. How does one define a "tradition"? As discussed in the chapter on his criminal justice decisions, Scalia tends to treat Eighth Amendment cruel and punishment issues as if they cannot be unusual if they were ever used in some state. Are traditions for accommodating religions to be assessed by the same standard? Such a standard gives judges significant leeway to recognize practices as "traditions," but obviously those "traditions" only operate in one direction: to favor governmental support for and accommodation of religions. If this is Scalia's approach, then it represents what is probably the lowest threshold for judicial protection of minority religions and a religious people in the Establishment clause context. This represents a formulation that, if applied as described by Scalia, could permit virtually anything short of a national religion. In some respects, it is consistent with Scalia's language of concession in acknowledging a broader meaning of the Establishment clause than simply coercing people to support and join a national religion. Scalia seems to really believe that the Establishment clause is no impediment to a wide variety of governmental accommodation of and support for religion and particular religions.

Conclusion

Scalia's fundamental view of the Establishment Clause and his reliance on traditional practices obviously advance his consistent theme of making constitutional rights subject to majoritarian political processes. The diminished judicial role advocated by Scalia in the Establishment Clause context fits neatly with the post-*Carolene Products* jurisprudence that is evident in Scalia's approach to other issues of constitutional rights. Instead of providing active judicial protection for discrete and insular religious minorities, Scalia would permit majoritarian interests to use their power over governmental policy-making to implement programs that accommodate and support majoritarian religious activities.

The deference to majoritarian political processes in most Establishment clause issues parallels the deference Scalia espouses in free-exercise cases. Scalia would subordinate the free-exercise interests of minority religions, such as Native Americans (*i.e.*, *Lyng v. Northwest Indian Cemetery Protective Association* 1989; *Employment Division of Oregon v. Smith* 1990), to the majoritarian policy preferences of democratic political processes with diminished judicial authority to identify and vindicate free exercise claims.

While the majoritarian deference of Scalia's post-*Carolene Products* jurisprudence unifies his vision of First Amendment religious rights, the inconsistency of his interpretive approaches for each religion clause reveals the result-oriented nature of his decision-making. In his dramatic free-exercise opinion in *Smith*, Scalia succeeded in reshaping constitutional jurisprudence in light of his own jurisprudential vision by gaining majority support for his opinion. Because his opinion gave scant attention to the textual and historical considerations that are the hallmarks of his jurisprudential rhetoric and instead relied on contrived mischaracterizations of precedent, the illusory nature of his purportedly principled interpretive methodology is easy to discern. By contrast, Scalia finds greater utility in the language of text and history for justifying the outcomes supported by his vision of the Establishment clause. However, as the challenge from Souter's textual and historical analysis revealed, Scalia seems less than fully committed to text and history when those methods might not advance his preferred outcomes. Instead, he can advance his consistent goal of placing individuals' constitutional rights in the hands of majoritarian political processes by focusing on the more ambiguous historical building-block of traditional practices rather than on Souter's more scholarly reference points in historical text development and original meaning.

Chapter 6

Freedom of Speech

Free speech, press, and association (hereinafter "SPA") are often described as necessary components of a democratic and liberal society. As far back as Milton's *Areopagitica*, John Locke's *Letter Concerning Toleration*, and John Stuart Mill's *On Liberty*, the Anglo-American liberal political tradition[1] has been ostensibly committed to free, open, and uncensored inquiry and to the belief that such inquiry is necessary either for the discovery of truth, individual self-expression, or the maintenance of open and accountable government. Within the American political tradition, legal scholars and democratic theorists such as Meiklejohn (1965), Ely (1980), Rawls (1971), Dahl (1991), Shiffrin (1990), Dworkin (1978; 1986), and Sunstein (1993) have described the importance of fostering free SPA as crucial to keeping America a free society.

Although expressive freedoms are important and have been canonized in the First Amendment, no consensus exists on what free SPA is, the breadth of these rights in a democratic society, or what the First Amendment is meant to protect. Some have argued that the First Amendment merely protects discourse directed against the government, and it was not meant to protect academic or artistic freedom or even the right to advocate the overthrow of the United States (Bork 1971). Yet Shiffrin has suggested that the spirit and meaning of the First Amendment represent a broad scope of protection for free expression, one that embodies a "romantic" image of the critic or dissenter (Shiffrin 1990: 142). Yet Shiffrin has also noted that judicial treatment of this amendment has resulted in an overly technical, cumbersome, and legalistic set of categories that departs from the role of the First Amendment as a "cultural symbol" (Shiffrin 1990: 90, 169) in support of American political freedom. As testament to the complexity of the First Amendment free-SPA jurisprudence, numerous treatises, texts, histories, and casebooks each year seek clarification of what facially ought

123

to be a simple subject.[2] Similarly, each year the Supreme Court revisits the First Amendment in its search to define the scope and meaning of our expressive freedoms.

Given the importance of the debates surrounding expressive freedoms, it is no surprise that Justice Scalia has figured prominently in recent First Amendment discussions. The next two chapters examine Antonin Scalia's opinions on the First Amendment both as judge of U.S. Court of Appeals and as associate justice of the United States Supreme Court. Although other aspects of the justice's jurisprudence have been examined, surprisingly little if any sustained attention has been singularly devoted to his First Amendment free SPA decisions.[3]

This chapter examines Scalia's philosophy regarding free speech, while the subseqent chapter turns to free press and associational rights in the context of the First Amendment. Several approaches to understanding Scalia's SPA decisions are employed. This chapter reviews his scholarly writings and decisions to ascertain philosophically what Scalia thinks free expression entails and what its importance is in a democratic society. After this discussion, a statistical profile of his holdings in the area of free SPA will be presented as one way of evaluating how sympathetic the justice is towards free expression claims. Following this, separate sections in this chapter and next will examine Scalia's major opinions involving free speech, press, and association while on the Court of Appeals and through the 1993 Supreme Court term. Within each of these sections, subsections representing traditional speech categories will also address Scalia's attitudes towards particular types of speech, including expressive conduct, obscenity, corporate speech, and pure political speech.

The conclusion of these two chapters is that Scalia's post-*Carolene Products* jurisprudence subordinates many types of expressive-activity claims to the need to protect the integrity of the majoritarian political process, since other values, beyond those of free SPA, are more important to the justice. This means that the Scalia does not have a philosophy of the First Amendment that depicts free speech, press, and association as fundamental values in a democracy that generally trump other values. While no Supreme Court justice, including former Associate Justice Hugo Black who espoused an "absolutist" view towards the First Amendment, is expected to favor expressive claims in all situations, some former justices such as William Brennan, were definitely more supportive of First Amendment claims because of the high value they placed upon free expression within a democracy. Scattered rhetorical comments not withstanding, Scalia has offered more reasons why free expression should be limited than why it should be sustained. For Scalia, many other competing and compelling state interests or values appear to trump free SPA rights. Hence, simply to claim that deference to governmental interests is what defines Scalia's First Amendment decisions is too simplistic. It is more accurate to state that Scalia's decisions are defined by a deference towards particular values that the state or the political process is seeking to enforce. Among these values are concern with maintaining the integrity of the electoral process, preventing political factionalization, supporting voluntary associations, and respecting the government's right to remain an active participant in the marketplace of ideas. While emphasizing these values, Scalia seems to attach little importance to individual participation and expression in the political system. Similarly, he generally ignores how the Court is supposed to protect individual political expression as critical to the maintenance of an open and representative system. Yet he does generally support corporate free speech rights, such support generally lending the impression that the justice may be a defender of the First Amendment. In actuality, Scalia endorses a political philosophy inconsistent with the high value on autonomy that Madisonian democracy demands, yet he places significant emphasis upon other political goals noted in the *Federalist Papers*, such as maintaining the political system against the threat of political factions.

A second conclusion will be that, as with his religious freedom jurisprudence, early on Scalia did not appear to be changing the basic divisions of First Amendment speech categorization. But his later treatment of these categories, especially in *R.A.V. v. St. Paul* (1993) indicates disagreement with current Court treatment of them. Scalia appears to be moving towards a more global view of the First Amendment, in which certain general rules apply to all types of speech regulation. Even if Scalia did not have a consistent philosophical view towards the First Amendment, he appears to be developing one in his recent opinions.

A final conclusion will be that although certain high profile decisions striking down laws on flag- or cross-burning as unconstitutional, such as *Texas v. Johnson* (1989), *U.S. v. Haggerty* (1990), *U.S. v. Eichman* (1990), and *R.A.V. v. St. Paul* (1992) have given him a reputation as a defender of free SPA, analysis of his decisions demonstrated the contrary. Instead, in the sixty-six identified cases involving free SPA,[4] he has voted against free SPA forty-one times and he has only authored one majority opinion sustaining or broadening First Amendment free SPA. Overall, he has only supported free SPA in thirty-eight percent of his decisions and, in some instances, such as with obscenity, he has never supported a free speech claim, while in cases of corporate speech, he has almost consistently supported these claims.

Philosophical Views

While Justice Scalia has concurred with holdings that have articulated some broader message or philosophical premise on the importance of the First Amendment and free SPA in America, such as in *Texas v. Johnson* (1989), he has not offered an extended discussion of his philosophical (as opposed to legalistic or constitutional) views towards free SPA. At best, his comments are fragmentary, confined to discussion of case law and precedent, or include only hints at what his broad philosophical view (if in fact he has one) of the First Amendment might be. Beyond these scattered comments, Scalia has offered little of a substantive philosophical vision of what the First Amendment's free SPA provisions mean.[5] While other scholars have claimed that his opinions reflect preference for "community interests to challenging litigant claims" (Brisbin 1990: 17), that "several of Scalia's First Amendment opinions upheld the tutelary power of the state" (Brisbin 1992b: 14), or that most doubts regarding the scope of the First Amendment will favor the government (Wilson 1986: 1197), none of these essays have successfully identified or constructed a comprehensive vision of Scalia's free SPA decisions that place them within a more comprehensive jurisprudential vision. No essay has singularly focused on Scalia's First Amendment decisions regarding free SPA, although at least one article has been directed towards Scalia's First Amendment church/state decisions (Schlosser 1986). Scalia's most extended discussion of First Amendment speech issues is found in *"A House with Many Mansions: Categories of Speech under the First Amendment"* (Scalia 1987c). Even here the former University of Chicago law professor eschews a developed theory about the First Amendment, declaring that:

> [T]here is really no such thing as a "First Amendment case." Lawsuits are not about the First Amendment, but about some concrete and fact-bound wrong that was allegedly inflicted upon the plaintiff. In the real world, it is less meaningful to talk about "First Amendment cases" than about libel suits by public figures; suits challenging the dismissal of public employees for their expression of views; suits challenging the proscription of commercial advertising on various grounds. Within these and many other areas of what might be termed the existential categories of common First Amendment cases, there may, and I think does, develop a consistency and uniformity that cannot be expected within the category of "First Amendment law" as a whole (Scalia 1987c: 19).

Here Scalia indicates that no coherent, overarching philosophical, political, or legalistic reading of the First Amendment, similar to efforts undertaken by Alexander Meikeljohn or Stephen Shiffrin, is possible. First

Amendment law is really about concrete and specific fact patterns that have been conceptually lumped together in a variety of categories. For Scalia, these categories or differences among types of speech include political, commercial, and symbolic speech, in addition to the speech plus category (Scalia 1987c: 13–17). Other categorizations of speech include distinctions based on who the speaker or audience is, the truth or falsity of speech, and its time, manner, and place. In general, this essay demarcates the existing distinctions the Court has made in seeking to define what speech is, yet Scalia steers away from offering much of his own views on the values of free SPA in the United States.

Despite this 1987 acknowledgment of the "existential" nature of First Amendment speech categories, in his 1992 *R.A.V. v. St. Paul* majority opinion Scalia appears to reject these categories in lieu of approaching the First Amendment from the point of proscribable or nonproscribable content. This new direction, hinted at in this case, would suggest a more global or comprehensive approach to the First Amendment that departs from viewing speech in terms of specific categories. Yet even the discussion here, his first Supreme Court majority opinion upholding a First Amendment claim, is surprisingly devoid of philosophical commentary on free expression.

Elsewhere Scalia has offered only scattered comments on this subject. In an essay "Economic Affairs as Human Affairs" (Scalia 1987), where the justice advocates renewed judicial and cultural support for economic liberties, political freedoms are linked to the free market and respect for economic autonomy (Scalia 1987: 32). Scalia declares that "I know of no society, today or in any era of history, in which high degrees of intellectual and political freedom have flourished with a high degree of state control over the relevant citizen's economic life" (Scalia 1987: 32). The marketplace of ideas and the economic marketplace are linked, and protection of the latter is the surest way to protect the former, including presumably free SPA. For Scalia, protecting our society against excessive economic regulation and defending property interests is a better way to support civil liberties than would it be for the Court to single out political freedoms of speech, press, and assembly alone. Free expression cannot survive on its own; it requires some institutions or forces, such as property rights, to sustain it. Perhaps, as will be noted in chapter eight, Scalia's strong support for property rights is indicative of the justice's efforts to support other individual rights, including expressive freedoms. Yet in none of those land use decisions has Scalia invoked the relationship between property and personal freedom in language similar to that found in some of his scholarly writings to support his defense of property rights. Nonetheless, Scalia's defense of property does seem important to him and his conception of a free society.

The justice comments on the First Amendment in his dissent in *Austin v. Michigan of Commerce* (1990). At issue in this case was a Michigan law, prohibiting independent corporate campaign expenditures. The majority opinion upheld the Michigan law which prohibited any direct corporate treasury funds from being spent to support or oppose any candidate for office. The Michigan law stated that corporations could make expenditures only from separate, segregated funds used solely for political purposes, in effect, creating political action committees or PACs. In attacking the majority decision Scalia claimed it represented "for the first time since Justice Holmes left the bench, that a direct restriction upon speech" is permissible (ibid: 1413) and that the aim of this legislation and the holding is inconsistent with the intent of the framers, the First Amendment, and Alexis de Tocqueville's observations on the role of voluntary associations in American democracy. Scalia stated that

> I doubt that those who framed and adopted the First Amendment would agree that avoiding the New Corruption, that is, calibrating political speech to the degree of public opinion that supports it, is even a desirable objective. . . . Those Founders designed, of course, a system in which popular ideas would ultimately prevail. . . . I am confident, in other words, that Jefferson and Madison would not have sat at these controls; but if they did, they would have turned them in the opposite direction (ibid.: 1415).

In his dissent, Scalia appeals to de Tocqueville and his discussion of the importance of voluntary associations in American society instead of appealing to Madison, *Federalist* 10 and 51, and the threats of factions to political stability. Instead of labelling corporations as factions, he links them to de Tocqueville's notions of political associations, democracy, and the expression of free ideas and indicates that "to eliminate voluntary associations— not only including powerful ones, but *especially* including powerful ones— from public debate is either to augment the always dominant power of government or to impoverish the public debate" (ibid.: 1416, Scalia's emphasis).[6] Similar thoughts about the necessity of organizations to the maintenance of free speech or expression is found in *Rutan v. Republican Party of Illinois* (1990) where, in dissent, Scalia sees patronage as useful to building political parties which serve as organizations for expressing political values though electoral competition. In both *Austin* and *Rutan*, competitive organizations are depicted as important forces defending political values including free speech.

Despite his views on the importance attached to associations and economics in maintaining to free expression, Scalia has also stated that there are cases where the "exercise of First Amendment rights may sometimes be quite wrong" (Scalia 1987a: 737). There are many constitutionally protected types of speech, such as cross burning, that are socially harmful and irresponsible and which should not be praised or encouraged (R.A.V. v. St. Paul 1993: 737). Some types of speech hide behind the First Amendment, eroding individual moral responsibility for actions (Scalia 1987a: 737). For Scalia, law in general and the First Amendment in particular, while supposedly enabling virtue, often discourage it and instead support types of speech that are not really socially desirable (ibid.: 736–738).

Scalia's philosophical views towards the value of speech in our society seem incomplete. He has told us that some types of speech are inherently more worthy than others and that social institutions such as respect for private property and voluntary associations are important to free expression. Yet the justice has not directly defended free SPA or shown why respecting it is necessary or desirable. Mere hints of a philosophical view are offered, and little beyond that can be discerned from his dicta, academic writings, or off-bench remarks to indicate that he is sympathetic to free SPA claims.

Statistical Profile of Scalia's
Free Speech, Press, and Association Decisions

Beyond linking political and economic freedom, competition, virtue, and voluntary associations, Scalia has offered little by way of a First Amendment philosophy. He has denied that the exercise of First Amendment rights is always a virtue. He has denied that such a coherent philosophy can be constructed except for subcategories of speech where certain types of issues are involved. Even with these categories, he has questioned their viability. Lacking a comprehensive philosophy, looking to a statistical profile of Scalia's free SPA holdings is useful to see what types of interests or free SPA he actually supports.

As a federal judge and through his service in the 1993 term as an associate justice, Scalia participated in sixty-six cases identified as involving free SPA issues. In those cases, he has voted against SPA claims forty-one times (sixty-two percent). If one were to look at Scalia's record just on the Supreme Court, he has only supported free SPA claims forty-one percent of the time. Another way to gain a statistical perspective of Scalia's free SPA decisions is to compare his record on the Supreme Court to thse of other justices. This in done in Tables I and II.

Tables I and II provide a breakdown of the number of decisions each of the justices participated in during their tenure on the court from 1986

TABLE I
Supreme Court Support for First Amendment
Free Speech, Press, and Association: 1986–1993 Terms

Rehnquist	32%
Thomas	41%
Scalia	41%*
O'Connor	47%
White	49%
Ginsburg	60%
Supreme Court	**61%**
Stevens	63%
Souter	64%
Kennedy	66%
Blackmun	77%
Brennan	90%
Marshall	92%

*Since becoming a federal judge and including his tenure as a Supreme Court justice, Antonin Scalia has participated in 66 free speech, press, and associations. He has supported the First Amendment in 25 of these decisions. Hence, his overall support stands at 38%.

TABLE II
Rehnquist Court Support for First Amendment
Free Speech, Press, and Association: 1986–1993 Terms

Justice	Court	Scalia	Rehnquist	White	O'Connor	Blackmun
total decisions	56	56	56	51	55	55
affirmed SPA	34	23	18	25	26	42
% support	61%	41%	32%	49%	47%	76%

Justice	Stevens	**Brennan**	**Marshall**	Kennedy	Souter	Thomas
total decisions	56	31	36	41	25	17
affirmed SPA	38	28	33	27	16	7
% support	63%	90%	92%	66%	64%	41%

Justice	Ginsburg
total decisions	5
affirmed SPA	3
% support	60%

through the 1993 terms (Justice Powell was not included on this list). During that period, the Supreme Court supported free SPA claims sixty-one percent of the time, with five members of the Court supporting free SPA claims less than half the time. Of these justices, only Thomas and Rehnquist have voting records less supportive of SPA claims than Scalia. These statistics hide some important trends. By that, Scalia's support for free speech claims has gone up sigificantly in the 1992 and 1993 terms. This is because five of the cases the Court has taken during that time addressed corporate or commercial free speech issues, with Scalia consistently supporting these claims. His overall support for commerical speech interests is seven out of nine cases (seventy-eight percent). Excluding these cases from Scalia's other cases, he has supported free SPA in thirteen of fifty-seven cases (twenty-three percent) overall, and in only sixteen of forty-seven cases (thirty-four percent) before him on the Supreme Court.

Still another way to examine Scalia is to break his decisions down into the categories of type of speech and speaker that were suggested by him in his "A House with Many Mansions: Categories of Speech under the First Amendment" (Scalia 1987c). When free speech, press, and association are distinguished, we find that eighteen of his forty-one free speech cases (forty-four percent) support free speech claims; two of eight (twenty-five percent) support freedom of association claims; and three of fifteen (twenty-percent) of his decisions support free press claims.

Looking at subcategories of speech, five of seven (seventy-one percent) are supportive of expressive conduct or symbolic speech claims. However, in none of the cases involving obscenity questions or sexually oriented businesses has he supported these businesses or held in favor of a narrower interpretation of obscenity or regulation. Scalia's most consistent support of speech claims occurred in the area of corporate or commercial speech. Here, he voted in favor of the corporation seven out of nine times (78%), voting against corporate speech only when it also implicated obscenity, as in *Alexander v. United States* (1993), and when it involved favoring a governmental institution over students in *Board of Trustees of SUNY v. Fox* (1989). But when the corporation was engaged in political speech through the creation of a Political Action Committee (PAC), he has voted to support the corporation in both of the decisions before him, i.e., *Federal Election Commission v. Massachusetts Citizens Concerned for Life* (1986) and *Austin v. Michigan Chamber of Commerce* (1990).

Examination of Scalia's free SPA decisions by speaker perhaps indicates an interesting pattern. Of the forty-nine decisions involving either a state or federal government or agency, Scalia supported the government thirty times (sixty-one percent). In those cases where he voted against the government, we find, among other decisions, that four involved flag- or cross-burning (*Texas v. Johnson* [1989], *U.S. v. Haggerty* and *U.S. v. Eichman* [1990], *R.A.V. v. St. Paul* [1992]), two decisions in opposition to campaign finance law that affected a right to life group and a business chamber of commerce (*Federal Election Commission v. Massachusetts Citizens Concerned for Life* [1986] and *Austin v. Michigan Chamber of Commerce* [1990]), decisions favoring corporate speech over the government (*Edenfield v. Fane* [1993], *City of Cincinnati v. Discovery Network* [1993], and

Turner Broadcasting v. F.C.C. [1994]), and one decision struck down a state law regulating the terms of party officers, which also banned them from making primary endorsements (*Eu v. San Francisco Court Democratic Central Committee* [1989]). Additionally, one decision struck down solicitation reporting requirements for nonprofit groups (*Riley v. National Federation of the Blind of North Carolina* [1988]), one decision voided a state law confiscating royalties from publications of convicted criminals describing their crimes (*Simon & Schuster v. New York State Crime Victims Board* [1992]), and one decision struck down a subway ban on a poster critical of the Reagan Administration (*Lebron v. Washington Metropolitan Area Transit Authority* [1984]). No clear pattern of subject-orientated voting appears, unless one argues that Scalia supports the government except when he is motivated to support some private interests favored by his political philosophy or ideology. Finally, of the nineteen cases where no government entity was involved, Scalia voted, inter alia, against the press in seven of eight cases involving libel or defamation and in favor of nonunion workers' speech rights over a union (*Lehnert v. Ferris Faculty Association* [1991]).

Several conclusions can be drawn from this statistical profile. First, Scalia is generally not supportive of First Amendment free SPA claims. He appears quite unsympathetic to freedom of association and press claims as well as First Amendment claims raised by sexually orientated businesses. Second, Scalia also seems quite willing to defer to governments to regulate speech and press, including the political process and elections. Finally, Scalia seems willing to support government regulation of speech when it come to a pro-choice voice, but unwilling to allow regulation when it is a pro-life voice. Although *Frisby v. Schultz* (1988), in which Scalia supported limits on anti-abortion protestors in front of a doctor's house in a private neighborhood, stands in contrast to this proposition. Similarly, his joining of the majority opinion of *National Organization of Women v. Schneider* (1994) to apply the federal Racketeer Influenced and Corrupt Organization (RICO) Act to anti-abortion protestors, despite possible First Amendment objections that application of the act threatened the rights of protestors, might also question this claim. However, one could argue that the Court did not see the latter case as a First Amendment case, but instead one involving an issue of legislative clarification of a act to which the Court had already given broad construction. Moreover, both cases involved demonstrations, and Scalia generally seems unsupportive of this type of political action, especially when the issue of public safety is invoked. Hence, political order and stability may have trumped expressive freedom claims in both of these, as well as in other cases before Scalia.

Despite his views in *Frisby* and *Schneider*, and while not arguing that the justice's holdings are necessarily controlled by who the speaker is, Scalia's sympathies, nonetheless, seem unsupportive of more liberal construction of free SPA except when it comes to defending pro-life, nonunion, government, or corporate political speech. In-depth analysis of Scalia's legal reasoning and holdings supports many of these claims, and also provides further insights into Scalia's jurisprudence.

Free Speech Decisions

As noted above, of all the areas of First Amendment free SPA, justice Scalia is most sympathetic towards free speech claims. Of the forty-one identified free speech cases, he has supported free speech claims eighteen times or in forty-four percent of his decisions. His support for speech claims is not universal across all speech categories. In the areas of pure speech, he opposes speech claims most of the time, and in the areas of obscenity he opposes claims in all his decisions. Yet in expressive conduct he opposes free speech claims only twenty-eight percent of the time. Examination of Scalia's freedom of speech decisions reveal several characteristics: 1) a generally narrow reading of what political speech is and what the First Amendment protects; 2) a limited notion of what constitutes governmental harm to free speech; 3) limited free speech rights or claims when the individual is a government employee or recipient of discretionary government largess or assistance; and 4) significant leeway given to governments to regulate speech to protect the integrity of the electoral process.[7]

Pure Speech

In the areas of pure speech Scalia has penned his own opinion in only a handful of cases, while joining majority decisions in several others. In *United Presbyterian Church v. Reagan* (1984) at issue was a constitutional challenge by several religious groups of an Executive Order that established intelligence-gathering functions against any domestic organizations deemed to be engaged in unlawful activities. Because the appellants alleged that such surveillance would have a "chilling effect" upon their political activities, including activities surrounding their support of some Central American political refugees, they claimed that the Executive Order violated their First Amendment free speech rights.

Judge Scalia, writing for a unanimous three judge panel, held that the appellants lacked the "injury-in-fact standing requirement imposed by Article III of the Constitution" (ibid.: 1378). Scalia held that for the Church to demonstrate a chilling effect upon their First Amendment activities they had to show some "concrete harm (past or immediately threatened) apart from the 'chill' itself" (ibid.: 1378). Scalia claims that the " 'harm of the chilling effect' is to be distinguished from the immediate threat of concrete, harmful action" (ibid.: 1380). The former will not support standing because there is no real harm, but the latter may involve threat of arrest and would grant standing to bring suit. Mere surveillance and whatever subjective threat one may feel from it is not harmful or chilly enough to the First Amendment to grant standing. Surveillance plus imminent threat of arrest or prosecution is required.

United Presbyterian articulates a narrow sense of what harm to First Amendment rights entails. A similarly narrow notion of harm is found in *Block v. Meese* (1986) where a movie distributor was challenging a State Department classification of two Canadian films critical of Reagan environmental policies as political propaganda pursuant to the Foreign Agents Registration Act of 1938. For our purposes, the two relevant claims by the distributor were that the Reagan Administration misinterpreted the statutory definition of "political propaganda" to apply to these documentaries, and that such a labelling of the films by the government constituted a form of governmental disapproval of these films and, thus, constituted a violation of the distributor's First Amendment free speech rights. Scalia dismissed both claims.

First, Scalia states that the distributor's claim that films can only be classified as propaganda if they are "subversive" or serve the interests of a foreign principal is false (ibid.: 1309–1310). Instead, relying upon dictionary definitions of propaganda, Scalia notes how while the ordinary usage of propaganda connotes this meaning, a broader meaning of the term also includes " 'ideas, facts, or allegations spread deliberately to further one's cause or to damage an opposing cause' " (ibid.: 1311, quoting *Webster's Ninth New Collegiate Dictionary* 1983: 942). Employing this broader meaning of the word, Scalia argued

> [I]t seems to us that in labelling something "propaganda" the government is not expressing its own disapproval but is merely identifying an objective category of speech of which the public generally disapproves (ibid.: 1312).

Even if the government were seeking to express its disapproval, the then-court of appeals judge contended that not "every government action which affects speech implicates the first amendment" (ibid.: 1312), and that the court knows of no case where "uninhibited, robust, and wide-open debate" consists of debate from which the government is excluded, or an " 'uninhibited marketplace of ideas' (is) one in which the government's wares cannot be advertised" (ibid.: 1313). In short, there is a long history of the government not remaining neutral but instead taking positions on topics such as polygamy or Hitler's Germany (ibid.: 1313). The mere taking of a position that expresses an opinion about two films is not a form of harm, coercion, or intimidation to dissuade people from seeing the film. The government is a participant in the intellectual marketplace of ideas and should be allowed to present its views.

Similar views about the government's nonneutrality regarding controversial issues is found in *Rust v. Sullivan* (1991). Although the majority opinion was written by Chief Justice Rehnquist, Scalia joined in upholding a regulation of the Secretary of Health and Human Services banning abortion counseling in federally funded Title X clinics. The Court claimed that the Secretary's regulations were made pursuant to 42 U.S.C. $\S \S$ 300–300a–6, which at 300a–4 1008 stated that "none of the funds appropriated under this subchapter shall be used in programming where abortion is a method of family planning."

In this case, Scalia agreed with the majority that the ban on abortion counseling is not a form of viewpoint discrimination against a particular position and not a violation of the First Amendment. In *Rust*, the majority rejected claims that congressional discretion to protect and regulate the way public money is spent denies the government the right to engage in the content restriction of speech. The regulation struck down was one that prevented federally-funded clinics from discussing abortion. The majority here did not see women or Title X employees giving up their First Amendment rights. Instead, the women and Title X workers retain their right to hold views on abortion (ibid.: 1775); however the "(g)overnment has no constitutional duty to subsidize an activity merely because it is constitutionally protected and may validly choose to fund childbirth over abortion" (ibid.: 1776). Finally, by not receiving information about abortion, the Court reasoned, a woman was no worse off than had Congress never enacted Title X (ibid.: 1778). Thus, the government had a right to express its views through government dispersement of funds, and the refusal to provide funds that support a contrary viewpoint does not violate the First Amendment. The government need not remain neutral, but it may join the ideological debate on a subject much as a private actor or agency would use its money to further a political position.[8]

Recognizing the legitimate use of private money to further a political cause and express a First Amendment viewpoint is exactly the logic behind Scalia's joining of the majority opinion in *Federal Election Commission v.*

Massachusetts Citizens for Life (1986) and his dissent in *Austin v. Michigan Chamber of Commerce* (1990). In both cases he votes to strike down applicable campaign finance reform legislation as a violation of the First Amendment free speech rights of the organizations in question.

In the first case, *Federal Election Commission v. Massachusetts Citizens for Life* (1986, hereinafter "*MCFL*") the Supreme Court was confronted with the application of a Federal Election Campaign Act (FECA) provision § 441b that "prohibits corporations from using treasury funds to make expenditures 'in connection with' any federal election and requires that any expenditure for such purpose be financed by voluntary contributions to a separate segregated fund." MCFL was a nonprofit, nonstock corporation supporting pro-life issues through a variety of activities including an infrequently published newsletter. In question was whether § 441b of FECA applied to an MCFL newsletter, published prior to an election primary, that urged Massachusetts citizens to vote for pro-life candidates even though the publication did not specifically say "vote for Smith" or whomever (ibid.: 620, 623). The Court did hold that this newsletter was a violation of § 441b. But this provision, as applied to MCFL, was unconstitutional because it excessively burdened the organization's First Amendment rights.

In reaching this holding, Scalia joined the majority in agreeing that preventing the "corrosive influence of concentrated corporate wealth" (ibid.: 627) was a compelling enough state interest to require separate segregated political funds to ensure that resources acquired in the economic marketplace do not have an unfair advantage in the political marketplace (ibid.: 627). However, justification for § 441b restrictions do "not uniformly apply to all corporations" (ibid.: 631). Some corporations, such as the MCFL, "have features more akin to voluntary political associations than business firms, and therefore should not have to bear burdens on independent spending solely because of their incorporated status" (ibid.: 631). Groups such as MCFL that were formed for ideological purposes, lacking shareholders and not acting as conduits for a business or a union are really political associations and not corporations (ibid.: 631). Therefore, the special accounting procedures and requirements that compliance with § 441b would entail are "more extensive than [they] would be if it (MCFL) were not incorporated" (ibid.: 626). Thus, because this segregated fund requirement is overly broad in its application to the MCFL, its application in this case is unconstitutional.

Scalia's joining of *MCFL*'s majority opinion stands in contrast to his *Austin v. Michigan Chamber of Commerce* dissent from a majority holding that upheld a similar segregated fund requirement in Michigan. The six-person majority held that corporations, even some nonprofit ones such as the Michigan Chamber of Commerce, which received its money from business members of the local chamber of commerce, could constitutionally be prohibited from using direct corporate treasury funds for independent expenditures to support or oppose candidates for office. Following arguments made in *MCFL* and *Buckley v. Valeo* (1976), the Court ruled that campaign finance laws may, to some extent, regulate the conditions affecting the marketplace of ideas to ensure that it functions fairly and efficiently. Scalia dissented, holding that the Michigan law interfered with the First Amendment rights of the chamber, which he labeled a voluntary political association (*Austin* 1416). To summarize the dissent here,[9] the justice's claim is that the majority holding is inconsistent with the First Amendment, by way both of its original intent and recent rulings on this amendment.

To support these claims, Scalia argues against the majority's position that legislatures can regulate corporate speech because "[s]tate law grants [corporations] special advantages" that allow them to amass wealth (ibid.: 1408). In citing *Pickering v. the Board of Education* (1968) and *Speiser v. Randall* (1958), Scalia reminds the majority that the "(s)tate cannot exact as the price of those special advantages the forfeiture of First Amendment rights" (*Austin* 1408).[10] The only way speech can be limited is by securing a compelling state need. In this case, the majority's contention that large corporate treasuries and corporate spending threaten public discourse is not narrowly tailored enough to justify limiting their ability to speak (ibid.: 1409, 1413). Additionally, as noted earlier in this chapter, Scalia also indicates that the Michigan Chamber of Commerce is more like a voluntary political association as described by the majority in *MCFL* and de Tocqueville in *Democracy in America* (ibid.: 1415–1416) than Madison's political faction. Although applying the three criteria of *MCFL* used to distinguish corporations from voluntary associations, i.e., voluntary associations are formed for ideological purposes, lack shareholders, and do not act as conduits for a business or a union, then it is debatable whether the chamber met any of these requirements very well or at all. Unfortunately, Scalia gives no argument to show how the *MCFL* rules apply to the Chamber of Commerce in Austin. Suppressing these voluntary associations, according to Scalia, is destructive and impoverishes public debate (ibid.: 1416) Thus, to burden the chamber with a segregated political fund requirement would be analogous to encumbering the *MCFL* with such a fund requirement. Such a requirement would place an excessive burden upon the free speech rights of the Chamber and thus would be unconstitutional.

When Scalia's views in *MCFL* and *Austin* are contrasted we find the justice making two distinct claims. The first one is that regulation appears to be a form of censorship. Second, he also appears to be moving towards the idea that all corporations are equivalent to de Tocqueville's notion of voluntary political associations. If we follow the direction of Scalia's thought in *Austin*, we see that elections represent the expression of political ideas, that all corporations are important vessels of political ideas, and, thus to regulate corporate spending in elections would be to suppress important First Amendment rights of free expression, which would result in censorship and damage to the electoral process. Hence, when we read *Block, Rust, MCFL*, and *Austin* together, we see that the government need not remain neutral in political debates. It is under no obligation to fund or support viewpoints that are contrary to its own preferences and, furthermore, it may not regulate other associations from expressing their viewpoints through the disbursement of money.

Scalia's support of other pure speech decisions similarly endorse the propositions that the government may not directly suppress speech it does not like, that individuals may not be forced to fund or listen to ideas they do not support, that government may regulate speech to ensure the integrity of the electoral process, or that government must permit its employees to hold viewpoints inconsistent with public mandates. In all of these cases, Scalia appears to be supporting broadly applied principles that endorse free speech. In reality, he endorses numerous restrictions based upon careful distinctions or contingencies associated with the First Amendment claims.

In *Boos v. Barry* (1988), Scalia joined the Court in voiding a District of Columbia ordinance making it unlawful, within 500 feet of a foreign embassy, to congregate or display any sign that seeks to bring the foreign government into public disrepute. The O'Connor majority opinion held that this ordinance was a "clearly content based *restriction on political speech in a public forum*" requiring strict scrutiny (1157, 1164, O'Connor's emphasis). The Court questioned whether the protection of the dignity of foreign diplomatic personnel was really a compelling state interest, yet it did not void the law on this ground but rather claimed that the regulation was not tailored narrowly enough to achieve the desired objective (ibid.: 1164, 1170). Because the ban on picketing near an embassy was not the least restrictive means to achieve the desired state objective, and because the ban broadly implicated fundamental speech rights (ibid.: 1169–70), the District of Columbia ordinance was declared unconstitutional.

In juxtaposition to striking down the District of Columbia ordinance because it was not narrowly tailored, Scalia supported another O'Connor majority opinion upholding a ban on protests in private residential neighborhoods. In *Frisby v. Schultz* (1988), at issue was a Wisconsin municipal ordinance that proscribed all picketing in residential neighborhoods, which was applied to forbid protestors from demonstrating in front of the home of a physician who performed abortions. While acknowledging that this picketing ban operated "at the core of the First Amendment" (ibid.: 2499), the Court refused to view the ban in the same way as the District of Columbia ordinance. Instead, the Court read the municipal law more narrowly (ibid.: 2501) and argued that it was a reasonable "place" restriction on speech to protect residential privacy and the unwilling listener (ibid.: 2502). The Court argued that residents in their neighborhood were unwilling "captives" to these protests, and that this ban on residential protesting was consistent with a line of past precedents seeking to protect unwanted speech. Hence, in dismissing claims by Brennan's dissent that the ban on all residential picketing was overbroad (ibid.: 2506–7), Scalia agreed with the majority that the city ordinance was narrowly tailored and represented a proper balance between the desire for neighborhood privacy and the speech rights of protestors.[11]

In the two *International Society for Krishna Consciousness v. Lee* cases (1992), Scalia also supported limits on the rights of individuals to engage in free speech activities in otherwise public areas in order avoid the duress that recipients of this unwanted speech may experience. In the first case, Scalia joined a Rehnquist majority opinion holding that the solicitation of money by individuals in a public air-terminal was a form of constitutionally protected speech (ibid.: 549). Yet the majority argued that the terminal was not a public forum; instead, the government as a proprietor of the facilities merely had to meet a reasonableness test in the construction of regulations that seek to maintain the order of the facility (ibid.: 549). Scalia supported limits on solicitation in airports because the terminals were not public forums and because the terminals had a duty to protect other individuals from unwanted requests. Similarly, in the second *Krishna* case, Scalia joined in a dissenting opinion holding that the mere leafletting in a public airport could be limited for the same reasons. In both these cases Scalia supported narrowly drawn conceptions of what constituted a public forum and the broad discretion of the government to protect individuals from unwanted speech.

Similarly, in *Forsyth County v. Nationalist Movement* (1992), Scalia dissented from the majority opinion that struck down a Forsyth County, Georgia ordinance that gave the county administrator the authority to adjust parade permit fees for groups depending on the expected amount of money required to maintain public order during the parade. For the Blackmun majority, this discretion to change fees was too broad, and it clearly allowed the administrator to alter the fee structure depending on whether he agreed with the viewpoint of the group asking for the permit (ibid.: 112–13).

Hence, the ordinance was facially invalid and a violation of the First and Fourteenth Amendment free speech rights. Joining Rehnquist's dissent, Scalia disagree with the majority claim that the potential for the administrator to abuse his discretion renders the ordinance facially unconstitutional. Instead, as in other cases where governmental authority is involved, Scalia seems willing to defer to the government to exercise its discretion until such time as clear instances of abuse occur. In this case, because there were no factual instances to indicate that the administrator had abused his discretion in the way the majority suggested, the ordinance was not unconstitutional. Potential abuses of First Amendment rights embedded in the language of ordinances do not seem to be enough for Scalia to declare a law unconstitutional. The government must actually abuse this discretion and commit harm before Scalia will declare the ordinance unconstitutional.

A good example of how the government must actually act unconstitutionally before Scalia will void a law is found in *Simon & Schuster v. Members of the New York State Crimes Victims Board*. (1991). Scalia again agreed with O'Connor's majority opinion striking down a New York State law confiscating the royalties earned when an author described the events or circumstances surrounding a crime or criminal activity. Here the majority held that although New York State had an interest in compensating crime victims, the law that confiscated the royalties of this type of speech and no other was not narrowly tailored because it could lead to the suppression of many classic and important works of literature (ibid.: 512). This law singled out a particular type of speech that the state does not like (ibid.: 508–9). Thus, the majority held that the state was directly burdening an idea it did not approve of, and this was clearly a violation of the First Amendment.

In *Eu v. San Francisco County Democratic Central Committee* (1989), Scalia joins Marshall's majority opinion striking down a California law that precluded party officials from making primary endorsements. Here, he argued that to deny a political party the right to endorse candidates prevents the party from undertaking the functions it must to mobilize political power and undertake its party functions related to articulating a particular political message (ibid.: 1021). For Scalia, political parties are voluntary associations and to deny them the right to endorse is to deny them their ability to contribute to the marketplace of ideas.

In contrast to *Eu*, where Scalia struck down legislative efforts to regulate the political process, in *Burson v. Freeman* (1992) and *Burdick v. Takushi* (1992) the associate justice upheld state bans on campaigning within 100 feet of polling places on election day and write-in voting, respectively. In both cases, Scalia was willing to uphold restrictions of free speech claims while merely employing rational basis and not heightened scrutiny tests. In *Burson* the majority argued that the ban on campaigning within 100 feet of a poll was a content-based restriction that had to pass a strict scrutiny examination and demonstrate that the State of Tennessee had a compelling state interest in restricting First Amendment rights. The majority held that Tennessee's interest in preventing voter fraud and intimidation was a compelling state interest to sustain the ban because the 100-foot restriction on campaigning was narrowly tailored to secure this important objective. Scalia concurs with the the majority holding but argues that campaigning bans like this one are traditional and date back to the early nineteenth century. Hence, no public forum exists, and no restriction of speech within a public forum has occurred. The Court merely needed to examine the statute on a rational basis standard and not employ an "exacting scrutiny" (ibid.: 4400).

Similarly, in *Burdick v. Takushi* (1992) Scalia joins Justice White's majority opinion upholding the State of Hawaii's ban on write-in voting. According to White, strict scrutiny is not applied to all laws that burden voting (ibid.: 256). To apply such a standard to all restrictions on voting would tie the hands of state legislatures seeking to "assure that elections are operated equitably and efficiently" (ibid.: 256). Instead,

[a] more flexible standard applies. A court considering the challenge to a state election law must weigh "the character and magnitude of the asserted injury to the rights protected by the First and Fourteenth Amendments that the plaintiff seeks to vindicate" against "the precise interests put forward by the State as justifications for the burden imposed by its rule," taking into consideration "the extent to which those interests make it necessary to burden the plaintiff's rights" (ibid.: 253, quoting *Tashjian v. Republican Party of Connecticut*, 213–14 (1986)).

Applying this standard, Scalia agreed with White that "when a state election law provision imposes only 'reasonable, nondiscriminatory restrictions' upon the First and Fourteenth Amendment rights of voters," then the state's regulatory interests will justify those restrictions (ibid.: 254). In the case of Hawaii, the state's need to ensure political stability (ibid.: 257), channel expressive activity (ibid.: 256), and prevent " 'unrestrained factionalism at the general election' " (ibid.: 257, quoting *Munro v. Socialist Party* 538 (1986)), outweigh any voter's interest in casting protest votes or otherwise using the ballot to express short-range and personal goals (ibid.: 257). In sum, some type of balancing test that is less than strict scrutiny sustains Hawaii's interests in running fair and efficient elections even though that legislation limits First Amendment expressive rights. *Burdick* and *Bunson*, along with several other of Scalia's decisions regarding the political process, suggest that a governmental need to protect the integrity of the political process by limiting factionalism generally outweighs any expressive interests voters, citizens, or parties have. Seemingly left unconsidered by Scalia is how the integrity of the political process can be sustained if numerous state interests continue to trump the rights citizens need to make intelligent and meaningful political choices.

However, in *Lehnert v. Ferris Faculty Association* (1991), Scalia does seem concerned with the rights of some individuals not to have their expressive rights limited. In this case, he agreed with the majority holding that in agency shop settings, unions could not charge nonunion members for the costs associated with articulating the union's political views. In his concurrence, Scalia argued that the limit to which a state law could mandate nonunion members to pay a service fee to a union was to eliminate the problems of "free-ridership" associated with nonunion members receiving union benefits without paying for them (ibid.: 1978). In reasoning that somewhat parallels the *Rust v. Sullivan* claim that the government is under no obligation to fund positions it disagrees with, Scalia here supports the majority's logic that no state can legislate an agency-shop fee that forces some people to subsidize political views that they do not support. The law can not financially compel people to support the opinions of a group or association; instead the contributions must be voluntary, as would the choice to join a union. For a state to mandate the payment of fees used for political purposes would be to move beyond neutrality and force people to support a particular organization.

A final restriction on speech is found in *Rankin v. McPherson* (1987) and to a lesser extent in *Waters v. Churchill* (1994). In *Rankin*, Scalia authors a bitter dissent against the majority opinion, which held that a government employee's free speech rights were violated when she was fired for her comment about Reagan's assassination attempt. Specifically, the employee stated that was that she hoped next time they would get him. Scalia saw absolutely no First Amendment protection in this speech (ibid.: 2903–4) and wrote that the government, in this case a law-enforcement agency, had no obligation to employ someone who "ride[s] with the cops and cheer[s] for the robbers" (ibid.: 2902). A government employee qua employee has fewer free speech rights than ordinary citizens (ibid.: 2902), and McPherson's speech has no "public value" whatsoever that entitles it to First Amendment protection (ibid.: 2903). Similarly, in *Waters*, Scalia also rules against a free speech claim involving a public employee fired for making comments that were overheard.

Overall, Scalia's views on pure speech do not support broad universal or absolutist views on the support for free speech. While pure political speech is important, numerous values qualify Scalia's endorsement of that principle. Employment in government service, the need to protect captive individuals from unwanted speech, the need to preserve the electoral process, and the location of the speech, among other concerns, all appear to define the limits of free speech claims. Scalia has also sought to make the government a participant in the marketplace of ideas and, accordingly, has sought to distinguish between cases in which the government directly suppresses speech from situations where it refuses to endorse or support it. The latter type of action is not a form of censorship or intrusion upon the First Amendment.[12] In these cases, Congress distinguishes between censorship and simply refusing to fund programs or projects it does not support. The distinction between suppression and refusal to support speech appears, Scalia's disclaimers notwithstanding, to be similar to the old distinction between rights and privileges as far as determining how the government treats specific individuals. For example, in McAuliffe v. New Bedford (1892), Holmes had argued that public employees "may have a constitutional right to talk politics, but . . . no right to be a policeman." In making the distinction between a right and privilege to public office, Holmes contended that occupying a public office was no more than a privilege. Certain rights, including those to engage in some political activities, may be curtailed in the interests of promoting reasonable control over government employees. Similarly, one could argue that while one has a constitutional right to express one's views free from government suppression, the government has no obligation to support that expression by giving one money or employment to express those beliefs.

Overall, the distinctions and principles that Scalia has articulated in the pure speech category are found throughout his decisions in other areas of the First Amendment, suggesting that some critics are correct in noting that the application of broad principles is important to Scalia (Savage 1992: 326). This application of broad principles covering all areas of the First Amendment intimates that Scalia is treating the First Amendment more coherently than he once thought it could be treated, and it also indicates a possible rethinking of the relationship of the basic categories of speech that the Court has created in the last seventy years. This is exactly what the justice appears prepared to do in R.A.V. v. St. Paul (1993) which is examined in the next section.

Expressive Conduct and "Political Correctness" Codes

Scalia's expressive conduct decisions reveal that he is willing to recognize Court precedent in Spence v. Washington (1974) and United States v.

O'Brien (1968) that certain types of conduct are forms of constitutionally protected speech. However, he is only willing to label certain types of conduct as expressive when the action is so inextricably connected to speech in the vast majority of the cases of that action such that it would be impossible to sort out nonspeech versus speech imbued instances of an action. He will only strike regulation or legislation affecting expressive conduct when the aim of the regulation or legislation is intentionally to suppress the expressive conduct and message being communicated. Finally, if Scalia's expressive conduct decision in *R.A.V. v. St. Paul* indicates the future direction of his First Amendment jurisprudence, the justice appears ready to alter the basic approach the Court has adopted to address the different categories of speech including expressive conduct.

Of his five holdings upholding speech claims, three addressed the same issue, i.e., flag-burning, and all three indicated the inherent expressive nature of the act in question, as well as the explicit purpose of the law to suppress that expression. In *Texas v. Johnson* (1989), *United States v. Eichman*, and *United States v. Haggerty* (1990, *Eichman* and *Haggerty* were rendered as one opinion), Scalia joined two majority opinions authored by Justice Brennan. The first case struck down a Texas statute that made flag-burning illegal. The second case involved the United States Flag Protection Act of 1989. This law was passed in response to the *Texas v. Johnson* decision and it criminalized anyone who "knowingly mutilates, defaces, physically defiles, burns . . ." a United States flag (103 Stat. 777, 18 U.S.C.A. § 700 [Supp.1990]).

In both decisions, Scalia agreed with the majority holding that application of the *O'Brien* test indicated that the act of flag-burning was expressive conduct, and that the singular aim of the Texas or United States statute was to suppress that form of expression (*Texas v. Johnson* 1989: 3549–50; *U.S. v. Eichman* 1990: 2408–9). Evidence of the legislation in both cases was aimed at expressive conduct and not at banning all forms of flag-burning was that the Texas statute only made flag-burning illegal when the aim of the burner was "to seriously offend one or more persons likely to observe or discover his action" (*Texas v. Johnson* 1989: 2537, n. 1), while the United States statute exempted flag-burning from prosecution in cases where the burning was done for the purposes of flag disposal (*United States v. Eichman* 1990: 2407). The only case of flag-burning that each of these statutes would prohibit would be those when the agent burning the flag sought to express a message through the act of flag-burning. Under both statutes, the aim clearly and singularly would be to suppress the constitutionally protected free speech rights of an individual.

In *Lebron v. Washington Metropolitan Area Transit Authority* (1984),

Scalia joined Judge Bork's majority opinion striking down a transit authority's decision to ban an artist from displaying a poster critical of the Reagan administration in a subway station. In this case, Scalia rejected the claim by the district court that the poster lacked speech content, or that the poster lacked constitutional protection because of a politically deceptive message. Application of the *O'Brien* test revealed the poster to be imbued with speech and the effort to prevent the display of the poster a clear case of prior restraint (ibid.: 895–6). Bork's opinion specifically notes a concern by Scalia that the judiciary had no business "passing upon the truth or falsity of political pamphleteering or advertising" (ibid.: 898), and that with the exception of obscenity, no case he know of supported content-based prior restraint (ibid.: 898). As with the flag-burning cases, the singular focus of this act was expressive, and the aim of the government was to suppress that constitutionally protected form of speech.

In juxtaposition to the above cases, in two opinions that Scalia did author, he held that neither of the actions in question was a form of expressive conduct. In *Community for Creative Non-Violence v. Watt* (1983, hereinafter "*Watt*") Scalia held that overnight camping in Lafayette Park across from the White House was not a form of expressive conduct, while in *Barnes v. Glen Theatre, Inc.* (1991) he similarly held that nonobscene nude dancing lacked First Amendment protection. In *Watt*, Scalia disagreed with the majority holding that a Park Service regulation banning overnight sleeping in Lafayette Park interfered with the First Amendment rights of individuals seeking to demonstrate the impact of Reagan's policy towards the homeless. Instead, Scalia did not see the overnight sleeping as an "integral and expressive part of a demonstration otherwise protected by the First Amendment" (ibid.: 608).

According to the dissenters (including Scalia's dissent) in *Watt*, not all or even very many forms of camping that would occur in parks would be undertaken for expressive purposes and that to expect the government to separate out "expressive camping" from nonexpressive camping would be difficult (ibid.: 610, 623, 626). Regulations that impose general bans on camping, as in this case, lack the singular aim of suppressing expressive conduct, unlike cases where bans on draftcard burning, wearing armbands, or affixing peace symbols to the flag (ibid.: 617). In those cases, most incidences of these actions would be inherently expressive, unlike camping where most cases would not be expressive (ibid.: 617–8). The government does not have a less restrictive means of enforcing a general ban on camping that could sort out the few instances of expressive camping (ibid.: 619–20). Overall, the regulation against overnight sleeping in the park is not aimed at suppressing speech but rather is a legitimate time, place, and manner restriction (ibid.: 613) that does not ban all forms of speech (ibid.: 623, 626); it is only an "accidental" and not a "purposive restraint of expression" (ibid.: 623).

A similar distinction between laws that generally ban a certain activity versus laws targeted at expressive conduct is made in *Barnes v. Glen Theatre, Inc.* (1991). At issue here was an Indiana public decency law that precluded establishments from providing totally nude dancing and instead required the dancers to wear pasties and a G-string. Glen Theatre, Inc., claimed that the ordinance violated the First Amendment and sued to enjoin its enforcement. While the majority opinion held that nonobscene nude dancing implicated some expressive conduct but nonetheless could be regulated (ibid.: 2462–3), Scalia argued that "the challenged regulation must be upheld, not because it survives some lower level of First Amendment scrutiny, but because, as a general law regulating conduct and not specifically directed at expression, it is not subject to First Amendment scrutiny at all" (ibid.: 2463).

Facially, according to Scalia, the ordinance is not at all directed at expression but instead is a general law regulating nudity and public decency (ibid.: 2464–2465). Moreover, Scalia notes that potentially every law prohibits some type of conduct, and that potentially all forms of action could be expressive (ibid.: 2466), yet not every law that restricts in fact restricts expressive conduct as protected by the First Amendment. Only when "the government prohibits conduct *precisely because of it communicative attributes*" (ibid.: 2466, Scalia's emphasis) is the restriction unconstitutional. In the case of the Indiana ordinance and Glen Theatre, Inc., the restriction is against conduct and not expression (ibid.: 2468).

Perhaps the most significant expressive conduct decision of Scalia's was *R.A.V. v. St. Paul*. This decision is important for two reasons. First, it is the only majority opinion Scalia has written upholding a First Amendment claim. Second, the argumentation in the decision reveals much about the justice's views on the First Amendment and how he may be articulating the new Rehnquist Court and conservative understanding of the free speech claims. Scalia's majority opinion was joined by Rehnquist, Kennedy, Souter, and Thomas (all Reagan-Bush appointees). Separate concurring opinions were filed by other members of the Court who, while agreeing with Scalia's holding, disagreed with his reasoning. At issue in this case was an individual charged with burning a cross on the front lawn of an African American family in violation of a City of St. Paul, Minnesota Bias-Motivated Crime Ordinance that states that

[W]hoever places on public or private property a symbol, object, appellation, characterization, or graffiti, including, but not limited to, a burning cross or

Nazi swastika, which one knows or has reasonable grounds to know arouses anger, harm or resentment in others on the basis of race, color, creed, religion, or gender commits disorderly conduct and shall be guilty of a misdemeanor (St. Paul, Minn. Legis. Code §292.02 (1990)).

All nine justices agreed that the ordinance was unconstitutional. While the concurrences would have voided the ordinance on the overbreadth doctrine first articulated in *Broadrick v. Oklahoma* (1973), Scalia rejects the overbroad approach and instead, seeks to strike the ordinance on the basis of the "proscribable content" of the ordinance (*R.A.V.* 1993: 318–9).

Specifically, Scalia commences his analysis in this case by reviewing past Supreme Court jurisprudence that has defined categories of speech, such as libel or obscenity, that have been viewed as falling outside of First Amendment protection (ibid.: 317). The justice then denies that the Court has really meant to create categories of speech through these distinctions; instead what these distinctions "mean is that these areas of speech can . . . be regulated because of their constitutionally proscribable content . . . [and] not because they are categories of speech entirely invisible to the Constitution" (ibid.: 318).

Once he has explained that First Amendment jurisprudence is simply governed by content (or by whether or not a type of speech falls within the Constitution or not), Scalia contends that the government may make these types of speech subject to regulation, but it may not make further distinctions within this content regulation. Scalia states that government may proscribe libel, but not the proscribe libel critical of the government (ibid.: 318). Similarly, in the case of the St. Paul ordinance, the city prohibits the use of "fighting words" that do lie outside of constitutional protection (ibid.: 319), yet it only prohibits the use of these words to "communicate messages of racial, gender, or religious intolerance" (ibid.: 324). The city does not similarly prohibit the same manner of expressing views supportive of tolerance towards these groups. Consequently, the city fails to grant even-handed and neutral treatment to different groups expressing views regarding a similar content of speech (ibid.: 320–24). Instead, it has "handicapp[ed] the expression of particular ideas" (ibid.: 324–5). If St. Paul is going to ban the use of fighting words or other modes of expression, it must do it categorically and not make special exemptions for some. In short, the city must use a general principle to regulate all uses of fighting words, not simply a subspecies of their use.

In dissent, Justice White chastises the majority opinion for inventing a new jurisprudence premised upon a notion of "underinclusiveness" (ibid.: 329–330). By that, White argues that Scalia's approach seems to set up an all-or-nothing proposition when it comes to the regulation of speech. For Scalia, legislatures must treat all types of speech within a specific content-area the same regardless of how (or where or when) they are used (ibid.: 330–331). This approach to the First Amendment, besides fundamentally distorting the seriousness or reality of the Court's past categorical distinctions (ibid.: 329), fails to appreciate how these categories "have provided a principled and narrowly focused means for distinguishing between expression that the government may regulate freely and that which it may regulate on the basis of content only upon showing a compelling need" (ibid.: 329). The categorical approach allows for the Court to take different approaches to the types of speech involved and also to make distinctions based on the contingencies surrounding the way the message is expressed (e.g., by means of time, manner, or place, among other things). Scalia's approach seems to obliterate all these distinctions and approach speech regulation in an all-or-nothing fashion.

Parenthetically, Scalia's opinion in R.A.V. stands in somewhat curious contrast to his joining of the unanimous Rehnquist opinion in *Wisconsin v. Mitchell* (1993). In *Mitchell*, at issue was a Wisconsin law that enhanced the maximum penalty of an offense when that offense was motivated by the victim's race, gender, or other specific characteristics. Arguably, if First Amendment considerations led to the invalidation of the St. Paul cross-burning ordinance, one's attitudes towards members of a specific racial group could also be considered unconstitutional content-punishment of one's views on race. However, the Court did not agree, instead, arguing that one's abstract views on race were not being punished; instead this was simply another factor to be weighed when considering the state of mind and intentionality of the defendant (ibid.: 444–6). Thus, the Court rejected the claim that R.A.V. was controlling and that the decision in this case was contrary to it. *Mitchell* and R.A.V. send somewhat contradictory signals when it comes to Scalia's views on the legal enforcement of P.C. or "politically correct" codes that punish individuals for their views towards members of specific racial or ethnic groups. On the one hand, cross-burning motivated by racial groups towards Blacks is protected by the First Amendment, but crimes motivated by hatred towards whites are not. Perhaps the resolution of the issue is that in R.A.V. the primary issue is how the Court focused on the abstract views or political message of the cross-burner as they were tied up in symbolic speech, while in *Mitchell* the focus was on the criminal harm resulting from animus directed towards another. Perhaps even other political considerations factor into Scalia's views here. Until the Court takes additional cases on this subject, clarification of Scalia's views remain merely speculation.

Scalia's rulings on expressive conduct suggest several tentative observations. First, the justice appeared willing until recently to accept the basic *O'Brien* test as far as identifying when something is expressive conduct. Yet to consider an action expressive, one must show that the conduct and message are almost always inextricably connected such that the aim of the prohibition necessarily limits speech communication. Further, Scalia appeared to read *O'Brien* as "supportive of my (Scalia's) view since it shows the importance of statutory purpose" (*Community for Creative Non-Violence v. Watt* 625). What this and Scalia's other opinions in the area of expressive conduct prior to *R.A.V. v. St. Paul* reveal is a reading of the *O'Brien* test as somewhat intent-based. To invalidate the legislation or regulation one must show that the intent of the law was aimed at suppressing speech. Unless one can demonstrate how the regulated conduct and speech are necessarily connected and thus show that obviously the regulation is aimed at the speech or the specific regulation it appears that the justice will uphold the regulation.

The *R.A.V.* opinion throws some of these claims into doubt. Scalia's rethinking of what the categories of the First Amendment are and his apparent "all-or-nothing" approach to speech raise questions about whether tests or distinctions like those formulated in *O'Brien* can continue to be used by the justice. This criticism is generally the one developed by Justice White in his *R.A.V.* concurrence. Moreover it remains to be seen how Scalia will reconcile his opinions in this case with the distinctions and tests formulated in the areas of pure speech that he has embraced in cases such as *Burson v. Freeman* (1992) and *Burdick v. Takushi* (1992) as little as one week prior to *R.A.V.* opinion.

Yet the First Amendment jurisprudence formulated in the *R.A.V.* is not completely surprising. Consistent with earlier expressive conduct cases, Scalia still focuses upon the overall intent of the legislation when seeking to regulate conduct, and he continues to look at the speech content that the legislation seeks to regulate even if his notion has changed of what constitutes content or how it is applied. All of the expressive conduct decisions seem to be developing a jurisprudence that eschews concentration upon particulars and instead looks towards how general laws or principles affect speech. This direction is consistent with his decisions in other areas of speech and critical commentary on his judicial philosophy (Savage 1992, 326). Finally, the rejection of categories as basic ontological units of the First Amendment seems at odds with earlier comments of Scalia's that acknowledge their existence (Scalia 1987c: 19). Perhaps Scalia's thinking has evolved or changed, or perhaps the decision was dictated by a concern to arrest growing demands for speech conduct codes on campus (Terry

1992, A10; *All Things Considered* [PBS radio broadcast, June 22, 1992]). In the PBS broadcast, Nina Totenburg suggested the decision was in part motivated by a reaction to the "P.C." ("politically correct") movements on campus, and the R.A.V. decision was an effort to stop university codes from endorsing them. Whatever the reason, R.A.V. raises interesting questions that will have to be addressed by Scalia in future First Amendment decisions.

Obscenity

In the area of obscenity and the regulation of sexually oriented businesses, Scalia has expressed the most explicit disagreement with current Court precedent. In *Pope v. Illinois*, (1987) Scalia agreed with the majority's clarification of the third prong of the *Miller* test for obscenity (*Miller v. California* (1973)) that required a jury to determine "whether the work, taken as a whole, lacks serious literary, artistic, political, or scientific value." He concurred that the determination of this prong should be judged not on the basis of an ordinary person in the community standard, but on the basis of an objective or reasonable person standard (ibid.: 1923). In his concurrence, the justice doubted whether reason had anything at all to do with esthetics (ibid.: 1923) and indicated that the attempts to fix a standard for judging obscenity "display the need for reexamination of *Miller*" (ibid.: 1923). Exactly how *Miller* should be redone, is suggested in some of Scalia's other decisions.

In *FW/PBS Inc. v. City of Dallas* (1990) at issue was a City of Dallas ordinance that sought through zoning, licensing, and inspections to regulate the secondary effects of crime and blight associated with sexually oriented businesses. The owners of an adult book store covered by this ordinance sought, among other things, standing to enjoin enforcement of the law. While Scalia joined part of the majority opinion (ibid.: 617), he dissented from the core of it and argued that the Dallas ordinance was constitutional (ibid.: 617).

Here Scalia argued that the current *Miller* test fails to provide local municipalities with the tools necessary to eliminate sexually oriented businesses if they so desire. This is because the *Miller* test requires a focus upon individual books, movies, or performances, rather than upon the general trade in which these businesses engage (ibid.: 618–19). Scalia thus returns to the "pandering" test articulated in *Ginsburg v. United States* (1966), seeking to merge it with the *Miller* test to produce a rule, which states:

[t]he Constitution does not require a State or municipality to permit business that intentionally specializes in, and holds itself forth to the public as specializing in, performance or portrayal of sex acts, sexual organs in a state of arousal, or live human nudity (*FW/PBS* 1990: 622).

The utility of this type of test is that it would allow a municipality to regulate sexually oriented businesses that pander without applying the "rigid test for obscenity that we apply to the determination whether a particular book, film, or performance can be banned" (ibid.: 625). This new test, while subject to claims of overbreadth in its application to other forms of speech (ibid.: 622), is meant easier to apply to businesses that on the whole pander to the prurient interest and, thus, make it easier for communities to regulate and prohibit sexually oriented businesses. Consequently, applying this test to the case before him, Scalia would have upheld the Dallas ordinance (ibid.: 622).

Scalia's new test in *FW/PBS* involves a significant increase in state authority to regulate obscenity and sexually oriented businesses in general. This and other decisions by Scalia in the area of obscenity and sexually oriented businesses suggest little sympathy for this area of speech. For example, in *Barnes v. Glen Theatre, Inc.*, discussed above, Scalia was unwilling to consider nonobscene nude dancing as a form of expressive conduct protected by the First amendment (*Barnes* 2465). Scalia went beyond the majority opinion holding that this dancing did marginally implicate the First Amendment but that it could still be regulated (ibid.: 2463). He held that this conduct had no speech value and could be regulated under public indecency laws (ibid.: 2466–67).

In two decisions prior to *FW/PBS*, Scalia also demonstrated little support for trimming back state regulation of sexually oriented businesses. In *Sable Communications of California, Inc. v. F.C.C.* (1989), Scalia concurred with the majority that a Federal Communications Commission ban on indecent sexually oriented speech as provided through "dial-a-porn" services was unconstitutional. He went on to say in his opinion that although certain sexually suggestive speech is protected, "we do not hold that the Constitution requires public utilities to carry it" (ibid.: 2840). The suggestion here, much like the claim given in *Rust v. Sullivan* is clearly that Congress, the Constitution, and other governmental units are under no obligation to support or fund a constitutionally protected form of speech if they object to or disagree with it.

The other case was *Massachusetts v. Oakes* (1989), and it involved a Massachusetts ordinance used to prosecute a stepfather for taking sexually suggestive photographs of his physically mature fourteen-year-old stepdaughter with the intent of sending them to adult magazines. While Scalia agreed to vacate the Massachusetts Supreme Court decision and return the case to that court for further proceedings, he also offered dicta suggesting a tightening of challenges to "Kiddy Porn" ordinances such as this one. Specifically, Scalia argued that if a person seeks to challenge one of these laws as overbroad in its restriction of constitutionally protected speech, then the "burden of the person whose conduct is legitimately proscribable, and who seeks to invalidate the entire law because of its application to someone else, [needs] to 'demonstrate from the text of [the law] *and from actual fact*' (Scalia's emphasis) that substantial overbreadth exists" (ibid.: 2641). In ordinances such as this, which Scalia saw as narrowly tailored to a specific type of action regarding minors (ibid.: 2641), the burden would not be on the state but the individual to show that the ordinance was overbroad and invalid. Undoubtedly such a switch in the burden of proof is unusual in cases involving a constitutional right where the burden usually shifts to the government to prove both a compelling state interest as well as that this is the least restrictive and only means available to secure that objective.

Justice Scalia's obscenity and sexually oriented business decisions, then, demonstrate a commitment to giving local governments more authority to regulate, as well as placing greater burdens upon litigants to challenge the validity of rules regulating sexually oriented speech and businesses. His decisions also intimate that while the Constitution may force governments to tolerate certain types of speech they do not like, they are under no obligation to assist or support such messages. Thus, distinctions similar to those found in *Rust v. Sullivan* and *Rankin v. McPherson*, where a line is drawn between active government suppression or support of a message versus not actively suppressing a message seems to be repeated in the case of sexually oriented businesses. Governments do not have to take any action to encourage or support this speech, but how far their actions may go before an actual suppression occurs is not clear. Perhaps the difference is much like what Holmes suggested in *Pennsylvania Coal Company v. Mahon* (1922). Here the difference between regulation and takings was noted to be only a matter of degree; i.e., at some point the regulation would be so severe that it would amount to a denial of use of property and, hence, a taking of the property. Yet the degree for Scalia between indifference or nonsupport of some speech versus active discouragement may eventually collapse with many forms of suppression, and turn into legitimate regulation except for a few narrow cases. For example, if, according to Scalia's opinion in *Rust v. Sullivan*, the government may favor childbirth over abortion, is there any reason the state could not favor some types of literature over that which is sexually explicit? While the government obviously could not directly suppress the latter, it perhaps could refuse to grant special zoning or land use or tax breaks to those types of establishments that engage in sexually oriented products.

Corporate Speech

Until the 1992 term, *Board of Trustees of State of New York v. Fox* (1989, hereinafter *"Fox"*) was the only clear case of commercial or corporate speech that Scalia had heard as a federal judge or justice. Two other cases, *Federal Election Commission v. Massachusetts Citizens Concerned for Life* (1986) and *Austin v. Michigan Chamber of Commerce* (1990), while involving corporations, were treated by Scalia as instances of pure political speech and not corporate speech. At issue in *Fox* was a State University of New York (SUNY) Resolution that banned the use of SUNY facilities for private commercial enterprises except as authorized by this resolution. Specifically, the resolution was enforced to prohibit students from holding "Tupperware" parties in dorms. Justice Scalia addressed two questions in his majority opinion upholding the resolution. First, the question was whether the parties were protected commercial speech and second what standards applied when constructing regulations aimed at commercial speech.

Scalia quickly answered the first question in the affirmative by stating that the " 'Tupperware' parties the students seek to hold 'propose a commercial transaction' " (ibid.: 3031). Next Scalia sought to analyze the Tupperware parties in terms of the four-part test the Court had proposed in *Central Hudson Gas & Electric Corporation v. Public Service Commission of New York* (1980) for ascertaining when commercial transactions were constitutionally protected speech:

> At the outset, we must determine whether the expression is protected by the First Amendment. For commercial speech to come within that provision, it at least must concern lawful activity and not be misleading. Next, we must ask whether the asserted governmental interest is substantial. If both inquiries yield positive answers, we must determine whether the regulation directly advances the government interest asserted, and whether it is not more extensive than is necessary to serve that interest (*Fox* 3032, quoting *Central Hudson* at 566).

Agreeing with the court of appeals that the speech here was lawful and not misleading, the court ruled that the transaction was a form of constitutionally protected free speech (ibid.: 3032). Next, Scalia sought to ascertain if the governmental interest to limit the speech—to promote an educational rather than a commercial atmosphere on campus—was substantial (ibid.: 3032). He held that it was.

Finally, the fourth prong of the test was examined to determine if the regulation was more extensive than necessary to serve that governmental interest. At this point, Scalia disagreed with the dissenters who argued that the test here necessitated a "least restrictive means" test (ibid.: 3038–39, Blackmun's dissent). Instead, the fourth prong merely required a "narrowly tailored" test (ibid.: 3033), which was less restrictive than the least restrictive means test. For Scalia, even though this Resolution might implicate some noncommercial speech, its possible overbreadth and application to noncommercial speech did not invalidate the facial validity of the resolution (ibid.: 3036). Instead, Scalia was unwilling to address the specific merits of the enforcement of this resolution to noncommercial speech and remanded the case back to the court of appeals for rehearing (ibid.: 3037–38).

In the 1992 term, the Court heard two corporate speech cases. In both, Scalia sided with the free speech claims of the business over the government. In *Cincinnati v. The Discovery Network* (1993), at issue was a municipal law banning the use of sidewalk newsracks to display and sell magazines. The purpose of the ban was to promote safe and attractive streets and sidewalks. Scalia joined Stevens's majority opinion invalidating the ban on First Amendment grounds. In distinguishing itself from *Fox*, the Stevens opinion did not see a "reasonable fit" between the interest in promoting safe streets and banning newsracks (ibid.: 108). Instead, the ban was not narrowly tailored, and it was not content neutral in that it arbitrarily distinguished between magazines and newspapers when the latter but not the former were banned as a means to promote safety and aesthetics (ibid.: 116–7).

Similarly, in *Edenfield v. Fane* (1993) Justice Scalia joined a Kennedy majority opinion striking down a Florida law banning in-person business solicitations by Certified Public Accountants. As with the *Cincinnati* case, Scalia concurred with the basic claim that commercial speech is protected by the First Amendment (ibid.: 551). Also, as in *Cincinnati*, the *Edenfield* decision held that the four-prong test of *Central Hudson* was the basic test to use to adjudicate restriction on commercial speech, and that the Florida ban was not a reasonable and narrowly tailored restriction upon speech meant to secure some substantial state interest (ibid.: 543).

These cases suggest several interesting observations about Scalia's approach to commercial speech. First, Scalia is unquestionably committed to the view that commercial speech is protected by the First Amendment. Subsequent decisions of Scalia's in the 1993 term, such as *Ibanez v. Florida Department of Business* and *Turner Broadcasting v. F.C.C.* upholding corporate speech rights, are evidence to this point. However, the adoption of a narrowly tailored test is clearly meant to be more permissive of government regulation of commercial speech than the least restrictive means test that had been articulated in previous Court cases on the subject, such as *Board of Airport Commissioners v. Jews for Jesus, Inc.* (1987), and *Houston v. Hill* (1987). This suggests that Scalia should be more willing to let the government restrict corporate as opposed to other types of speech. Yet his holdings more consistently supporting commercial interests appear to indicate that Scalia de facto is not more, but less willing to give the government slack when regulating business speech. Given Scalia's views on other types of nonpolitical speech, i.e., his decisions on commercial speech seem odd, unless we argue that his affirmation of free speech is motivated by specific policy concerns.

Scalia's opinions in *Federal Election Commission v. Massachusetts Citizens for Life* and *Austin v. Michigan Chamber of Commerce* further reinforce the general theme that the justice is willing to find reasons to support commercial speech. In these cases, Scalia found some pure political speech interests implicated and, thus, the commercial speech was subject to the compelling state interest tests as articulated in *O'Brien*. Overall, then, Scalia's jurisprudence acknowledging the First Amendment protections to commercial speech appears to parallel his property law decisions that have given ownership rights increased protections against government regulation (Schultz, 1992a). In short, while government interests may be more important than many types of speech claims, commercial speech claims are de facto looked at more favorably than governmental interests.

Conclusion

As noted in the introduction to this section on freedom of speech, Scalia's decisions demonstrate a generally narrow reading of what political speech is and what the First Amendment protects. Within that is a limited notion of what constitutes government harm to free speech and only direct and intentional suppression of expression is considered unconstitutional. Many values may be considered legitimate limits on free expression, including government employment, protection of a community against sexual pandering, maintenance of the electoral process, protecting captive audiences from unwanted speech, and fostering an educational environment. Yet while dismissing other speech claims, commercial speech warrants protection under the First Amendment. The justice sees an important role for the government in articulating its political viewpoint, and that articulation is not considered suppression of free speech when the government refuses to fund or support views with which it does not agree. While these decisions tell us what values are important to Scalia when it comes to limiting the First Amendment, what he does not offer us is a definition or explanation of where citizen or individual expression fits into his political vision of American politics. Instead, the individual seems eclipsed by other concerns. As the next chapter indicates, the same conclusion can be reached in regard to Scalia's decisions affecting free press and association claims.

Notes

1. For a discussion of the liberal basis to American political thought, see: Hartz (1961); Diggins (1986); Dworetz (1990); and Schultz (1991 and 1993).

2. For recent titles on the subject of the meaning of the First Amendment free SPA see: Van Alstyne (1991); Graber (1991); Shiffrin (1990); Greenawalt (1989); and Kalven (1988).

3. See: Wilson (1986: 1186–97); King (1988: 24–33); Brisbin (1990: 17–19); and Parmet and Brown (1992: 17), for discussion of selected legal aspects of Scalia and the First Amendment.

4. *Renne v. Geary* (1991), which potentially could have raised a First Amendment issue, is not included in the cases identified here because the majority opinion disposed of the case on a standing issue without addressing the free speech questions involved. However, similar issues to the ones raised in this case were addressed in *Eu v. San Francisco County Democratic Central Committee* (1989).

5. King (1988: 24), offers a similar view, stating "Scalia's academic writings give no hint of his First Amendment views."

6. Although de Tocqueville did not have corporations in mind when he was discussing voluntary associations.

7. Compare to the discussion of Scalia's views on the regulation of the political process and his support on limits of free speech to protect third parties from unwanted speech.

8. Perhaps also important to Scalia's joining of the majority opinion in this case was the appeal to *Chevron v. N.R.D.C.* as a means of deferring to administrative construction of legislative meaning when Congressional and statutory meaning is unclear. Chapter three discussed Scalia's principles of statutory construction and the use of *Chevron* in depth.

9. For an extend analysis of Scalia's dissent in this case, see Shockley and Schultz (1992) as well as discussion earlier in this chapter. For a general discussion of judicial treatment and interpretation of campaign finance reform after *Austin v. Michigan Chamber of Commerce*, see Lowenstein (1992).

10. Note though that in both *Pickering* and *Speiser*, the rights in question were those of individuals seeking public employment and not corporations participating in the political process.

11. Yet in *Masden v. Women's Health Center* (1994), Scalia was unwilling to apply

similar logic to support limits on pro-life protestors picketing outside of clinics where abortions are performed. Apparently, residents in a residential neighborhood are captive audiences, yet doctors and women seeking health services (other than abortions) at clinics where abortions are performed are not considered captive audiences.

12. Parenthetically, this distinction is at the basis of congressional legislation denying or limiting funding to the arts or public television or radio.

Chapter 7

Freedom of Press and Association

As noted in chapter six, Scalia is generally not very sympathetic towards First Amendment free speech claims, except in a few special situations, such as those implicating corporate speech rights. He has sought to reorder expressive freedom law and has found numerous reasons or interests to trump these rights to serve majoritarian interests. Beyond his hostility to religion and speech, he shows a similar indifference in his decisions regarding freedom of the press and association. Throughout Scalia's career, he has expressed deep skepticism towards the press, seeking to loosen restrictions that make it difficult to sue reporters or newspapers for defamation. Scalia has also found numerous reasons why free association can be compromised, arguing that such compromises are necessary to serve other goals important to the political process. Overall, while many would contend that both a vigorous press and broad freedom of association are necessary to the functioning of a democratic society, Justice Scalia has seen fit to narrow many previous precdents and open up both types of rights to more stringent regulation by the political process.

Freedom of Press Decisions

Scalia has participated in fifteen cases directly involving freedom of the press as both a judge on the court of appeals and an associate justice on the Supreme Court through the 1993 term. In virtually all of these cases he ruled against free press claims by supporting government regulation and denial of access to court records, or by easing the standards necessary for individuals to sue the press for libel or breach of contract. These rulings demonstrate that it is Scalia's wish to put the press on notice that it often acts irresponsibly, and that it does not enjoy quite as privileged a position in our democracy as it thinks.

For example, in *Arkansas Writers' Project Inc. v. Ragland* (1987), at issue was a 1935 Arkansas state law that imposed a tax on receipts from the sale of tangible personal property, including general interest magazines, but which exempted newspapers and "religious, professional, trade and sports journals and/or publications printed and published within this State . . ." (Ark.Stat.Ann. § 84–1904[f] [1980 and Supp. 1985]). Arkansas Writers' Project, a general interest magazine, challenged the tax exemption claiming it violated the First Amendment. The majority of the Court agreed, arguing that the determination of the tax exemption was "content based" (*Arkansas Writers' Project* 1987: 1722) or based upon the contents of the magazine. To retain such a basis for tax exemption, the Court required Arkansas to defend it by showing that the "regulation is necessary to serve a compelling state interest and is narrowly drawn to achieve that end" (ibid.: 1728). Arkansas failed to do so, and the Court invalidated the tax.

In dissent, Scalia contended that the granting of a tax exemption on the basis of content, as in the Arkansas ordinance, was not a violation of the First Amendment. The distinction between general and special interest and religious magazines was really a way to distinguish between larger presses and smaller publishers with limited audiences and advertising revenues (ibid.: 1731). For Scalia, a genuine content-based distinction is one based on a "particular viewpoint of political concern" (ibid.: 1731) and not broad subject matter. Hence, the Arkansas distinction between general and special interest presses had a rational basis to it, did not implicate the First Amendment, and therefore the burden of analysis to be used was not the one suggested by the majority but instead a "reasonably related" test (ibid.: 1731).

Arkansas Writers' Project is important because Scalia, anticipating his efforts in *R.A.V. v. St. Paul* (1993), redefines what content-based distinctions are, at least in reference to the press, and he narrows the scope of the First Amendment that is extended to press or speech. In Scalia's words, "it is realistically quite impossible, to extend to all speech the same degree of protection against exclusion from a subsidy that one might think appropriate for opposing shades of political expression" (ibid.: 1732). Implicitly his dissent also hints at increased deference towards government taxation of the press as long as the tax is not clearly aimed at a particular *political* viewpoint.

A second area where Scalia has narrowed press rights is in access to court records in civil cases, such as in *In re Reporters Committee for Free Press* (1984). Although the Supreme Court held in *Richmond Newspapers, Inc. v.*

Virginia (1980) that the press had a Sixth Amendment right to observe the operations of criminal trials (ibid.: at 575), it had not ruled on whether that right applied to civil trials. In part, *In re Reporters Committee* addresses this question.

In this case, a reporters' group sought access to the discovery documents in a civil case sealed indefinitely by a district court. The material concerned a libel suit between the *Washington Post* and the president of Mobil Oil Company prior to the final judgment of the court. The reporters' group sued the court, contending that the order violated their First Amendment right to public access to the court records. Writing for the court of appeals, Judge Scalia disagreed.

Scalia indicated first that no Supreme Court decision had yet addressed the public's First Amendment rights to civil court records (*In re Reporters Committee for Free Press* 1984: 1331). To resolve this issue, two questions had to be answered in the affirmative: (1) whether civil proceedings have historically been open; and (2) whether the right of access to civil proceedings plays an essential role in the proper functioning of the judicial process and government (ibid.: 1331). In answer to the first question Scalia held that there was a tradition of access to court records even in civil suits, but the right of access was not absolute (ibid.: 1333). In civil suits, that access may apply to post judgment scenarios, but it has never applied to pre-judgment situations as in the present case (ibid.: 1333–35). Since the release of these records was sought prior to a verdict, their release would not enhance the quality of justice or the functioning of the judicial process (ibid.: 1335, 1337). Hence, the answer to both of the questions Scalia posed was no and the reporters' access was denied.

Had Scalia's decision stopped here the ruling would have simply been confined to pre-judgment releases, while keeping open the possibility for post-judgment access. Yet Scalia similarly limited this right and ruled that as long as a hearing was held on the sealing of the records, access could be denied (ibid.: 1339). As opposed to extending the holding of *Richmond Newspapers, Inc. v. Virginia* to apply to civil trials, Scalia drew a limit to it and confined press access to court records of a case of significant public interest.

Another example of Scalia's refusal to recognize special privileges for the press can be found in the justice's unwillingness to exempt it from many legal constraints that apply to other organizations. As a result, the press may be subject to rules that compromise its ability to undertake its activities. For example, often an individual will speak to the media on the condition of confidentiality, which the press will grant so that they can print the story. However, what if the press promises to maintain confidentiality but then publishes the name of the source? In *Cohen v. Cowles Media Corporation* (1991), Scalia joined a majority of the Court in holding that an individual could sue the media for breach of promissory estoppel.

During the closing days of a Minnesota gubernatorial campaign, Dan Cohen, a political informant, approached two local newspapers with information about a candidate for lieutenant governor. He offered this material on the condition of anonymity. The newspapers agreed, but after more research both papers independently decided to publish his name. Cohen sued under the Minnesota doctrine of promissory estoppel. The case was eventually appealed to the Supreme Court which held in favor of Cohen. According to the Court, the First Amendment is not a bar against a cause of promissory estoppel against the newspapers. This is because although the case was private, promissory estoppel is a state doctrine invoking state action in this case (ibid.: 2517–8).

The Court rejected the claim that this case was controlled by a line of precedent supporting limits on government intrusion on free press publication rights (ibid.: 2518). The Court reasoned that the case is governed by a "well established line of decisions holding that generally applicable laws do not offend the First Amendment simply because their enforcement against the press has incidental effects on its ability to gather and report the news" (ibid.: 2518). Here the Court argued that the Minnesota doctrine of promissory estoppel was of general application and not specifically directed towards the press or media in regards to news-gathering functions (ibid.: 2518–9). Allowing Cohen's suit was not a means of punishing the press and thus not controlled by *Smith v. Daily Mail Publishing Company* (1979).

Important to Scalia's joining the majority opinion was the question of whether to apply the general concept that was not specifically aimed at the press's news-gathering functions. Much as Scalia's arguments about expressive conduct seem to distinguish between general prohibitions of some general conduct versus intentional suppression of a specific act of speech, the reasoning in this case hangs on the same claim about the press. Laws that are general in scope but are applied to the press are valid as long as they impinge on the press's news-gathering functions only incidentally and not intentionally.

Besides expressing his willingness to hold the press to its promises, Scalia has also advocated changes in constitutional doctrine to make it easier to sue the press for libel. The landmark case of *New York Times v. Sullivan* (1964) established the basic criteria that must be met before a newspaper can be sued for libel.[1] When the plaintiff is a public figure, she cannot prevail in a libel suit unless she shows by clear and convincing evidence that the defendant published material with malice, or more specifically, with "knowledge that it was false or with reckless disregard of whether it was false or not" (*New York Times* 1964: 279–80). *New York Times* is recognized as an important defense of a free press because it placed limits upon the ability of individuals to sue the press, and it liberated the press to undertake critical and probing exploration of the news without constant fear that every little mistake it may make in a story will result in a lawsuit. Although Scalia has not rejected the basic *New York Times* standards and framework, he has expressed concern that the First Amendment incorrectly protects "wrongful destruction of someone's reputation" (Scalia 1987a: 737). He has also refashioned *New York Times* in several libel cases, such as *Liberty Lobby v. Anderson* (1984), *Tavoulareas v. Piro* (1985), *Ollman v. Evans* (1984), *Flynt v. Falwell* (1988), *Harte-Hanks Communications v. Connaughton* (1989), *Milkovich v. Lorain Journal* (1990), and *Masson v. New Yorker Magazine* (1991) to make it easier to bring libel suits against the press. The impact of Scalia's decisions has been towards a de facto hollowing out of *New York Times* at the expense of press freedom.

In *Liberty Lobby v. Anderson* (1984), Scalia wrote a majority opinion that proved a mixed blessing for press freedom. In this case an alleged right-wing group brought libel action against a publisher regarding a story written about it. Among other claims was the contention that some of the facts and conclusions based on these facts were false, and the publisher knew that they were false. Liberty Lobby also claimed that a directed verdict by the judge against them before their entire case was presented violated their rights. In defense, the publisher argued that many of the facts printed had been previously published elsewhere, that some of the errors were journalistic inaccuracy and not malice, and that many of the claims were opinion and thus not actionable as libel. Judge Scalia, writing for the court, supported some of Liberty Lobby's claims while denying others.

Scalia held that mere opinion (ibid.: 1572) and journalistic inaccuracies (ibid.: 1574) were not subject to libel action, yet prior publication of some facts and reliance upon sources of questionable reputation for information left the press open for libel action and charges of malice (ibid.: 1568–73). Finally, Scalia argued that the issuance of a summary judgment was incorrect, and that the clear and convincing standard to establish actual malice for a summary judgment would increase the burden of proof on the plaintiff which would necessitate numerous changes in court procedure (ibid.: 1570.) Judges can not issue summary judgments in libel cases that dispose of the suit prior to the presentation of all facts (ibid.: 1571). Such judgments would make it harder to prevail in libel suits and clearly disadvantage the plaintiff. In effect, *Liberty Lobby* forestalls the ability of the judiciary to halt a libel case against a newspaper by establishing heightened standards for summary judgments.

Scalia also seeks to relax libel hurdles in his court of appeals dissent in *Ollman v. Evans* (1984). Here, a marxist professor of political science claimed that he was libeled by the nationally syndicated columnists Evans and Novak. The majority of the court held that the article about Ollman was political opinion and protected by the First Amendment (ibid.: 982–985).

Scalia dissented, contending that the Evans and Novak essay was "a classic and coolly crafted libel" meant to disparage Ollman's professional reputation (ibid.: at 1036). Scalia disagrees with the concurring opinion of Bork's that sought to construct a means to weigh fact versus opinion in political commentary (ibid.: 1010). Scalia also disagreed with Bork's assertion that even in political debates, a certain number of defamatory statements are permitted because such statements are discounted in the heat of the debate (ibid.: 1038). For Scalia, forcing judges to determine how much defamation is permissible in political debate or opinion runs the "risk of judicial subjectivity." This risk he finds unacceptable (ibid.: at 1038). Making determinations regarding how much defamation is permitted is a job not for judges but for legislatures (ibid.: 1038–9), suggesting broad legislative authority to regulate the press and other Bill of Rights guarantees.

More important than his disagreement with Bork is Scalia's suggestion of a new constitutional principle—the willful false disparagement of professional reputation in the context of political commentary—(ibid.: 1039) to check journalistic excesses. These excesses include the tendency of an irresponsible media "to descend from discussion of public issues to destruction of private reputations" (ibid.: 1038) and the media are "capable of holding individuals up to public obloquy from coast to coast and then reap[ing] financial rewards commensurate with that power" (ibid.: 1039).[2] Thus, Scalia's dissent in *Ollman* indicates his general feeling towards much of contemporary journalism, e.g., that it is destructive and irresponsible, and that perhaps the only solution to this irresponsibility is some recognition of increased libel action or malice against the media.

Given this opinion and animosity towards willful destruction of a reputation, Scalia's joining of the majority opinion in *Flynt v. Falwell* (1988) is odd. *Flynt* is the only libel or freedom of the press case in which Scalia votes to support a First Amendment claim. Here, the justice joins a majority opinion overturning a damage award to Jerry Falwell, leader of the religious group the Moral Majority, who was found in a jury trial to be libeled by Larry Flynt and *Hustler* magazine. In this case, Larry Flynt testified that he intended to destroy Jerry Falwell through his political parody of the latter in a sexually oriented and graphic magazine. To accomplish this goal, *Hustler* depicted Falwell in a parody of a commercial advertisement showing him in an outhouse discussing incestuous acts. Scalia agreed with the majority that the *New York Times v. Sullivan* precedent only applied when malice was intended in the context of the use of actual facts or events. Since no person could reasonably construe the parody as fact rather than opinion (*Flynt* 1988: 882–3), the First Amendment shielded Flynt from libel.

Flynt notwithstanding, it is no surprise that on the Supreme Court Scalia has sought to relax requirements to prove malice. Many of his decisions have demonstrated that he distrusts the press and is otherwise unwilling to give the media special protections or status in our society. *Tavoulareas v. Piro* (1985), and *Harte-Hanks Communications v. Connaughton* (1989) are two other libel cases that illuminate Scalia's views. Tavoulareas discussion addresses the procedures for issuing special *n.o.v.* motions, and Scalia's concurrence in *Harte-Hanks* similarly discusses this technical issue. Similarly, *Milkovich v. Lorain Journal* (1991) addresses issues that are more technical in nature and will be passed over here.

The major import of these three cases is that Scalia upheld libel judgments against the press. The final case in which Scalia moves to enhance the ability of public figures to bring libel suits against the press is found in *Masson v. New Yorker Magazine* (1991). In this case, a reporter interviewed Jeffrey Masson, a former director of the Freud Archives, and wrote an article in which, as a narrative device, she enclosed lengthy passages in quotation marks in such a way that it appeared that Masson had made these statements even though he had not. Masson informed the publisher prior to the printing of the article that many of the passages contained errors, and that these passages portrayed Masson in an unfavorable light. Masson sued, claiming malice, and the Supreme Court eventually upheld his claim. The majority opinion of the Court held that

> Deliberate alteration of the words uttered by a plaintiff does not equate with knowledge of falsity for purposes of *New York Times v. Sullivan* . . . unless the alteration results in a material change in the meaning conveyed by the statement. The use of quotations to attribute words not in fact spoken bears in a most important way on that inquiry, but it is not dispositive in every case (ibid.: 2433).

The use of this narrative technique could be, but it is not necessarily, a sign of falsity necessary to establish libel, and the Court remanded the case for further proceedings consistent with this ruling.

In a partial concurrence and dissent, Scalia disagreed with the majority opinion that the above-described alteration of words was not necessarily malice (ibid.: 2437). The justice argued that fabricating quotes "(b)y any definition of the term, this was 'knowing falsehood'" (ibid.: 2437–8). Any intentional fabrication of quotes always (and not just in some occasions, as the majority contended) constituted malice.

Scalia's dissent in *Masson* places a burden on reporters to ensure that all quotations are completely accurate and true even though, as the majority noted (ibid.: 2431–2433), it is often difficult to ensure that level of accuracy. Holding the press to such a stringent standard might "hinder the First Amendment values of robust and well-informed public debate by reducing the reliability of information available to the public" (ibid.: 2431). Scalia's standard would contribute to a chilling effect upon press freedom and news-gathering functions.

Finally, besides narrowing protections for the press in general, Scalia has also participated in decisions that specifically narrow the rights of student newspapers. In *Tinker v. Des Moines Independent School District* (1969), the Supreme Court upheld the right of high-school students to wear black armbands to express their opposition to the Vietnam War. In that case, the Court argued that students in public schools do not "shed their constitutional rights to freedom or expression at the schoolhouse gate" (ibid.: 506). *Tinker* was an important statement that students in public schools enjoy significant First Amendment rights that can not be easily suppressed by schools in the name of discipline.

In *Hazelwood School District v. Kuhlmeier* (1988) the Court distinguished the case of a principal censoring a high-school newspaper from the lofty rhetoric of *Tinker* and held that this action did not violate the First Amendment. In this case, Scalia signed on to White's majority opinion that held that this act of apparent censorship was not really a form of censorship. Crucial to this claim were several important facts. First, the publication of the student newspaper did not constitute the establishment of an unregulated public forum because the writing and production of the paper were part of a class curriculum where extensive school review and supervision occurred (ibid.: 568). This meant that the newspaper was less a newspaper than an educational project sponsored by the school. Second, the Court argued that even if this case did involve some type of censorship, the school district, as the publisher and funding source of the newspaper, had a legitimate right to determine the contents of the paper (ibid.: 568–70). Third, unlike *Tinker* in which the school sought the actual suppression of political views, here the school was not really censoring but simply refusing to fund forms of speech that the school did not wish to support (ibid.: 569). Hence, as in *Rust v. Sullivan* and other cases where the Court had recently argued that the government is not obligated to fund or support speech it does not agree with, *Hazelwood* distinguishes between the action a school takes to punish a student for her expression and the action it takes not to support student speech it does not like. For the majority in *Hazelwood*, the First Amendment rights of the students in the former scenario are governed by the *Tinker* standard which affords greater protections for students than in the latter situation (which is not controlled by *Tinker*). *Hazelwood School District v. Kuhlmeier* not only represented a retreat from the *Tinker* ruling that gave public school students significant constitutional rights, but for Scalia it was an example of a winnowing away of important free press rights for students.[3]

Overall, other scholars have noted that Justice Scalia is not a strong defender of the press (Nagareda 1987; Meaux 1987), and that he mistrusts the press as an institution and gives little weight to the value of the press in our society as far as it contributes to a free society. While these conclusions were based mostly upon Scalia's tenure as a court of appeals judge, analysis of his decisions on the Supreme Court (as well as some off bench remarks noted earlier) confirms these early claims. As with his freedom of speech decisions, many values, including the right not to have one's character destroyed, trump free press claims. Moreover, while Scalia generally states support for *New York Times v. Sullivan*, the reality is that his record supporting libel decisions against the press indicates that the principles of this case are not as significant a protection of press freedom as the case is supposed to represent. While giving lip service to what *New York Times* stands for, his holdings and dicta suggest otherwise.

Freedom of Association Decisions

Antonin Scalia's freedom of association decisions demonstrate general hostility towards associational claims, especially when those claims affect government regulation of the political process. An earlier chapter demonstrated that Scalia is skeptical of legislative power and that this skepticism influences his interpretation of statutes, but his freedom of association decisions do reveal a deference to government regulation of the political process in order to avoid the threat of political factionalism or judicial preemption of legislative authority to govern campaigns, elections, or the staffing of the bureaucracies. All of these values reflect a commitment to legislative regulation of many fundamental political rights that stand in contrast to the assumptions of a *Carolene Products* type of jurisprudence.

Earlier chapters discussed Scalia's views on the political process in some depth. Yet several of Scalia's association decisions address legislative control of the political process and are worth reviewing again in context of the justice's First Amendment jurisprudence. Two of these decisions clearly demonstrate Scalia's apparent unwillingness (at least when he agrees with the decision) to second guess legislatures or Congress in their control of the political process. In *Morgan v. United States of America* (1986), Scalia wrote the majority opinion denying judicial authority to review the House of Representatives's determination of who won a particular House race. According to the judge, it was "difficult to imagine a clearer case of 'textually demonstrable constitutional commitment' of an issue to another branch of government to the exclusion of the courts" (*Morgan* 1986: 447, quoting *Baker v. Carr* 217 [1962]). In this instance, Article I, Section 5, clause 1 of the Constitution commits to each House the role as final judge of its own elections, and there is no indication either from the framers or by subsequent commentary that judicial review of House determinations in this area was envisioned (ibid.: 447).

Rutan v. Republican Party of Illinois (1990) also demonstrated clear judicial deference to legislatures. The case grew out of a challenge to the Illinois governor's use of party affiliation when hiring, rehiring, transferring, and promoting individuals. Civil servants challenged this patronage practice, and the majority opinion on the Court struck down the practice as an unconstitutional infringement of the First Amendment rights of the civil servants. Scalia's dissent attacked the majority's anti-patronage position by arguing that while the merit principle is clearly the "most favored" way to organize governments, it is neither the only way and nor does it enjoy exclusive constitutional protection (ibid.: 2747). In referring to George Plunkitt in his discussion of patronage, Scalia describes spoils as part of the American administrative/political tradition, but he backs off from claiming that it is of "landmark status or one of our accepted political traditions" (ibid.: 2748).[4]

As noted in chapter two, Scalia's dissent argues that the strict-scrutiny standard employed by the majority in this case, as well as in *Elrod* and *Branti*, to protect the rights of federal employees is inappropriate and ought to be rejected in favor of a balancing-of-interests test (ibid.: 2749, 2752).[5] He asserts that the restrictions on the speech of governmental employees have been held to differ from the restrictions that may be placed on the general citizenry (ibid.: 2749). This means that the government has more latitude to act with regard to its own employees; it merely needs to show a rational basis to regulate. While this decision seemed supportive of political party rights and associational claims, it is also a decision that subordinates individual rights to government regulation.

However supportive of political parties *Rutan* *seems* to be, three other decisions limit party autonomy or formation in the interest of preventing political confusion or factionalism. In *Munro v. Socialist Workers Party* (1986) and *Norman v. Reed* (1991) what was at issue were respective State of Washington and Illinois laws that mandated that minor party candidates in Washington receive one percent of the vote before their names appear on the ballot, and that in Illinois, new political parties that field candidates for statewide offices must receive 25,000 signatures from eligible voters from each political district. Scalia voted with the majority in *Munro* to uphold the Washington statute, while he dissented in *Norman* also to uphold the Illinois law.

The majority in *Munro* noted how the associational rights of access to the ballot had been previously recognized in *Williams v. Rhodes* (1968), yet other cases such as *Storer v. Brown* (1974) indicated that these rights were not absolute (*Munro* 1986: 536–7) and that a state may require a " 'preliminary showing of substantial support in order to qualify for a place on the ballot' " (ibid.: 537, quoting *Anderson v. Celebrezze*, 788–9 [1983]). Among the substantial state interests that a state would have in placing a threshold limit for ballot access are the "existence of voter confusion, ballot overcrowding, or the presence of frivolous candidates" (ibid.: 537). The majority concluded that legislatures "should be permitted to respond to potential deficiencies in the electoral process with foresight . . . provided that the response is reasonable and does not significantly impinge on constitutionally-protected rights" (ibid.: 538).

In his *Norman* dissent, Scalia also sees the signature requirement as advancing a legitimate state interest (ibid.:710). However, unlike *Munro*, in which that interest was perhaps to prevent voter confusion, crowded ballots, or the presence of frivolous candidates, the interest here was to "prevent the dangers of factionalism" (ibid.: 711). In referring to James Madison and *Federalist* 10, Scalia notes the dangers of the political splintering and factionalism that occur when many different parties emerge and compete (ibid.: 711). By insisting that parties meet minimum signature or support requirements, the state is doing no more than acting to prevent political parties from breaking up or factionalizing. Hence, the threat of factionalism outweighed any freedom of association rights involved. Similar fears of factionalism seem also to control the justice's dissent in *Tashjian v. Republican Party of Connecticut* (1986).

In *Tashjian*, the State of Connecticut had a closed primary law requiring voters in a political primary to be members of that primary. The Republican Party in Connecticut, in an effort to broaden its political base, sought to open up the primary to independent voters who were not registered with any party. The majority of the Court voided the Connecticut law, claiming that the law violated the freedom of association rights of the Republican party and its members. It rejected arguments by the state that the law was necessary to protect the Republican Party from undertaking actions destructive to its own interests (ibid.: 554). Instead, they held that the "Party's determination of the boundaries of its own association, and of the structure which best allows it to pursue its political goals, is protected by the Constitution" (ibid.: 554).

In Scalia's own dissent (as opposed to the Stevens dissent that he joined), he first questioned whether this party rule was supported by any majority of the state Republican Party since this decision was not made by a democratic ballot but by a minority of party officials (ibid.: 560). The justice then argued that "a major purpose of state-imposed party primary requirements [was] to protect the general party membership against this sort of minority control" (ibid.: 560). Scalia thus adopted the state's argument that it was seeking to protect the Republican Party from pursuing actions destructive to its own interests. These were actions that the justice felt would lead to political factionalism or domination of a majority by a political minority. In effect, the associational rights of the party are outweighed by the interest the state has in maintaining the integrity of democratic party structures that would be threatened by party initiated open primaries.

In contrast to *Tashjian*, in which Scalia upheld state regulation of party governance and organization, the justice voted with the majority in *Eu v. San Francisco County Democratic Central Committee* (1989) to strike down state laws that limited the terms and composition of some party officer positions. Searching for some compelling state interest that would justify regulation of the party structure, i.e., to preserve the integrity of primary elections or ensure fair and honest elections, Justice Marshall could find none, and his majority opinion concluded instead that free association claims should be respected to allow the party to develop a "structure which best allows it to pursue its political goals" (ibid.: 1024). It would seem in *Eu* that existing party organization did not appear to be factionalizing or thwarting the maintenance of party mobilization. Presumably, the state law, by telling who could be officers and for how long, interferred with the mobilization of majorities that would be necessary to overcome internal organizational problems and sectarianism. However, Scalia could have dissented here and argued that state laws limiting officer terms, etc., would prevent one group from dominating the party and using its power to suppress dissent. Such a scenario would be a majority faction tyrannizing a minority. Why such a reasoning was not employed is a mystery, given that Scalia fears the spectre of factions, with majority factions, as James Madison argued, being the most dangerous.

Overall, the threat of factionalism, the need to maintain party structures, and the deference to legislatures to determine how best to staff the government are all factors that dominate Scalia's associational decisions regarding the political process. Given these concerns, it is not hard to see why Scalia agreed with the holding in *Eu v. San Francisco County Democratic Central Committee*. Although the decision did strike down a state law, it did so in order to enhance the ability of party leaders to perform the essential party function of mobilizing support and coalitions in order to run candidates for election. In *Eu*, allowing primary endorsements enhanced party integrity and performance, while in *Tashjian*, open primaries threatened to create political factionalism and damage democratic structures.

A final case addressing associational claims is *Molerio v. F.B.I.* (1984). This case involved several questions, but most germane here was whether an applicant who was denied employment with the F.B.I. in part because of his father's political beliefs and association with a pro-Fidel Castro group had been denied his constitutional rights. The plaintiff asserted that his "father's lawful political activities gives [sic] Molerio standing to assert a First Amendment violation" (ibid.: 824) that would allow him to challenge the decision by the F.B.I. not to hire him. Scalia's majority decision, while noting the F.B.I.'s acknowledgement that his father's activities in part were responsible for their personnel decision (ibid.: 825), denied that the hiring decision implicated any First Amendment concerns (ibid.: 825). Crucial to Scalia's decision here was the assertion by the F.B.I. of the "state's secret doctrine" (ibid.: 825) and the need of the government to screen out from certain areas of government employment those whose political associations, although lawful, may pose a perceived risk to national security. In this case, the F.B.I. acknowledged that the pro-Castro political activities of Molerio's father were a cause of concern, but Scalia just ignored the First Amendment claim here out of deference to government discretion.

Summary

In *Molerio*, national security concerns perhaps outweigh freedom of association claims. The emphasis is on "perhaps" because Scalia does not present a full analysis in this case of when national security is more important than free association claims. We do not have a full discussion of how the justice reads the case law here, or how he would respond if a First Amendment free association claim directly confronted national security. However, a survey of Scalia's free association decisions reveals that numerous factors, including threats of factionalism, needs of party maintenance and structure, and national security all outweigh these rights, at least in some circumstances. Scalia's decisions follow Supreme Court precedents indicating more sympathy for the maintenance of the major two parties than for alternative or third-party candidates.[6] His decisions in the area of free association also parallel decisions in the areas of free speech and press, where numerous values appear to eclipse First Amendment claims.

Conclusion

In a 1988 essay that examined Scalia's record through his first year on the Supreme Court, Michael Patrick King concluded that "Scalia has formed no absolutist views in the areas of speech and expression" (King 1988: 32). Examination of his record through the 1993 term in this and the previous chapter suggest a similar conclusion about his attitude towards expressive freedoms. If, as other commentators have indicated, Scalia is ambivalent towards democracy (Kannar 1991: 1861), he is equally ambivalent to those forces—free speech, press, and association—that sustain democratic action and values. His decisions in the areas of free SPA indicate that the justice is not a friend of individual expression and criticism and that instead, he supports numerous restrictions that endorse what he perceives to be a majoritarian position in society.

One can not explain Scalia's understanding of the First Amendment SPA by simply saying he defers to the government when in doubt (Brisbin 1992b: 14). After all, free SPA is only one value in the equation of numerous other values considered, including his political philosophy, when adjudicating a case. As noted throughout these last two chapters, values such as the need to prevent political factionalism, to protect the integrity of the electoral process, or to protect captive audiences from unwanted speech consistently appear to trump First Amendment free SPA claims. A hierarchy of values seems to structure Scalia's First Amendment jurisprudence, with support of free SPA falling lower on the hierarchy than other values. While Scalia's decisions stress the importance of supporting many institutions and values in society, including private property, his vision has a notable blind spot when it comes to defining the role and importance of individual and press expression. Both seem conspicuously absent from his vision of society and government, as well as from more recent applications of judicial power to protect fundamental rights. This is especially curious given Scalia's preoccupation with the Founders and *their* concern to defend individual liberty against factions, especially those which include the majority. According to Madison, "(w)hen a majority is included in a faction, the form of popular government, on the other hand, enables it to sacrifice to its ruling passion or interest both the public good and the rights of others" (Madison 1937, 57).

Were we to describe a comprehensive philosophy that Antonin Scalia has towards the First Amendment, it would be one that considers a hierarchy of values that places individual expressive efficacy quite low, thus limiting judicial supervision and second-guessing of legislatures and other institutions that may have organizational needs to limit expressive freedoms. Free expression is not viewed as the sine qua non of his vision of a democratic and liberal society, but rather merely one value in many that can be sacrificed for any one of several social or political interests. However, any theory of society that systematically allows for social values to consistently trump free speech claims is a theory that fails to respect individual liberty. According to John Rawls, "(j)ustice denies that the loss of freedom for some is made right by the greater good shared by others" (Rawls 1971: 28).

Scalia's jurisprudence clearly demonstrates the lack of concern for free expression and autonomy. This jurisprudence is best described by a quote of the justice's that has been cited several times in this chapter; i.e., "The exercise of First Amendment rights may sometimes be quite wrong" (Scalia 1987a: 737). The use of one's free SPA is not always appropriate for Scalia.

Notes

1. Powe (1992: 110–140) offers a discussion of *New York Times v. Sullivan* (1964) and the evolution of Supreme Court treatment of libel law.

2. Compare this claim to Scalia (1987: 737), where the justice argues that "a wrongful destruction of someone's reputation . . . (is) irresponsible."

3. When *Hazelwood* and *Fox v. SUNY* are considered together, it appears that Scalia believes that students as a group have less expressive rights in school, in part because of the institutioanl needs of order required to promote educational goals. Similarly, as chapter seven will show, prisoners also have fewer rights than do other individuals because of the security needs of prisons. Later in chapter seven Scalia's opinion in *Rutan v. Republican Party of Illinois* (1990) will indicate that he also believes the government employees are entitled to expressive rights that are also limited by the needs of the organization of government. Arguably, Scalia's approach to individuals located within certain institutions is that they enjoy constitutional rights that are qualified or otherwise limited by other institutional values that are seldom overridden by Bill of Rights claims. Given that almost all individuals must interact within some type of institutional structure, the logic of Scalia's opinions indicates that rights can be limited to serve diverse governmental and organizational values.

4. Brinkley (1991: 725) claims that Scalia thinks the Court ought to respect long-standing traditions that are not found in the Constitution's text. Compare this to Scalia in *Rutan v. Republican Party of Illinois* (1990: 2748).

5. Johnson (1991: 422) discusses Scalia's claim that a lesser level of scrutiny should be applied to government management and operations, including patronage.

6. See Epstein and Hadley (1990) for a discussion of this point.

Chapter 8

Criminal Justice
and the Majoritarian Process

In the realm of criminal justice, Justice Scalia's votes and opinions generally reflect his "reluctan[ce] to let the practice of rights interfere with majoritarian choices" (Brisbin 1993: 914). Despite the "conservative" label that Scalia can wear as a justice who usually supports the government when criminal defendants and prisoners assert claims of constitutional rights, Scalia has produced notable "liberal" opinions supporting individuals in selected criminal justice cases. These opinions that supporting claims by criminal defendants do not necessarily embody an unconscious contradiction in Scalia's normal decisional patterns. Instead, they illustrate Scalia's individualistic pursuit of his vision of the Constitution's text and history, as well as reflecting how his interpretive methods interact with that vision.

As noted by other scholars, Scalia believes that "[t]here is to be criminal due process, but due process should not threaten the majority's sense of what constitutes a secure society" (Brisbin 1990: 27–28). Yet Scalia's emphasis on the text and history of constitutional provisions can lead him to support individuals' claims when he sees their asserted constitutional rights as clearly protected by the words and original meaning of the Constitution. Although he frequently allies himself with conservative colleagues, Scalia appears less inclined than those colleagues to support the government for practical policy reasons. George Kannar (1990: 1323) characterized Scalia's criminal justice opinions as "demonstrat[ing] an unflinching belief that inequity, or at least 'policy' irrationalities, have to be accepted as the price—or at least the result—of being 'strong enough to obey' . . . strict textual self-discipline." Scalia's textualist focus can lead him to support either defendants or the government depending on the meaning and clarity—in his mind's eye—of the constitutional provision at issue.

175

Justice Scalia's opinions concerning criminal justice issues must be understood in the context of recent Supreme Court history. In most criminal justice cases, the Court is tackling familiar issues. Thus, instead of analyzing novel issues, a new set of justices is reassessing, altering, or reaffirming jurisprudential trends initiated during the Warren and Burger Court eras. As a result, Scalia frequently finds himself confronting—and criticizing—precedents and reasoning established by predecessors who did not share his values or judicial philosophy. That adverse precedents exist made it harder, but not impossible, for Scalia to advance his vision of the Constitution and appropriate judicial policy.

During the Warren Court era, the Supreme Court had a significant impact upon the criminal justice system by interpreting the Bill of Rights in new ways that provided greater protections for criminal defendants and convicted offenders. As described by David Bodenhamer:

> Between 1961 and 1969 the Warren Court accomplished what previous courts had stoutly resisted: it applied virtually all of the procedural guarantees of the Bill of Rights to the states' administration of criminal justice. . . . The result was a nationalized Bill of Rights that dimmed the local character of justice by applying the same restraints to all criminal proceedings, both state and federal. (1992: 113)

Notable Supreme Court decisions affected the policies and practices of law enforcement agencies and courts by, for example, requiring police officers to inform arrestees of their rights (*Miranda v. Arizona* 1966). They also forced local courts to provide attorneys for indigent criminal defendants (*Gideon v. Wainwright* 1963) and jury trials for defendants facing incarceration on serious charges (*Duncan v. Louisiana* 1968).

President Richard Nixon responded to the popular perception that the Court had gone "too far" in protecting criminal defendants and in interfering with criminal justice agencies by attempting to appoint new justices during the 1970s who would take a narrower view of constitutional rights. For example, Warren Burger was nominated to be Chief Justice specifically because of Nixon's expectation that Burger would implement the President's goal for "law and order" judicial policies (Abraham 1985: 297–298). Nixon ultimately appointed four justices (Burger, Blackmun, Rehnquist, and Powell) who were initially more conservative than their predecessors. During the Burger Court era (1969–1986), the justices narrowed some protections for criminal defendants by, for example, creating exceptions to the "exclusionary rule" (e.g., *United States v. Leon* 1984; *New York v. Quarles* 1984). Although they declined to expand established rights, they did not completely erase landmark decisions. In fact, they expanded the scope of several rights by endorsing judicial supervision of conditions in correctional institutions (*Hutto v. Finney* 1978) and narrowing the applicability of capital punishment (*Coker v. Georgia* 1977).

By contrast, the conservative justices on the later Rehnquist Court demonstrated a much greater inclination to change precedents with which they disagreed. While the Burger Court justices essentially diluted the Warren Court's exclusionary rule, the Rehnquist Court majority accelerated the pace of change by altering and refining decisions affecting a variety of criminal justice issues, including search and seizure, capital punishment, cruel and unusual punishment, and habeas corpus. Justice Scalia demonstrated a willingness to part company with his conservative colleagues in order to support individuals' claims in specific criminal justice cases, but generally he was an active participant in the process of creating new decisions that limited the scope of criminal defendants' and prisoners' rights.

Patterns and Approaches

How has Justice Scalia participated in the Supreme Court's Rehnquist-era criminal justice decisions? As indicated by Table I, Scalia consistently joined the other conservative justices as a relatively dependable vote against assertions of rights by criminal defendants and prisoners.

TABLE I

Percentage of Justices' Decisions Against Individuals in Criminal Justice Cases, 1986–1993 (includes 4th Amendment, 5th Amendment, 6th Amendment, 8th Amendment, Death Penalty, and Habeas Corpus)

Justice	Percentage (N)	
Thomas	89%	(24)
Rehnquist	87	(139)
Scalia	81	(139)
Powell	81	(26)
Kennedy	75	(109)
O'Connor	74	(138)
White	73	(139)
Souter	56	(45)
Blackmun	35	(138)
Stevens	22	(139)
Brennan	8	(92)
Marshall	3	(111)

The evident consistency of Scalia's voting pattern on criminal justice cases does not prove that Scalia necessarily votes in a lock-step fashion with other conservatives in every case. Subsequent sections of this chapter will discuss how Scalia's independent views have led him to disagree with his conservative colleagues and to join the liberal justices in cases concerning particular issues. Scalia also frequently distinguishes his views from those of his conservative colleagues by writing concurring opinions in cases in which he shares other justices' views about the proper outcomes for cases but disagrees with their reasoning.

Although this chapter will focus primarily on Scalia's approach to constitutional interpretation with respect to criminal justices issues, Scalia has also applied his approach to interpreting statutes to legislative enactments that affect criminal justice. As discussed in preceding chapters, with respect to statutory interpretation, Scalia has been labeled the leader of the movement toward "the new textualism," which "posits that once the Court has ascertained a statute's plain meaning, consideration of legislative history becomes irrelevant " (Eskridge 1990: 623). Although Scalia has yet to persuade a majority of justices to adopt his approach, he is gaining influence and, simultaneously, forcing members of Congress to rethink their approach to creating new statutes. For example, Scalia influenced the development of a crime bill in Congress during 1991:

> When the House Judiciary Committee was drafting an anti-crime bill two weeks ago, some members suggested resolving a dispute by putting compromise language into a committee report, which accompanies a bill to the floor. But Barney Frank, D-Mass., warned off his colleagues with just two words: "Justice Scalia." ("Congress Keeps" 1991: 2863)

Scalia has also advanced his textualist approach to statutory interpretation in criminal justice cases. For example, in a case concerning the omission of a precise definition of "burglary" in a sentence-enhancement statute for repeat offenders, Scalia's concurring opinion chided his colleagues for their reliance on legislative history to determine the statute's meaning: "I can discern no reason for devoting ten pages of today's [majority] opinion to legislative history, except to show that we have given this case close and careful consideration" (*Taylor v. United States* 1990: 2162).

As the following section on constitutional interpretation will discuss, Scalia's advocacy of textualism as well his version of originalism can, at times, apparently overcome any philosophical predisposition he may possess to decide cases in the government's favor. For example, Scalia's approach to statutory interpretation presumably influenced his decision to part company with fellow conservatives (Rehnquist, Souter, White, and O'Connor) and join, without issuing a concurring opinion, a majority opinion by Justice Marshall stating that the federal sentencing statute requires judges to notify defendants before departing upward from the established sentencing range (*Burns v. United States* 1991). The "prodefendant" outcome of the case went against Scalia's usual decisional pattern, but Scalia's interpretation of the statute's text apparently overrode his usual tendency to endorse the prosecutors' arguments. Unlike Justice Thomas and Chief Justice Rehnquist, who rarely support the claims of defendants or prisoners unless virtually the entire Court recognizes a constitutional claim (e.g., *Austin v. United States* 1993) or identifies a trial judge's error (*Sochor v. Florida* 1992), Scalia will sometimes follow his interpretive principles when they lead him to vote against the government.

Scalia's emphasis on textualism has had its most significant impact upon his criminal justice decisions with regard to constitutional interpretation. Scalia does not always decide cases in the manner of the other conservative justices, who are inclined to balance competing interests or advance policy preferences in deciding criminal justice cases against defendants and prisoners. In creating a "public safety" exception to the "exclusionary rule," Rehnquist asserted that "the [police officers'] need for answers to questions in a situation posing a threat to public safety outweighs the need for the prophylactic rule protecting the [defendant's] Fifth Amendment privilege against self-incrimination." (*New York v. Quarles* 1984: 657). Such reasoning is based on an explicit policy choice derived from weighing competing values. By contrast, because Scalia is "[s]olid in his conviction that the text or texts can answer almost every question, he has not been hesitant to apply his view of their meaning on behalf of criminal defendants whenever the constitutional language or the language of authoritative precedent seems to dictate that he do so" (Kannar 1990: 1321). Despite his consistency in deciding criminal justice cases against the claims of defendants and prisoners (see Table I), Scalia's textualist approach to constitutional interpretation has provided the basis for notable deviations from the decisions of his conservative colleagues.

Fourth Amendment

In search-and-seizure cases, Scalia has generally joined the other conservatives in loosening restrictions placed upon law enforcement officers. In asserting his views in written opinions, Scalia applied his reasoning on behalf of individuals as well as on behalf of the government. From 1986 through

1993, Scalia supported individuals' claims in only eight of the Supreme Court's thirty-three Fourth Amendment cases, yet four of his eleven opinions supported criminal defendants' arguments (*Arizona v. Hicks* 1987; *National Treasury Employees Union v. Von Raab* 1989; *County of Riverside v. McLaughlin* 1991; *Minnesota v. Dickerson* 1993).

Scalia surprised many observers during his freshman term by writing an opinion in *Arizona v. Hicks* (1987) on behalf of Justices Brennan, Marshall, White, Blackmun, and Stevens that supported the exclusionary rule. Scalia's majority opinion preserved against further erosion the probable cause requirement for warrantless searches conducted in conjunction with the "plain view doctrine." In this case, police officers improperly moved stereo equipment to look at serial numbers during a warrantless search for weapons in an apartment from which shots had been fired. The state argued that the officers should not need probable cause to examine the stereo equipment without a warrant. Scalia referred to his emphasis on the Constitution's text when he endorsed the reaffirmation of the "exclusionary rule" in this case: "[T]here is nothing new in the realization that the Constitution sometimes insulates the criminality of the few in order to protect the privacy of us all. Our disagreement with the dissenters pertains to where the proper balance should be struck; we choose to adhere to the textual and traditional standard of probable cause" (*Arizona v. Hicks* 1987: 329). This did not necessarily mean either that Scalia intended to endorse the exclusionary rule or that he completely distinguished himself from other justices' tendencies to assess the exclusionary rule purely in policy, as opposed to jurisprudential, terms.

Scalia dismissed Arizona's assertion that the stolen stereo equipment discovered during the search should be admitted into evidence through a "good faith" exception to the exclusionary rule because "[t]hat was not the question on which certiorari was granted, and we decline to consider it" (ibid.). Scalia's opinion reflected a restrained approach to addressing the narrow issue presented to the Court (i.e., whether to maintain the probable cause requirement for the plain view doctrine) rather than an endorsement of the exclusionary rule in any general sense.

The policy-oriented basis of the dissenters' views was evident in the first sentence of Justice Powell's dissenting opinion: "I join Justice O'Connor's dissenting opinion, and write briefly to highlight what seems to me the *unfortunate consequences* of the Court's decision" (ibid.: 330; emphasis supplied). Although Scalia did not join the dissenters, Powell, O'Connor, and Rehnquist, his own policy preferences lurked beneath his decision to support the defendant's claim. As a practical matter, a decision permitting the police to move the stereo equipment a few inches in order to locate the serial numbers could have unleashed a flurry of cases raising separate questions concerning whether, under the plain view doctrine, objects observed by the police may be moved two feet, three feet, four feet, or turned upside down. One of Scalia's primary goals is to diminish the number of cases brought before the federal courts; a bright-line rule requiring probable cause for moving observed objects under the plain view doctrine spares judges from the prospect of entertaining claims raising myriad contexts in which police might otherwise move or open an item during a warrantless search (Smith 1989a: 131–133).

Scalia's opinion in *Arizona v. Hicks* did not indicate that he placed any special value on the validity or importance of the exclusionary rule because Scalia subsequently participated in eroding the rule in other cases. For example, in *Illinois v. Rodriguez* (1990), Scalia's majority opinion endorsed a warrantless search of an apartment based on the consent of a third party (i.e., a girlfriend of the defendant) who the police erroneously believed to be a resident of the apartment. In effect, Scalia's opinion expanded the "good faith" exception to the exclusionary rule by declaring that such warrantless searches are "reasonable" and therefore constitutionally permissible if the officers reasonably believe that they have permission from someone with authority over the premises. In this particular case, the girlfriend occasionally spent nights at the apartment. She never went there when the defendant was not there; she did not contribute rent money; and she admitted that she took the key without the defendant's knowledge. Thus, in spite of Scalia's conclusion that "the Appellate Court's determination of no common authority over the apartment [by the girlfriend] was obviously correct" and therefore she lacked the authority to give the police permission to enter (*Illinois v. Rodriguez* 1990: 182), Scalia was concerned only with the reasonableness of the police officers' belief in the girlfriend's authority over the apartment.

Scalia also wrote a majority opinion endorsing the warrantless search of a probationer's home based on a state statute authorizing such searches if based on "reasonable grounds," where the grounds were a police officer's statement that the probationer's apartment might contain a handgun (*Griffin v. Wisconsin* 1987). In both cases, Scalia evinced a textualist concern that the warrantless searches must be "reasonable" in order to be constitutionally permissible. His assessment of reasonableness did not evince much skepticism about police motivations. He also did not discuss the cases from the perspective of the defendants by emphasizing their constitutionally protected expectations of privacy.

In cases in which the Court was deeply split, Scalia tended to cast decisive votes that favored law enforcement actions over individuals' assertions of Fourth Amendment rights and the exclusionary rule. For example, Scalia endorsed: the admissibility of evidence seized during a warrantless search that relied on an unconstitutional statute (*Illinois v. Krull* 1987); the finding that helicopter surveillance is not a "search" (*Florida v. Riley* 1989); and an illegal warrantless arrest as not requiring exclusion of incriminating statements made by the defendant after being arrested (*New York v. Harris* 1990). In cases concerning stops and searches of vehicles and their contents, Scalia provided a dependable vote for the Rehnquist Court's expansion of police officers' authority to conduct warrantless searches (*Colorado v. Bertine* 1987; *Alabama v. White* 1990; *Michigan Department of State Police v. Sitz* 1990; *California v. Acevedo* 1991). Thus, Scalia's support for law enforcement practices and the narrowing of Fourth Amendment rights was so consistent and therefore unremarkable that the intriguing aspects of his Fourth Amendment jurisprudence arise in attempting to understand the few cases in which he supported individuals' claims.

In two notable cases, Scalia's textualist and originalist approaches led him to join the liberal justices in supporting individuals' rights. In *National Treasury Employees Union v. Von Raab* (1989), Scalia was among four dissenters (Brennan, Marshall, and Stevens) who objected to the Court's endorsement of drug testing for Customs Service employees when there is no basis for suspicion of wrongdoing by the employees. In his dissenting opinion, Scalia recognized that the scope of Fourth Amendment rights has frequently been limited when balanced against competing interests. Thus, Scalia would not require individualized suspicion for drug testing of railroad employees involved in accidents or for searches of prisoners within correctional institutions (see *Skinner v. Railway Labor Executives Association* [1989]). Scalia condemned the Customs Service's drug-testing practices as "a kind of immolation of privacy and human dignity in symbolic opposition to drug use" (*National Treasury Employees* 1989: 681). According to Scalia, "the impairment of individual liberties cannot be the means of making a point . . . symbolism, even symbolism for so worthy a cause as the abolition of unlawful drugs, cannot validate an otherwise unreasonable search" (ibid.: 687).

In this case, Scalia's concern with the requirement of "reasonableness" as a basis for searches stems directly from the text of the Fourth Amendment and its prohibition against "unreasonable searches and seizures." Scalia virtually concedes that policy considerations govern the Court's definition of "reasonableness": "[T]he question comes down to whether a particular search has been 'reasonable,' [and] the answer depends largely upon the social necessity that prompts the search" (ibid.). Although Scalia amply demonstrated in other cases that he would not scrutinize closely the policy justifications offered by the government to justify the reasonableness of searches, he distinguished himself from his conservative colleagues in the *National Treasury Employees* case by, in effect, declaring that the text's reasonableness requirement demanded some specific justification for the searches. In Scalia's words:

> What is absent in the Government's justifications—notably absent, revealingly absent, and as far as I am concerned dispositively absent—is the recitation of *even a single instance* in which any of the speculated horribles actually occurred: an instance, that is, in which the cause of bribetaking, or of poor aim, or of unsympathetic law enforcement, or of compromise of classified information, was drug use [by Customs Service employees]. (ibid.: 683)

In the second example, *County of Riverside v. McLaughlin* (1991), Scalia joined the three most liberal justices (Marshall, Blackmun, and Stevens) in opposing the Court's decision permitting arrestees to be held for up to forty-eight hours before a probable cause hearing. The case raised the issue of the Fourth Amendment's requirement of a prompt determination of probable cause. Scalia's blistering dissent emphasized his belief that the "Court's constitutional jurisprudence . . . alternately creates rights that the Constitution does not contain [e.g., abortion] and denies rights that it does contain [*e.g.*, confrontation of accusing witnesses]" (*County of Riverside v. McLaughlin* 1991: 65). According to Scalia, the majority's decision on jailing suspects "repudiate[s] one of [the Fourth Amendment's] core applications so that the presumptively innocent may be left in jail" (ibid.: 72). Scalia distinguished this case from the search-and-seizure issues in which, according to his opinion, "[t]here is assuredly room for [policy-oriented balancing] approach in resolving novel questions" (ibid.). Under his concern for preserving the Constitution's original meaning, Scalia saw probable cause determinations for detainees as resting on "a clear answer [that] already existed in 1791 and has been generally adhered to by the traditions of our society ever since" (ibid.). Scalia argued that the Court should enforce the long-standing tradition of requiring probable cause determinations for detainees within twenty-four hours rather than forty-eight hours.

The two foregoing examples provide a basis for acknowledging Scalia's independence as a decisionmaker, but they do not reveal any clear jurisprudential vision concerning the Fourth Amendment. Scalia's textualist concern with the "reasonableness" requirement for searches apparently precludes him from accepting some hollow justifications presented by the government as the basis for searches. But his votes and opinions in other search cases do not indicate that he examines closely the basis or consequential implications of the government's justifications for warrantless searches in most contexts. His desire for prompt probable cause determinations illustrates his concern about preserving long-standing (i.e., two-centuries-old) understandings of Fourth Amendment concepts. Because it is relatively unusual for pretwentieth century definitions of criminal defendants' rights to be broader than those recognized by the Rehnquist Court, it is not surprising that Scalia's historical approach seldom asserts itself on behalf of individuals in Fourth Amendment cases.

Aside from the elements of Scalia's jurisprudential building blocks that are evident in these two unusual cases, namely textualism (*National Treasury Employees*) and originalism (*County of Riverside*), another common thread is woven through these cases that may lead Scalia, consciously or unconsciously, to display greater defensiveness about the preservation of rights. In the many Fourth Amendment cases in which "challengeable" law enforcement practices, such as stops of cars without probable cause and warrantless searches, produce incriminating evidence, Scalia almost always endorses the law enforcement practice (*Arizona v. Hicks* excepted) as constitutionally permissible. By contrast, Scalia's emphasis in *National Treasury Employees* and *County of Riverside* was on preserving rights for *innocent* citizens. When faced with claims from guilty defendants (i.e., those caught with drugs or other illegal contraband), Scalia generally supports the government and demonstrates little skepticism about law enforcement officers' motives or the consequences of their actions (Smith 1990). When faced with governmental intrusions on protections for the innocent, the risk of governmental abuse is suddenly of grave concern to Scalia.

In *National Treasury Employees*, Scalia expresses opposition to "this invasion of [the Customs Service employees'] privacy and affront to their dignity" (*National Treasury Employees* 1989: 686), a concern that is noticeably absent in his opinions for cases concerning individuals who have been caught in illegal activities through warrantless searches. Similarly, Scalia's *County of Riverside* dissent is directed toward protecting innocent citizens:

> One hears the complaint, nowadays, that the Fourth Amendment has become constitutional law for the guilty; that it benefits the career criminal (through the exclusionary rule) often and directly, but the ordinary citizen remotely if at all. By failing to protect the innocent arrestee, today's opinion reinforces that view. . . . While in recent years we have invented novel applications of the Fourth Amendment to release the unquestionably guilty, we today repudiate one of its core applications so that the presumptively innocent may be left in jail. (1991: 72)

Perhaps most telling of all, Scalia, the former University of Virginia law professor, includes in his opinion an anecdote from the *Washington Post* concerning a University of Virginia student who was arrested for failing to pay a restaurant's required $5 minimum fee when he tried to leave after looking unsuccessfully for some friends in the dining area. While Scalia's use of the anecdote was an obvious effort to tap the reader's empathy for the innocent "everyman" drawn into the criminal justice system, did the anecdote reveal Scalia's empathy as well? It is difficult to identify a particular jurisprudential vision asserted by Scalia in the realm of the Fourth Amendment. Thus, one cannot help but wonder whether Scalia is most inclined to employ his tools of textualism and originalism in the service of innocent citizens with whom he empathizes rather than on behalf of guilty defendants, although even these people do not forfeit all of their constitutional rights merely because they have been caught violating criminal laws.

Fifth Amendment

In Fifth Amendment cases, Justice Scalia seldom supported claims of individuals and he wrote few opinions. In cases questioning the voluntariness of confessions, Scalia cast the decisive fifth vote to acknowledge that a prisoner's incriminating statements were coerced when an undercover officer posing as a prisoner promised to protect him from other prisoners if he would talk about a past crime (*Arizona v. Fulminante* 1991). However, in the same case, Scalia switched sides on a separate issue to provide an equally decisive fifth vote for establishing for the first time ever that a coerced confession may be regarded as a "harmless error" that would not justify the reversal of a conviction. Thus, Scalia provided the pivotal vote for weakening defendants' claims that violations of their constitutional rights entitled them to new trials. After the decision, David Kairys complained that "[i]t is as if the Constitution were amended to read, after the Bill of Rights and succeeding amendments, 'but no violation of the foregoing rights of persons accused of crime matters if a majority of the Supreme Court is convinced that the defendant was guilty and the violation is no big deal!' " (1993: 175).

Scalia voted consistently, with one exception, to support the government in cases that narrowed the definition of Fifth Amendment protections established by *Miranda v. Arizona.* Scalia endorsed permitting officers to change the *Miranda* warnings given to suspects before questioning (*Duckworth v. Eagan* 1989). When six justices said that police cannot reinitiate interrogation of a defendant without the defendant's counsel present, Scalia's dissenting opinion in *Minnick v. Mississippi* (1990) argued that the police should not be precluded from urging defendants to waive their right to counsel and to confess their crimes. Scalia displayed little skepticism about the risks of coercive effects from permitting police to initiate questioning outside of the presence of counsel. Moreover, while his Fourth Amendment opinions favoring individuals seemed motivated by his concern for the innocent, his narrower view of the Fifth Amendment also appeared guided by his diminished concern for protecting rights when guilty individuals are involved:

> The procedural protections of the Constitution protect the guilty as well as the innocent, but it is not their objective to set the guilty free. . . . While every person is entitled to stand silent, it is more virtuous for the wrongdoer to admit his offense and accept the punishment he deserves. (*Minnick v. Mississippi* 1990: 166–167)

Scalia voted during his second term to forbid police from interrogating suspects concerning a separate, unrelated offense when they are already represented by counsel for a different offense (*Arizona v. Roberson* 1988). His *Minnick* dissent two years later, however, provided an indication that Scalia's thinking about the issue had changed. The change appeared complete in 1991 when Scalia wrote a majority opinion in *McNeil v. Wisconsin* (1991) purporting to distinguish the invocation of a Fifth Amendment right to counsel from the invocation of a Sixth Amendment right to counsel. In *McNeil*, a defendant requested and received representation from a public defender during a bail hearing for a robbery charge. Scalia's opinion for the Court declared that the defendant's request for Sixth Amendment counsel at a judicial proceeding did not constitute a Fifth Amendment request for counsel that would preclude the police from questioning him outside of the presence of counsel on an unrelated murder charge. Scalia's opinion was harshly criticized by commentators as "a dizzying display of dancing around precedent, principle, and common[-]sense policy" (Decker 1992: 77). Drawing from a statement in Scalia's opinion, John Decker accused Scalia of saying, in effect, that "it is appropriate to have some suspects exercise their rights some of the time but inappropriate to have it 'seriously impede law enforcement' " (ibid.: 78).

Scalia wrote his largest number of Fifth Amendment opinions (i.e., three) concerning the right against double jeopardy. Unlike the tone of other opinions that emphasized constitutional protections for the innocent, Scalia's first double jeopardy opinion explicitly endorsed protections for the guilty: "Whenever [the Double Jeopardy Clause] is applied to release a criminal deserving of punishment it frustrates justice in the particular case, but for the greater purpose of assuring repose in the totality of criminal prosecutions and sentences" (*Jones v. Thomas* 1989: 396). Although Scalia deserted his usual conservative allies in expressing these liberal sentiments in a dissenting opinion, he returned to the fold in a subsequent controversial case, *Grady v. Corbin* (1990), in which a five-member majority precluded a prosecution for vehicular homicide after the defendant entered a guilty plea for two traffic tickets concerning the same conduct that caused the death. Scalia applied his textualist and originalist analysis to argue that the Double Jeopardy Clause protects against multiple trials for the same *offense*, not multiple charges based on the same conduct. Scalia's dissent predicted that, "A limitation that is so unsupported in reason and so absurd in application is unlikely to survive" (*Grady v. Corbin* 1990: 543). The subsequent retirements of two members (Brennan and Marshall) of the slim five-member majority and their replacement with appointees by President Bush led to the fulfillment of Scalia's prediction about the decision's survival—albeit because of new personnel rather than the decision's purportedly patent absurdity. Three years later, with the support of Justice Marshall's replacement, Clarence Thomas, Scalia wrote the majority opinion in *United States v. Dixon* (1993) which overruled the Grady case.

The clearest component of Scalia's jurisprudential vision discernible in the Fifth Amendment cases was his successful application of textualist and originalist analysis to reverse a recent precedent (*Grady v. Corbin*) and thereby focus the Double Jeopardy Clause on specific offenses rather than on conduct. Scalia also helped to permit police to initiate questioning of defendants who are represented by attorneys on separate charges. It is not clear whether his complicated and controversial separation of the Fifth and Sixth Amendment rights to counsel actually follows from his usual approaches to constitutional analysis or whether it reflects the advancement of policy preferences regardless of textualism and originalism. Despite his willingness to adhere to his interpretive approaches even if they produce liberal outcomes in some criminal justice cases, as indicated by the discussion in previous chapters, Scalia seems to ignore originalism in favor of his policy preferences in other kinds of cases.

Sixth Amendment

The Sixth Amendment specifies a variety of familiar rights associated with criminal trials: right to counsel; right to speedy and public trial; right to trial by impartial jury; right to confront adverse witnesses; and right to compulsory process for obtaining witnesses. As in cases concerning other criminal defendants' rights, Scalia supports the government in most Sixth Amendment cases. During the Rehnquist Court era it has been relatively unusual to find any justices other than Stevens, Blackmun, and, when they were on the Court, Brennan and Marshall, supporting individuals in Sixth Amendment cases. Other than a few unanimous decisions in which the entire Court recognized errors by trial judges in giving jury instructions,[1] the Sixth Amendment cases generally divided the justices along predictable lines. In fact, Scalia, along with Thomas, demonstrated that he was less inclined than other justices to recognize individuals' Sixth Amendment rights by dissenting in a 7-to-2 decision that had declared that a state cannot forcibly administer antipsychotic drugs to a defendant during a trial (*Riggins v. Nevada* 1992).

With respect to one issue, the Confrontation clause, Scalia had occasion to part company with his usual allies when he felt that the Rehnquist Court majority's decisions clearly impinged on the text and meaning of the Sixth Amendment. In *Cruz v. New York* (1987), Scalia, joined by the four most liberal justices—Brennan, Marshall, Stevens, and Blackmun—wrote the majority opinion in a Confrontation Clause case that deeply divided the Court. Scalia's opinion held that a nontestifying codefendant's confession incriminating the defendant is not admissible at their joint trial. In *Coy v. Iowa* (1988), Scalia, joined by Brennan, White, Marshall, Stevens, and O'Connor, wrote the Court's majority opinion declaring that a defendant accused of raping two minor girls had his Sixth Amendment Confrontation clause rights violated by the placement of a one-way mirror/screen between the defendant and the victims during the victims' testimony in court. Justice Blackmun's dissenting opinion adopted a policy argument by asserting that the Court should balance competing public policies in attempting to reduce the trauma of courtroom confrontations for children who are victims of sex crimes. Subsequently, when a majority of justices (O'Connor, Rehnquist, Kennedy, Blackmun, and White) approved the use of one-way closed-circuit television broadcasts for taking children's testimony during child sex-abuse cases in *Maryland v. Craig* (1990), Scalia wrote the dissent, joined by more liberal justices (Brennan, Marshall, and Stevens), which emphasized the clear text of the Sixth Amendment:

> Seldom has this Court failed so conspicuously to sustain a categorical guarantee of the Constitution against the tide of prevailing current opinion. The Sixth Amendment provides, with unmistakable clarity, that '[i]n all criminal prosecutions, the accused shall enjoy the right . . . to be confronted with the witnesses against him. (*Maryland v. Craig* 1990: 3171)

Scalia's opposition to the conservatives' arguments in this series of cases was a manifestation of his independent interpretation of the Confrontation clause, rather than an indication of his agreement with the Court's liberals. In other Confrontation clause cases, Scalia wrote majority opinions with which the Court's most liberal justices disagreed. In *Richardson v. Marsh* (1987), Scalia's opinion declared that the admission of a nontestifying co-defendant's confession was permissible as long as specific references to the defendant were deleted. Over dissenting opinions by Justices Brennan and Marshall, Scalia's majority opinion in *Richardson v. Marsh* approved the admissibility of a prior, out-of-court identification by a witness unable to explain its basis due to memory loss. Scalia's strong belief in an immutable core contained within the confrontation right of the Sixth Amendment did not necessarily lead him to take an especially broad view of the Confrontation Clause's meaning. Instead, Scalia's textualist emphasis merely precluded his agreement with some policy-oriented decisions of his conservative colleagues, especially when they sought to protect child-victim witnesses in *Coy v. Iowa* and *Craig v. Maryland*. Scalia viewed these efforts as clashing directly with the command of the Sixth Amendment's very words.

Eighth Amendment and Capital Punishment

Through 1993, Justice Scalia sided with individuals in only five of the more than fifty cases concerning the Eighth Amendment, capital punishment, and habeas corpus. Four of the cases were unanimous decisions,[2] including one that had a plausible conservative philosophical basis that involved protecting property rights through application of the Eighth Amendment's Excessive Fines clause to government seizures of property in drug cases (*Austin v. United States* 1993). The other case, concerning the introduction of evidence on a defendant's membership in a racist organization when the crime was unrelated to racial animus, would have been unanimous if not for Justice Thomas's solo dissent (*Dawson v. Delaware* 1992). Among the Rehnquist Court justices, only Thomas supported individuals in a smaller percentage of these cases than Scalia. Scalia has supported arguments of defendants and prisoners only in exceptional cases in which there was consensus among the Court's justices. Unlike his decisions on other provisions of the Bill of Rights that affect criminal defendants and prisoners, Scalia's textualist and originalist approaches did not benefit individuals when applied to the Eighth Amendment and capital punishment. Instead, Scalia applied his interpretive approach and energies to undo precedents favoring individuals. With respect to the Eighth Amendment and capital punishment, more than with any other issues affecting criminal justice, Scalia worked to effectuate a particular jurisprudential vision that, consistent with other elements in his judicial philosophy, advocated the primacy of authoritative decision-making by state legislatures, corrections officials, trial judges, and juries. Scalia's approach to the Eighth Amendment and capital punishment comports with Brisbin's characterization of Scalia's pattern of decision-making. According to Richard Brisbin (1990: 5), Scalia "believes in popular control of public policy through representative institutions and in respect for the majority's policy choices."

Justice Scalia, along with his colleague Justice Thomas, distinguished himself as possessing the Court's most restrictive view of the Eighth Amendment. Indeed, it is not clear from the Supreme Court's cases precisely when, if ever, Scalia (or Thomas) would recognize a government action as violating the Eighth Amendment's prohibition on cruel and unusual punishments. Initially, Scalia's nonjudicial writings indicated that he would be willing to deviate from his usual emphasis on originalism in Eighth Amendment cases. In a speech that was later published in the *Cincinnati Law Review*, Scalia advocated his consistent theme that judges and justices should look to the text and original meaning of the Constitution as the primary sources for interpretive guidance. Scalia indicated, however, that he believed that the Eighth Amendment should not require the same faithful adherence to original meanings as the rest of the Constitution. Scalia said:

> What if some state should enact a new law providing public lashing, or branding of the right hand, as punishment for certain criminal offenses? Even if it could be demonstrated unequivocally that these were not cruel and unusual measures in 1791, and even though no prior Supreme Court decision has specifically disapproved them, I doubt whether any federal judge—even among the many who consider themselves originalists—would sustain them against an [E]ighth [A]mendment challenge. . . . I am confident that public flogging and hand[-]branding would not be sustained by our courts, and any espousal of originalism as a practical theory of exegesis must somehow come to terms with that reality. . . . I hasten to confess that in a crunch I may prove a faint-hearted originalist. I cannot imagine myself, any more than any other federal judge, upholding a statute that imposes the punishment of flogging. (1989: 864)

Despite the strong indication that the Eighth Amendment, like the Confrontation Clause, might be a specific constitutional provision that Scalia would view as requiring judicial action to protect individuals' rights, Scalia's

Eighth Amendment decisions provide no indication that he would actually limit the government's policies and practices that affect criminal offenders. In two cases, in fact, Scalia wrote important opinions seeking to alter Eighth Amendment jurisprudence in order to reduce protections for individuals. In *Wilson v. Seiter* (1990), Scalia wrote a majority opinion that changed the standard for judicial action in cases contesting the conditions of confinement in correctional institutions. In previous cases, the Court had "endorsed judicial intervention when an examination of the 'totality of conditions' revealed 'wanton and unnecessary infliction of pain' or 'unquestioned and serious deprivation of basic human needs' " (Smith 1992–93: 207). This represented an *objective* standard that sought to examine whether the conditions of confinement in an institution violated the Eighth Amendment by constituting cruel and unusual punishment. After Scalia's majority opinion in *Wilson v. Seiter*, however, the Court had suddenly switched to a *subjective* standard that examined whether challenged conditions had resulted from the "deliberate indifference" of corrections officials. Scalia reinterpreted precedents concerning conditions of confinement in correctional institutions in order to assert that the standard of review applied to claims of deficient medical care for prisoners should be applied to all claims concerning conditions that allegedly violate the Eighth Amendment.[3] According to Justice White's dissent, Scalia's new standard not only was contrary to the Court's clear line of precedents, it also created the likelihood that judges would no longer intervene to correct inhumane conditions:

> [T]he majority's intent requirement . . . likely will prove impossible to apply in many cases. Inhumane prison conditions often are the result of cumulative actions and inactions by numerous officials inside and outside a prison, sometimes over a long period of time. In those circumstances, it is far from clear whose intent should be examined and the majority offers no real guidance on this issue. . . . The majority's approach is also unwise. It leaves open the possibility, for example, that prison officials will be able to defeat a [civil rights] action challenging inhuman conditions simply by showing that the conditions are caused by insufficient funding from the state legislature rather than by a deliberate indifference on the part of prison officials. (*Wilson v. Seiter* 1991: 310–311)

In *Harmelin v. Michigan* (1991), Scalia's opinion expressing the judgment of the Court sought to eliminate the Eighth Amendment's proportionality requirement for noncapital cases. Scalia used originalism to note that, unlike some state constitutions, "those who framed and approved the Federal Constitution chose, for whatever reason, not to include within it the guarantee against disproportionate sentences" (*Harmelin v. Michigan*

1991: 2696). In approving Michigan's mandatory life-imprisonment-without-possibility-of-parole penalty for a first offender convicted of possessing more than 650 grams of cocaine, Scalia concluded that "[s]evere, mandatory penalties may be cruel, but they are not unusual in the constitutional sense, having been employed in various forms throughout our Nation's history" (ibid.: 2701). Three concurring justices and four dissenting justices took issue with Scalia's argument that the Eighth Amendment contains no general proportionality requirement. Scalia succeeded, through his assertiveness in writing opinions, in laying his arguments out for consideration by future justices.

By joining Justice Thomas's opinions in other cases, Scalia continued his advocacy for a very narrow conception of Eighth Amendment rights. In *Hudson v. McMillian* (1992), two Louisiana corrections officers beat a handcuffed prisoner. The prisoner "suffered minor bruises and swelling of his face, mouth, and lip . . . [and] loosened . . . teeth and [a] cracked . . . partial dental plate" (*Hudson v. McMillian* 1992: 156). The prisoner sought to file a civil rights lawsuit against the corrections officials, and the Supreme Court faced the question of whether excessive use of force can constitute an Eighth Amendment violation of cruel and unusual punishment when the prisoner does not suffer serious injuries. Seven justices, including Chief Justice Rehnquist, agreed that the prisoner presented a valid Eighth Amendment claim, and they reconfirmed that Eighth Amendment claims are "contextual and responsive to 'contemporary standards of decency' " (ibid.: 167). The Eighth Amendment had been consistently interpreted in light of developing and changing social standards since the Warren Court defined the Amendment's meaning as evolutionary in *Trop v. Dulles* (1958). This conceptualization of Eighth Amendment standards as flexible and evolutionary clashed directly with Scalia's usual originalist stance. Thus, it was not surprising to find Scalia, along with his consistent ally Thomas, as the lone dissenters.

Thomas's dissenting opinion, joined by Scalia, initially made the argument that the Eighth Amendment was originally aimed at preventing only cruel and unusual *criminal sentences*, not mistreatment of prisoners. Although the opinion did not advocate outright abandonment of prisoners' Eighth Amendment claims about their treatment and conditions of confinement, it clearly implied that Thomas and Scalia believe such claims are not valid under their originalist approach to interpreting the Constitution. Thomas ultimately concluded that "primary responsibility for preventing and punishing [improper] conduct [by corrections officers] rests not with the Federal Constitution but with the laws and regulations of the various States" (*Hudson v. McMillian* 1992: 180). In effect, Thomas and Scalia argued for a return to the "hands-off" approach that had traditionally been applied by judges to correctional institutions prior to the 1960s and 1970s. By turning back the clock, the policy advocated by Thomas and Scalia would once again place the "actualization of prisoners' constitutional rights . . . in the hands of the same elected legislative and executive branches that [historically] created and maintained civil rights violations in the first place" (Smith 1986: 150). Scalia and Thomas evince scant recognition of the potential consequences of the withdrawal of judicial enforcement of Eighth Amendment protections for prisoners, a group that under the Warren Court had been given new protections as a result of their relative powerlessness in society against majoritarian wishes. American history demonstrates many examples of the kinds of shockingly inhumane conditions that can be produced in prisons when there is no threat of judicial supervision (see, e.g., Berkson 1975).

In *Helling v. McKinney* (1993), a prisoner filed a civil rights action asserting an Eighth Amendment violation when he was placed in a cell with another prisoner who smoked five packs of cigarettes per day and thereby exposed him to health risks from second-hand tobacco smoke. In an opinion by Justice White, a seven-member majority ruled that the prisoner had raised a colorable Eighth Amendment claim that corrections officials' deliberate indifference (under Scalia's *Wilson v. Seiter* standard) had led to the prisoner's exposure to an unreasonable risk of serious harm to his health. In Thomas's dissenting opinion, joined by Scalia, the conservative duo followed their originalist interpretive approach by questioning whether the Eighth Amendment should apply to anything other than an actual criminal sentence made by judges and juries, not to the treatment of prisoners by corrections officials. Thomas further argued that only actual serious injuries should be considered if the Eighth Amendment were to be applied to the corrections context. Again, Thomas and Scalia established themselves as advocates for a return to the "hands-off" judicial policy of yesteryear with respect to prison conditions and the treatment of convicted offenders.

Consistent with his view that federal courts should defer to the policies and judgments of state government officials, Scalia generally opposed judicial scrutiny of and interference with the imposition of the death penalty. In a careful study of Scalia's decisions on capital punishment, Steven Gey (1992: 102) concluded that "Scalia seems to believe that there are virtually no constitutional limits on a state's imposition of the death penalty," notwithstanding Scalia's claims about the death penalty that he made in his essay "Originalism" (Scalia 1989b).

Scalia's initial written opinion concerning the death penalty in *Hitchcock v. Dugger* (1987) was a unanimous majority opinion reversing and remanding for reconsideration a death sentence imposed without consideration of nonstatutory mitigating factors. This was by no means an indication that Scalia had doubts about the propriety of how the death penalty was generally applied. After all, he was among the five justices in the majority who refused to consider powerful statistical evidence of systemic racial discrimination in Georgia's death sentences as an indication of constitutional infirmity in *McCleskey v. Kemp* (1987). The *Hitchcock* case merely failed to tap Scalia's growing concerns about judicial interference with states' imposition of the death penalty.

Beginning in his first term as a justice, Scalia began to criticize the Court's decisions that controlled what information could be considered by judges and juries in deciding whether or not to impose the death penalty. When the Court decided in 1987 that victim-impact statements were impermissible in the sentencing phase of capital cases because they may improperly lead to arbitrary and capricious imposition of the death penalty, Scalia spoke on behalf of the four dissenters in *Booth v. Maryland* (1987). Scalia implied that capital sentencing procedures that permit the introduction of mitigating factors show favoritism to defendants and reiterated his familiar theme that policy decisions, including those affecting capital punishment, should be decided by branches of government other than the judiciary:

> Many citizens have found one-sided and hence unjust the criminal trial in which a parade of witnesses comes forth to testify to the pressures beyond normal human experience that drove the defendant to commit his crime, with no one to lay before the sentencing authority the full reality of human suffering the defendant has produced—which (and *not* moral guilt alone) is one of the reasons society deems his act worthy of the prescribed penalty. Perhaps these sentiments do not sufficiently temper justice with mercy, but that is a question to be decided through the democratic processes of a free people, and not by the decrees of this Court. There is nothing in the Constitution that dictates the answer, no more than in the field of capital punishment than elsewhere. (*Booth v. Maryland* 1987: 520)

Scalia's advocacy for shifting the sentencers' emphasis from moral guilt to subjective perceptions of the degree of harm raises risks that discriminatory applications of the death penalty would result when some victims' lives are considered by jurors to have been more valuable than other victims' lives—a result perfectly consistent with Scalia's participation in the majority in *McCleskey v. Kemp* (1987). In *McCleskey*, detailed statistical studies had demonstrated that convicted murderers were much more likely to receive the death penalty for killing white victims than for killing black victims (Baldus, Woodworth, and Pulaski 1990). A slim five-member majority rejected the use of statistics to show systemic discrimination, in part because they did not wish to interfere with discretionary decision-making within the criminal justice system. The four dissenters were dismayed that the majority could overlook evidence of racial discrimination in order to avoid threatening the continuation of capital punishment. When the Thurgood Marshall papers were made available to the public at the Library of Congress in 1993, it was revealed that Scalia, alone among the members of the *McCleskey* majority, had recognized that the statistics presented do, indeed, demonstrate the existence of racial discrimination. However, rather than apply this recognition to invalidate Georgia's capital punishment procedures as violative of the Equal Protection Clause, Scalia wrote in a memo to his colleagues, "[I]t is my view that the unconscious operation of irrational sympathies and antipathies, including racial, upon jury decisions and (hence) prosecutorial [ones], is real, acknowledged by the [cases] of this court and ineradicable. . . ." (Dorin 1994: 1038). After such an acknowledgement, how could he vote to perpetuate the disciminatory system of capital punishment in Georgia? According to Dennis Dorin, Scalia "trivializ[ed]" African-Americans' concerns about racism and discrimination "by saying, in a single-paragraph memo, that they were merely an unavoidable and legally unassailable part of life for African-Americans. Apparently for Scalia, the capital punishment system's valuing a white life significantly above a black one did not implicate any constitutional provisions" (ibid.: 1077). Thus, Scalia has supported the perpetuation of discretionary, subjective decision-making that inevitably exacerbates discrimination problems in the criminal justice system.

Two years later, when another case raised the issue of victim-impact statements and the Court narrowly reconfirmed its decision in *Booth*, Scalia was unusually blunt about his eagerness to overturn the Court's precedents. Scalia's opinion raised questions about his regard for the concept of *stare decisis*, and about the manner in which political changes in the composition of the Court produce changes in constitutional interpretation:

> It has been argued that we should not overrule so recent a decision, lest our action "appear to be . . . occasioned by nothing more than a change in the Court's personnel,". . . . I doubt that overruling *Booth* will so shake the citizenry's faith in the Court. Our overrulings of precedent rarely occur without a change in the Court's personnel. . . . In any case, I would think it a violation of my oath to adhere to what I consider a plainly unjustified intrusion upon the democratic process in order that the Court might save face. (*South Carolina v. Gathers* 1987: 824–825)

Only two more years passed before the retirement of Justice Brennan and President Bush's appointment of Justice Souter gave Scalia just the change in composition that he had been waiting for to permit the introduction of victim-impact statements in *Payne v. Tennessee* (1991). Scalia seized the opportunity in a concurring opinion to counterattack against Justice Marshall's assertion that the conservative majority had no respect for *stare decisis* when it reversed precedents that were only two and four years old. Scalia noted instances in which Marshall had participated in reversing precedents concerning other issues. Scalia also emphasized his view that society, rather than judicial officers, should decide on appropriate punishments for criminal offenders (*Payne v. Tennessee* 1991: 833): "[The Eighth Amendment] permits the People to decide (within the limits of other constitutional guarantees) what is a crime and what constitutes aggravation and mitigation of a crime"; and "[The *Booth* decision] conflicts with a public sense of justice keen enough that it has found voice in a nationwide 'victim's rights' movement" (ibid.: 834).

Scalia's desire to end judicial limitations on the factors that sentencers can consider in deciding whether to impose the death penalty was presented most forcefully in a concurring opinion in *Walton v. Arizona* (1990). The Burger Court decisions concerning capital punishment during the 1970s initially abolished capital punishment in *Furman v. Georgia* (1972) because the death penalty was being imposed arbitrarily and capriciously. Shortly thereafter, the Court permitted reinstatement of capital punishment when states enacted revised death penalty statutes that provided mechanisms for channeling the discretionary decisions of judges and juries, such as separate hearings on the issue of sentencing and consideration of aggravating and mitigating factors (Epstein and Kobylka 1992). Scalia argued that there was an inherent conflict between *Furman v. Georgia's* effort to channel sentencers' discretion and later cases, such as *Woodson v. North Carolina* (1976) and *Lockett v. Ohio* (1978) that required sentencers to consider mitigating evidence rather than imposing mandatory sentences and prevented states from limiting the kinds of mitigating circumstances that could be considered. According to Scalia, "[T]he practice which in *Furman* had been described as the discretion to sentence to death and pronounced constitutionally prohibited, was in *Woodson* and *Lockett* renamed the discretion not to sentence to death and pronounced constitutionally required" (*Walton v. Arizona* 1990: 662). Scalia even applied his characteristic biting sarcasm to ridicule the two doctrines that he viewed as in conflict:

> To acknowledge that "there perhaps is an inherent tension between this line of cases and the line stemming from *Furman*" . . . is rather like saying that

there was perhaps an inherent tension between the Allies and the Axis Powers in World War II. And to refer to the two lines as pursuing "twin objectives" . . . is rather like referring to the twin objectives of good and evil. They cannot be reconciled. (ibid.: 664)

Scalia also took the opportunity to enunciate a narrow view of the Eighth Amendment that, consistent with his other opinions, provided little basis for judges to identify violations:

When punishments other than fines are involved, the Amendment explicitly requires a court to consider not only whether the penalty is severe or harsh, but also whether it is "unusual." If it is not, then the Eighth Amendment does not prohibit it, no matter how cruel a judge might think it to be. Moreover, the Eighth Amendment's prohibition is directed against cruel and unusual *punishments*. It does not, by its terms, regulate the procedures of sentencing as opposed to the substance of punishment. . . . Thus, the procedural elements of a sentencing scheme come within the prohibition, if at all, only when they are of such a nature as systematically to render the infliction of cruel punishment "unusual." (ibid.: 670)

Scalia went on to say that mandatory death sentences for crimes tradition-ally punished by death "cannot possibly violate the Eighth Amendment, because it will not be 'cruel' (neither absolutely nor for a particular crime) and it will not be 'unusual' (neither in the sense of being a type of penalty that is not traditional nor in the sense of being rarely or 'freakishly' im-posed)" (ibid.: 671). Because, in Scalia's view, the "*Woodson-Lockett* line of cases . . . bears no relation whatever to the text of the Eighth Amendment" (ibid.), he rejected any claim that they might deserve protection under *stare decisis*. In other cases, Scalia has continued his attacks on judicial require-ments and limits (i.e., the "channeling" of mitigating discretion) on the factors considered by judges and juries in sentencing (*McKoy v. North Caro-lina* 1990; *Sochor v. Florida* 1992; *Johnson v. Texas* 1993).

Scalia may be correct that the Court's death penalty jurisprudence that seeks to require, through the use of mitigating and aggravating factors, indi-vidualized decisions in capital cases creates an inherent conflict with the *Furman* decision's concerns about the excessive application of discretion. However, by advocating the permissibility of mandatory death penalty stat-utes, Scalia fundamentally misapprehends the complex factors and multi-ple discretionary decision points that can produce capriciousness and dis-crimination. Scalia focuses on the sentencing decision itself and argues that problems caused by *Furman*'s clash with *Woodson-Lockett* would be re-solved by eliminating the sentencer's discretion. This myopic preoccupation with the application of discretion at a single decision point ignores the consequences of discretion at earlier stages in the proceedings, such as the prosecutor's decision about whether to seek the death penalty, the prosecutor's trial strategy and arguments, selection of the jury, judges' jury instructions, and the jury's biases in making determinations about guilt. Moreover, a focus on the sentencer's decision ignores the consequences of inadequate legal representation that may affect poor defendants in especially harsh ways (Bowers 1983). The formalistic view of the criminal justice process evident in Scalia's arguments about discretion blind him to the cumulative impact of discretion and other factors on capital punishment decisions. Because scholars have documented how Supreme Court justices' backgrounds affect the attitudes that shape their decisions (see, e.g., Tate 1981), George Kannar (1990: 1300–1320) has argued that Scalia's religious background as an especially devout Catholic has contributed to his formalistic approach to legal decisions, including criminal justice issues.

A footnote in Justice Blackmun's dissenting opinion in *Walton v. Arizona* (1990: 545 n.2) accused Justice Scalia of threatening "the integrity of this Court's adjudicative process" by attacking settled Eighth Amendment doctrines that were not briefed and argued in the case. According to Blackmun, "It is disturbing that the decisive vote in a capital case should turn on a single Justice's rejection of a line of authority that both parties to this controversy, and eight Members of this Court, have accepted" (ibid.). Sometimes Scalia avoids issues that were not briefed and argued by counsel, as evidenced by his summary rejection of Arizona's arguments for a "good faith" exception in the exclusionary rule case of *Arizona v. Hicks* (1987). His textualist and originalist vision for the "true" meaning of the Eighth Amendment apparently overrides his consideration for such jurisprudential matters as *stare decisis* and issues that are not properly raised before the Court, perhaps reflecting stronger policy preferences in Eighth Amendment cases than in Fourth Amendment cases and other issues.

Scalia's preference for permitting states to make their own decisions about criminal punishment without excessive supervision by the federal courts was also in evidence in the Court's decision concerning the death penalty for juveniles and people with mental retardation. Scalia dissented in the Court's 1987 decision declaring that the application of the death penalty to a fifteen-year-old defendant constituted an Eighth Amendment violation (*Thompson v. Oklahoma*). Consistent with his concern for deferring policy judgments to majoritarian preferences, Scalia's dissenting opinion, like O'Connor's majority opinion, emphasized the question whether a national consensus existed against executing people who committed murders while under the age of sixteen.

In reexamining the issue of executing juveniles, Scalia attracted majority support for a decision endorsing the application of capital punishment to individuals convicted of committing murders at sixteen and seventeen years of age (*Stanford v. Kentucky* 1989). Scalia's opinion relied on both the originalist approach and majoritarianism emphasis that he regularly favors. Scalia said that capital punishment was permitted for teenagers at the time that the Bill of Rights was drafted and adopted, and he observed that a majority of states that authorize capital punishment permit such punishment for murderers at age sixteen and above. Thus, Scalia rejected the defendants' claims that public opinion polls demonstrate a national consensus against execution of juvenile offenders. According to Scalia, "We decline the invitation to rest constitutional law upon such uncertain foundations. A revised national consensus so broad, so clear, and so enduring as to justify a permanent prohibition upon all units of democratic government must appear in the operative acts (laws and the application of laws) that the people have approved" (ibid.: 377).

In the Court's 1989 decision in *Penry v. Lynaugh* that the Eighth Amendment did not preclude the execution of mentally retarded persons convicted of murder, Scalia's opinion (concurring in part and dissenting in part) emphasized that such executions violate neither the original intent of the Eighth Amendment nor evolving standards of decency. He also pressed his argument that the Court should not require juries to consider mitigating factors.

Notwithstanding Scalia's speech published in the *Cincinnati Law Review* that acknowledged that public flogging would violate the Eighth Amendment despite its acceptance in 1791, it is highly questionable whether Scalia would recognize an Eighth Amendment violation in any situation other than a case of "excessive fines." Scalia's repeated emphasis on his view that punishments must be "cruel *and* unusual" and his rejection of a proportionality requirement in the Eighth Amendment would apparently permit approval of all punishments no matter how cruel or disproportionate as long as they are not "unusual." As Scalia wrote in *Harmelin v. Michigan* (1991: 2701): "[s]evere, mandatory penalties may be cruel, but they are not unusual in the constitutional sense, having been employed in various forms throughout our Nation's history." Because of Scalia's originalist orientation and his deference to elected officials, it appears that a punishment can virtually never be "unusual" if it existed when the Bill of Rights was ratified or if it was approved by a legislative body. Thus, the Eighth Amendment's prohibition on "cruel and unusual punishments" becomes virtually meaningless for any judicial supervision of statutorily permitted punishments because legislative action favoring a punishment makes that punishment *ipso facto* not unusual in Scalia's eyes. One must wonder whether Scalia's rationale could be extended to preclude Eighth Amendment review of punishments created through discretionary judicial orders if those punishments were created by state judges who gained office through partisan or nonpartisan elections. From Scalia's perspective, the decisions of these judges may reflect society's values and therefore be considered *not* unusual.

One of the dominant trends affecting criminal punishment and the death penalty during the Rehnquist Court era has been the concerted efforts of Chief Justice Rehnquist and like-minded justices to expedite the process of appeals and collateral review of convictions (Yackle 1993). On his own, Scalia has acted to reduce the Supreme Court's burden of death penalty appeals. Prior to 1991, Justice White was the Circuit Justice for the Fifth Circuit Court of Appeals covering Texas, Louisiana, and Mississippi— states that apply the death penalty more than most others. White routinely granted extensions to the ninety-day filing deadline for death row inmates who did not have attorneys to prepare their submissions for Supreme Court review. In February 1991, however, Chief Justice Rehnquist shuffled the justices' circuit responsibilities and made Scalia the Circuit Justice overseeing the Fifth Circuit. Scalia immediately announced that he would not give extensions for the filing deadlines, even for prisoners who were forced to attempt to represent themselves because they lacked professional assistance in seeking Supreme Court review (Greenhouse 1991). Because most indigent prisoners are incapable of adequately representing themselves due to problems with illiteracy, learning disabilities, limited education, psychological problems, and the inherent complexity of legal research and the judicial process for lay advocates, Scalia's efforts to limit the flow of cases may produce especially harsh consequences for some prisoners who might otherwise assert claims that are worthy of review.

As a component of this effort to reduce the opportunities for prisoners, and especially death row prisoners, to contest their convictions, the Rehnquist Court has created new procedural rules for habeas corpus petitions. The Court's habeas jurisprudence is particularly relevant to capital punishment issues because, according to Joseph Hoffmann (1993: 832), "[T]he Court is not yet prepared to hop off the endless merry-go-round that it boarded when it first chose to interpret the Eighth Amendment in death-penalty cases primarily in procedural, rather than substantive, terms." Recent Supreme Court decisions have limited prisoners' access to federal judicial review by requiring all claims to be filed in a single habeas petition (*McCleskey v. Zant* 1991), regarding even inadvertent violations of state appellate procedures as constituting defaults for federal claims (*Coleman v.*

Thompson 1991), limiting retroactive application of decisions recognizing constitutional rights (*Butler v. McKellar* 1989), and denying a right to representation for death row inmates pursuing habeas petitions (*Murray v. Giarratano* 1989). According to Welsh White (1991: 21), "[T]he Court's habeas decisions undoubtedly have had and will continue to have a dramatic effect on the administration of capital punishment."

Scalia has cast his votes in support of these developments when deciding relevant cases, but he has not been prominent in writing opinions for most of these decisions. Justice Scalia's primary contribution to habeas reform was a concurring opinion, joined by Thomas, in a case brought forward by a death row inmate who claimed that new evidence demonstrated that he was actually innocent of the crime (*Herrera v. Collins* 1993). Unlike the three dissenters (Blackmun, Stevens, and Souter), who asserted that it would violate the Eighth Amendment to execute an innocent person, Scalia stated that, "There is no basis in text, tradition, or even in contemporary practice (if that were enough), for finding in the Constitution a right to demand judicial consideration of newly discovered evidence of innocence brought forward after conviction" (ibid.: 874–875). Scalia reaffirmed his faith in elected officials and his desire to keep the federal judiciary out of policy decisions by asserting that, "[I]t is improbable that evidence of innocence as convincing as today's opinion requires would fail to produce an executive pardon" (ibid.).

The current reduction in federal judicial review for capital cases, which comports with Scalia's views and reflects recent changes in habeas jurisprudence, increases the risk that innocent people may be executed. Chief Justice Rehnquist stated during an interview for the PBS film *This Honorable Court* that, "The Supreme Court of the United States should be reserved . . . for important disputes and questions of law, not for individual injustices that might be corrected and should be corrected in other courts." It is clear that Justice Scalia agrees with this assessment. In his *Herrera* opinion, Scalia noted that the Constitution provides no right for innocent persons to gain reconsideration of their cases after they have been tried and convicted. Scalia's belief that post-trial discovery of evidence of innocence will produce executive pardons clashes with the reality that governors, as elected officials, may be reluctant to pardon someone if public opinion is divided (as it frequently is) about the clarity of the evidence of innocence. Indeed, news media investigations of death penalty cases have raised disturbing questions about the risks that innocent people may be executed in specific cases that were denied judicial review in the current trend toward reducing federal judicial supervision of state courts (Marcus 1990; Willwerth 1993).

Conclusion

Justice Scalia's consistent support for government and generally narrow conceptualizations of constitutional rights for criminal defendants and prisoners reflect his overriding philosophy of deference to legislatures and the other institutions and actors produced by majoritarian political processes. Scalia's jurisprudential emphasis on textualism and originalism are clearly discernible in many of his opinions in criminal justice cases. On occasion, his interpretive approaches lead him to part company with his usual allies among the Court's conservatives in order to join with the Court's liberal justices in supporting an individual's constitutional claim. The Confrontation Clause cases in which Scalia's interpretive approaches clashed with the conservative justices' policy-oriented initiative to protect child-victim witnesses illuminate the potential for Scalia to demonstrate his independence when addressing specific issues.

Scalia does not articulate a clear vision of the constitutional provisions affecting criminal justice except with respect to the Eighth Amendment and capital punishment. Although Scalia's opinions clearly indicate that he believes that the text and original meaning of the Bill of Rights provide the basis for *some* protections for individuals under the Fourth, Fifth, and Sixth Amendments, his opinions make it difficult to discern a comprehensive vision of what these amendments mean. For example, the message underlying his three opinions defending the Confrontation Clause is muddied by other Confrontation Clause opinions supporting the government when varying factual circumstances arise. By contrast, Scalia's opinions on the Eighth Amendment and capital punishment are forceful, relatively consistent, and grounded in his interpretation of the Constitution's text and original meaning. The existence and strength of Scalia's vision for the Eighth Amendment and capital punishment are evident in his aggressive efforts to abolish myriad precedents and reshape constitutional doctrine in a manner that will comport with his view of the Eighth Amendment's meaning.

Scalia's vision of the Eighth Amendment is, in many respects, quite different than that developed by case decisions since the Warren Court era and that which is reflected in the decisions of most justices on the Rehnquist Court. Because Scalia sees the Eighth Amendment as applying only to sentencing decisions and not to conditions in correctional institutions, as prohibiting only "unusual" punishments that also happen to be cruel, and as being defined essentially by eighteenth-century standards, his views are shared only by Justice Thomas. Despite his minority viewpoint within the Rehnquist Court, Scalia has scored victories in his effort to remake constitutional rights affecting criminal punishment. His deft and persuasive pen redefined fifteen years' worth of precedents in establishing a new, more relaxed standard for assessing the constitutionality of prison conditions in *Wilson v. Seiter*. Moreover, his repeated attacks on precedents with which he disagrees and frequent references to the Court's authority to alter constitutional precedents may help to smooth the way for other justices who might otherwise have been concerned about *stare decisis* in, for example, quickly undoing recent precedents on the admissibility of victim-impact statements (*Payne v. Tennessee*). Scalia's future success in shaping the meaning of the Eighth Amendment will depend significantly on the nature of changes in the Court's composition. Despite the everpresent uncertainty about the Court's future, it is apparent that Scalia will aggressively continue to lay the groundwork for doctrinal change by seizing opportunities in concurring and dissenting opinions to elaborate and reiterate his vision of the authoritative text and history of the Eighth Amendment.

Notes

1. See *Satterwhite v. Texas* 1988 (improper failure to give defendant advance notice of psychiatric examination evidence); *Carella v. California* 1989 (improper mandatory presumptions in jury instructions); *Yates v. Evatt* 1991 (erroneous presumption instructions); *Sullivan v. Louisiana* 1993 (erroneous jury instructions do not constitute harmless error).

2. *Hitchcock v. Dugger* 1987 (death penalty cannot be imposed in state sentencing hearing in which the judge barred consideration of nonstatutory mitigating factors); *Maynard v. Cartwright* 1988 (aggravating circumstances provision of the Oklahoma death penalty statute, referring to "especially heinous, atrocious, or cruel" murders, found to be unconstitutionally vague as applied); *Johnson v. Mississippi* 1988 (Eighth Amendment required re-examination of Mississippi death sentence following reversal of New York felony conviction that was used by Mississippi as an aggravating circumstance in imposing the death sentence).

3. In *Estelle v. Gamble* (1976), over the objections of Justice Stevens, the Court applied a "deliberate indifference" standard to claims concerning unconstitutionally deficient medical care for prisoners.

Conclusion

A Different Kind of Conservative

Each justice on the U.S. Supreme Court casts but one of nine votes in any case decided by the nation's highest court. The equality of the justices' formal power as voters within a group masks the different influence and impact that individual justices may generate through the force of their intellect, persuasiveness, and strategic interactions with colleagues. While many justices are remembered for individual opinions authored or votes cast in important cases, relatively few of the Supreme Court's members have been noted for consistently sustaining a comprehensive, articulated judicial philosophy. Justice Antonin Scalia stands out among the Rehnquist Court's justices for his efforts to shape law and judicial philosophy according to a visionary framework. As indicated by the foregoing analysis of Scalia's opinions, Scalia's jurisprudential vision is beset with biases and inconsistencies. Such defects are not surprising and would undoubtedly be present and weaken the appearance of coherence in any justice's jurisprudential pattern when examined in microscopic detail in the hands of legal scholars.

Although Scalia has not achieved a consistent jurisprudential vision, the mere fact that he aspires to develop and propagate such a vision gives him significant potential influence over constitutional law. Most other justices apparently react to legal issues in an ad hoc fashion as they produce their preferred rules and outcomes for each situation. Meanwhile, Scalia lies in wait, armed with the elements of his jurisprudential vision as he looks for opportunities to reshape precedents in conformity with the persistent themes of his judicial philosophy.

Our analysis in this book reveals many consistent themes in Justice Scalia's decision-making. Scalia is supportive of property rights, corporate interests, the death penalty, and the loosening of the restrictions imposed by the exclusionary rule and *Miranda v. Arizona* (1966). He is hostile to *Roe v. Wade* (1973), a constitutional right to privacy that encompasses a woman's right to an abortion, and a variety of speech, press, religious, and associational rights recognized in the last fifty years as important to American democracy. Scalia is also generally skeptical of legislative power, yet supportive of the majoritarian process over individual rights. He has applied his preferred interpretive methodology, his understanding of the constitutional framers, and his views of separation of powers to redefine the basic structure of American politics and political institutions, including that of the federal judiciary. With respect to the formal outcomes advocated by Scalia, he supports the kind of conservative agenda that one might have expected from a justice appointed to the high court by President Reagan.

Many observers may conclude, then, that this book has produced no surprises and that it merely demonstrates that Justice Scalia is, in fact, the conservative people thought, hoped, or feared he would be. His generally conservative voting record, one that has led him consistently to agree with Chief Justice Rehnquist over seventy percent of the time each term, masks important differences that distinguish Scalia from other conservatives appointed by Presidents Reagan and Bush. If one simply says that his preferred outcomes support a conservative agenda, then the nuances of Scalia's thought will be overlooked. These nuances distinguish him from other conservative thinkers on the bench and define the scope of influence that the justice has had on the Court.

As we have noted throughout the previous chapters, Scalia has frequently concurred with the decisions in many cases, yet failed to join majority opinions penned by other conservatives. His decision to write his own separate opinions can provide a source of disagreement and conflict with usual allies who share many of his values and policy preferences. For example, in *Webster v. Reproductive Health Services* (1989), Scalia's strident concurring opinion led him into a bitter disagreement with Justice O'Connor and others as he sought to overturn *Roe v. Wade* in a single swift ruling. In other opinions concerning such issues as criminal punishment and separation-of-powers issues, Scalia has become the sole voice or leader of a small minority (when joined by Justice Thomas) in staking out unique views on specific constitutional and political issues. Despite his consistent support for politically conservative outcomes, in scattered cases dealing with such issues as flag burning, the Confrontation clause, and mandatory drug testing, Scalia has parted company with the conservative bloc and joined the liberals in affirming specific Bill of Rights protections. The independence that Scalia has displayed in making decisions and writing opinions demonstrates both his notable effort to define a jurisprudential vision and the inadequacy of the simple label "conservative" as an accurate characterization of the performance of a Supreme Court justice who is distinctively different from other justices who generally share his outcome preferences.

Scalia espouses a conservatism that distinguishes him from Chief Justice Rehnquist and Justices O'Connor and Kennedy. Unlike Rehnquist, O'Connor, and Kennedy, who seem content simply to advance their policy preferences through the advocacy of conservative case outcomes, Justice Scalia seeks to accomplish broader ends by rethinking the political philosophy and values that have defined American constitutional jurisprudence since the New Deal. We have described Scalia's new thinking as the articulation of a post-*Carolene Products* jurisprudence.

Scalia's post-*Carolene Products* jurisprudence is not a blanket rejection of the assumptions behind the logic of judicial review that have grown out of footnote number four of *United States v. Carolene Products* (1938) and the opinions of the Warren Court. As we have noted, in many of his scholarly writings, Scalia invokes the logic of *Carolene Products* to argue that the job of the judiciary is to protect the Bill of Rights or otherwise protect the rights of minorities. While advancing this approach in some cases, he has in other cases rerouted the logic of *Carolene Products* to redefine what rights and values deserve protection, how they will be protected, and what level of protection will be given to each. In Scalia's hands, the logic of Justice Stone's famous footnote has not been invoked to protect or defend affirmative action, racial minorities, or prisoners—political minority interests that received the benefit of judicial scrutiny applied to government policies during the Warren and Burger Court eras. Instead, Scalia has invoked the *Carolene Products* approach to defend whites, corporations, and property owners.

Scalia's post-*Carolene Products* approach does not merely provide judicial protection for a different sets of interests. Instead, Scalia advances a selective application of judicial protectiveness for rights in conjunction with a broader advocacy of deference to majoritarianism and the political process. The justice has been reluctant to oversee the political process in order to ensure that it respects rights—unless cases raise issues concerning his set of preferred rights, such as those that defend property interests.

In pursuing his jurisprudential objectives, Scalia has been willing to call into question two of the most fundamental legal assumptions of the post-New Deal *Carolene Products* jurisprudence, namely broad respect for delegation of power and the contrasting levels of analysis given to property rights and civil rights. In the case of delegation, Scalia would enforce separation-of-powers principles scrupulously in order to maintain what he believes the constitutional framers considered in the *Federalist Papers* to be the heart of the American political system. While Scalia has not explicitly called for a resurrection of the logic of *Schechter Poultry Corporation v. United States* (1935), his opinions portray an image of desired outcomes that is not far removed from the logic of that earlier controversial era in constitutional history. In the case of the property-and-individual-rights dichotomy, Scalia's opinions have supported the gradual elevation of judicial scrutiny from rational basis to an intermediate level analysis in examinations of property and land use regulation. At the same time, he has supported the retreat from heightened scrutiny in examining more traditional Bill of Rights complaints by deferring to majoritarian political processes.

Scalia's legal philosophy, as we indicated in the introduction, is the product not simply of political or jurisprudential values, but a combination of substantive political, methodological, and interpretive values. As we have tried to indicate throughout this book, several values are important to Scalia's political vision, and these values compete with one another to produce his jurisprudence. Scalia's central values include a commitment to respect for the majoritarian process, protection of property, a use of a specific political methodology, and a qualified respect for a textualist-originalist judicial defense of traditional Bill of Rights claims. All of these commitments are influenced and shaped by a generally conservative ideology that determines how tradeoffs are made among these four values, including defining those situations when the legislative or majoritarian process should or should not be trusted.

Scalia has sought to impose his jurisprudential vision upon the Court. He is not a justice who sees himself providing input in an interactive process of deliberations among thoughtful, reasonable, respectable colleagues. Indeed, he often seems to regard his colleagues with the disdain that one would reserve for people considered unquestionably inferior in intellectual or reasoning abilities. Instead of conveying an image of someone who is a respectful participant in a larger deliberative process, he evinces a strong belief in the clarity and correctness of his vision, and this strong belief drives him to present his views at every opportunity and to criticize harshly those who disagree with him. His outspokenness seems to reflect a kind of self-righteous individualism that makes him stand out among the Rehnquist Court's justices. By subordinating persuasiveness to stridency, his interpretive approach and expressive style emphasize the dissemination of ideas at the expense of maximizing the number of successful outcomes. Many people have observed that Scalia would rather be right than win. This is, in some respects, an admirable image of principled advocacy. However, when the ultimate objective is the shaping of law and policy, then putatively principled advocacy that hinders its own possibilities of success may be more unwise in practice than it is praiseworthy in the abstract.

If "success" is defined in terms of writing majority opinions, getting other justices to agree with him, or in articulating opinions and doctrines that later would be the basis for majority opinions (Murphy 1984), then Scalia has achieved mixed results. He has been influential in redefining the law regarding property rights, free exercise of religion, and the Eighth Amendment. Scalia has been relatively unsuccessful in getting other justices to adopt his interpretive methodology, especially his views on legislative intent and history, affirmative action, abortion, free speech, and religion. Initially, it appeared that Kennedy and O'Connor would be close allies of Scalia. These justices, as well as Souter, have broken with Scalia concerning reasoning and outcome in several critical cases. Scalia has only Justice Thomas as a relatively dependable ally. Moreover, in cases where he has succeeded, such as in *Employment Division v. Smith's* (1990) alteration of freedom of religion, and in *Lorance v. AT&T Technologies'* (1989) restrictions on discrimination litigation, Congress has acted to lessen the impact of Scalia's opinions. Thus, Scalia has yet to translate his visionary jurisprudence into consistent influence over law and policy.

The appointments of Democratic justices Ruth Bader Ginsburg and Stephen Breyer have not enhanced Scalia's potential influence in the short term. Justices Ginsburg and Breyer tend to approach the issues of reproductive rights, discrimination, statutory interpretation, *Chevron v. NRDC* (1984), and administrative delegation quite differently than does Scalia. These differences are certain to produce new voting alignments, disagreements, and doctrines to which Scalia will need to react. Several of Scalia's colleagues are likely to retire and be replaced in the foreseeable future. The appointment of new justices, along with the emergence of new legal and policy issues, will test Scalia's fidelity to his core values and interpretive methods. Scalia has already shown a penchant for manipulating his interpretive methods in order to advance particular rules and outcomes concerning his most salient policy preferences. In rewriting free-exercise jurisprudence in *Employment Division of Oregon v. Smith* (1990), for example, Scalia eschewed textual and historical approaches in favor of seizing upon a weak precedential base as the foundation for persuasively mischaracterizing existing doctrines. The emergence of new issues could elicit similar responses in which Scalia casts aside elements of his interpretive approach to advance more explicitly his preference for the dominance of majoritarian political processes. As Scalia responds to new developments, future appointments stemming from changes in presidential administrations could enhance Scalia's power if additional new justices are attracted to Scalia's values and methods.

While we have sought to define Scalia's jurisprudence up to the present, and we assume that it will remain consistent in the future, we are mindful that justices' philosophies do evolve. This was most evident in Justice Blackmun's move from the conservative to the liberal end of the Court's spectrum during the 1970s and 1980s. Yet, if Scalia's past performance is any indication of the future, it will be somewhat surprising if the justice moderates his tone or style to become more accommodating toward other justices in the hope that he can persuade them to agree with his reasoning. Scalia appears to be firmly and self-righteously committed to his jurisprudential vision. Barring a dramatic philosophical conversion, Scalia's insistence on presenting his views in an uncompromising and undiluted fashion is likely to hamper his success in convincing a majority of his colleagues that they should share his jurisprudential vision.

Bibliography

Abraham, Henry J. *Freedom and the Court.* 5th ed. New York: Oxford University Press, 1988.

Abraham, Henry J. *Justices and Presidents: A Political History of Appointments to the Supreme Court.* New York: Oxford University Press, 1992.

Ackerman, Bruce. "Beyond Carolene Products." *Harvard Law Review* 98 (1985): 713–746.

Ackerman, Bruce. *We the People: Foundations.* Cambridge: Harvard University Press, 1991.

All Things Considered. (PBS radio broadcast, June 22, 1992).

Ball, Howard. *Courts and Politics: The Federal Judicial System.* 2nd ed. Englewood Cliffs, N.J.: Prentice-Hall, 1987.

Barrett, Paul M. "Independent Justice: David Souter Emerges as Reflective Moderate on the Supreme Court," *Wall Street Journal,* A1 (February 2, 1993).

Baugh, Joyce A., Christopher E. Smith, Thomas R. Hensley, and Scott Patrick Johnson. "Justice Ruth Bader Ginsburg: A Preliminary Assessment." *University of Toledo Law Review* 26 (1994): 1–34.

Baum, Lawrence. *The Supreme Court,* 4th edition. Washington,D.C.: Congressional Quarterly Press, 1992.

Baum, Lawrence. *The Supreme Court,* 3rd ed. Washington, D.C.: CQ Press, 1989.

Baum, Lawrence. *American Courts: Process and Policy.* 2nd ed. Boston: Houghton Mifflin, 1990.

Becker, Carl. *The Declaration of Independence.* New York: Vintage Books, 1961.

Berkson, Larry C. *The Concept of Cruel and Unusual Punishment.* Lexington, Mass.: Lexington Books, 1975.

Bickel, Alexander M. *The Least Dangerous Branch: The Supreme Court at the Bar of Politics* New Haven: Yale University Press, 1986.

Biskupic, Joan. "Abortion Dispute Entangles Religious Freedom Bill." *Congressional Quarterly* 49 (1991): 913–917.

Blasi, Vincent, ed. *The Burger Court: The Counterrevolution that Wasn't,* New Haven: Yale University Press, 1983.

Bodenhamer, David. *Fair Trial: The Rights of Accused in American History.* New York: Oxford University Press, 1992.

Bork, Robert H. *The Tempting of American: The Political Seduction of the Law,* New York: Simon & Schuster, Inc, 1990.

Bork, Robert H. "Neutral Principles and some First Amendment Problems. *Indiana Law Journal* 47 (1971): 1–35.

Bosselman, Fred P. "Scalia on Land" in David L. Callies, ed., *After Lucas: Land Use Regulation and the Taking of Property without Compensation.* Chicago: American Bar Association, (1993): 82–101.

Bowers, William J. "The Pervasiveness of Arbitrariness and Discrimination Under Post-*Furman* Capital Statutes." *Journal of Criminal Law and Criminology* 74 (1983): 1067–1100.

Bowman, Cynthia. " 'We Don't Want Anybody Anybody Sent': The Death of Patronage Hiring in Chicago," *Northwestern University Law Review* 86 (1991): 57–95.

Brest, Paul. "The Misconceived Quest for the Original Understanding." *Boston University Law Review* 60 (1980): 204–234.

Breyer, Stephen. "Judicial Review of Questions of Law and Policy." *Administrative Law Review* 38 (1986): 363–399.

Brinkley, Martin. "Despoiling the Spoils." *North Carolina Law Review* 69 (1991): 719–740.

Brisbin, Richard A., Jr. "Antonin Scalia, William Brennan, and the Politics of Expression: A Study of Legal Violence and Repression." *American Political Science Review* 87 (1993): 912–927.

Brisbin, Richard A. Jr. "'Administrative Law is not for Sissies:' Justice Antonin Scalia's Challenge to American Administrative Law." *Administrative Law Review* 44 (1992): 107–129.

Brisbin, Jr., Richard A. "The Rehnquist Court and the Free Exercise of Religion." *Journal of Church and State* 34 (1992a): 57–76.

Brisbin, Richard A. Jr. Justice Antonin Scalia and the Politics of Repression: A Study of the Law's Violence." (March 18–21, 1992. Unpublished manuscript presented at the 1992 Annual Meeting of the Southwestern Political Science Association, Austin, Texas, 1992).

Brisbin, Richard A. Jr. and Edward V. Heck. "The Battle over Strict Scrutiny: Coalitional Conflict in the Rehnquist Court." *Santa Clara Law Review* 32 (1992): 1049–1105.

Brisbin, Richard A. Jr. "Justice Antonin Scalia, Constitutional Discourse, and the Legalistic State." *Western Political Quarterly* 4 (1991): 1006–1038.

Brisbin, Richard A., Jr. "The Conservatism of Antonin Scalia." *Political Science Quarterly* 105 (1990): 1–29.

Burt, Robert A. "Precedent and Authority in Antonin Scalia's Jurisprudence." *Cardozo Law Review* 12 (1991): 1685–1698.

Caldeira, Gregory. "Neither the Purse Nor the Sword: The Dynamics of Public Confidence in the Supreme Court." *American Political Science Review* 80 (1986): 1209–1226.

Callies, David L. ed. *After Lucas: Land Use Regulation and the Taking of Property without Compensation.* Chicago, American Bar Assocaition, 1993.

Cardozo, Benjamin N. *The Nature of the Judicial Process,* New Haven: Yale University Press, 1969.

Casper, Gerhard. "An Essay in Separation of Powers: Some Early Versions and Practices." *William & Mary Law Review* 30 (1989): 211–261.

Chemerinsky, Erwin and Larry Kramer. "Defining the Role of the the Federal Courts." *Brigham Young University Law Review.* (1990): 67–95.

Cofer, Donna P. *Judges, Bureaucrats, and the Question of Independence.* Westport, Conn.: Greenwood Press, 1985.

Collier, Calvin J. "Oversight and Review of Agency Decisionmaking." *Administrative Law Review* 28 (1976): 661–695/.

"Congress Keeps Eye on Justices As Court Watches Hill's Words." *Congressional Quarterly Weekly Report* 49 (1991): 2863–2867.

Cook, Bethany A. and Lisa C. Kahn. "Justice Scalia's Due Process Model: A History Lesson in Constitutional Interpretation." *Journal of Legal Commentary* 6 (1991): 263–285.

Coyle, Dennis J. "The Reluctant Revival of Landowner Rights." (Unpublished Convention Paper presented in Chicago at the 1987 American Political Science Association Annual Convention, 1987).

Coyle, Dennis J. *Property Rights and the Constitution: Shaping Society Through Land Use Regulation.* Albany: SUNY Press, 1993.

Craig, Barbara Hinkson. *Chadha: The Story of an Epic Constitutional Struggle.* Berkeley, Calif.: University of California Press, 1988.

Dahl, Robert. *Democracy and its Critics.* New Haven: Yale University Press, 1991.

Dahl, Robert. *Democracy in the United States.* Boston: Houghton Mifflin, 1981.

Davis, Sue. *Justice Rehnquist and the Constitution.* Princeton: Princeton University Press, 1989.

Decker, John F. *Revolution to the Right: Criminal Procedure Jurisprudence during the Burger-Rehnquist Court Era.* New York: Garland, 1992.

Diggins, John Patrick. *The Lost Soul of American Politics.* Chicago: University of Chicago Press, 1986.

Dolbeare, Kenneth M. *Directions in American Political Thought.* Chatham: Chatham House, 1969.

Domino, John. *Civil Rights and Liberties: Toward the 21st Century.* New York: HarperCollins, 1993.

Dworetz, Stephen M. *The Unvarnished Doctrine: Locke, Liberalism, and the American Revolution,* Durham, North Carolina: Duke University Press, 1991.

Dworkin, Ronald. *Taking Rights Seriously.* Cambridge: Harvard University Press, 1978.

Dworkin, Ronald. *Law's Empire.* Cambridge: Harvard University Press, 1986.

Easterbook, Frank H. "The Role of Original Intent in Statotory Construction." *Harvard Journal of Law and Public Policy* 11 (1988): 59–66.

Edelman, Peter B. "Justice Scalia's Jurisprudence and the Good Society: Shades of

Felix Frankfurter and the Harvard Hit Parade of the 1950s." *Cardozo Law Review* 12 (1991): 1799–1816.

Elliott, E. Donald. "Why Our Separation of Powers Jurisprudence Is So Abysmal." *George Washington University Law Review* 57 (1989): 506–532.

Ely, James W. Jr. *The Chief Justiceship of Melville W. Fuller, 1888–1910*. Columbia, South Carolina: University of South Carolina Press, 1995.

Ely, James W. Jr. *The Guardian of Every Other Right: A Constitutional History of Property Rights*. New York: Oxford University Press, 1992.

Ely, John Hart. *Democracy and Distrust*. Cambridge: Harvard University Press, 1980.

Epstein, Richard A. "*Lucas v. South Carolina Coastal Council*: A Tangled Web of Expectations." *Stanford Law Review* 45 (1993): 1369–1392.

Epstein, Richard A. *Takings: Private Property and the Power of Eminent Domain*. Cambridge: Harvard University Press, 1985.

Epstein, Aaron. "A War on Individual Rights? Courts Smile on Tactics Once Discouraged." *Akron Beacon Journal*, June 10, 1990: A14.

Epstein Leon and C.D. Hadley. "On the Treatment of Political Parties in the U.S. Supreme Court, 1900–1986." *Journal of Politics* 52 (1990): 413–432.

Eskridge, William N., Jr. "The New Textualism." *U.C.L.A. Law Review* 37 (1990): 621–691.

Farber Daniel A and Philip P. Frickey. *Law and Public Choice: A Critical Introduction*. Chicago: University of Chicago, 1991.

Fisher William W. III. "The Trouble with *Lucas*." *Stanford Law Review* 45 (1993): 1393–1410.

Fisher, Louis. *American Constitutional Law*. New York: McGraw-Hill, 1990.

Freitag, J. "Takings 1992: Scalia's Jurisprudence and Fifth Amendment Doctrine to Avoid *Lochner Redivivus*." *Valparaiso University Law Review* 28 (1994): 743–783.

Friedelbaum, Stanley H. *The Rehnquist Court: In Pursuit of Judicial Conservatism*. Westport: Greenwood Press, 1994.

Friedman, Milton. *Capitalism and Freedom*. Chicago: University of Chicago Press, 1962.

Friedman, Richard D. "Putting the Dormancy Doctrine Out of Its Misery." *Cardozo Law Review* 12 (1991): 1745–1762.

Gadamer, Hans-Georg. *Truth and Method*, New York: Crossroad Publishing, 1986.

Garrow, David J. "Justice Souter Emerges," *The New York Times Magazine* (September 25, 1994): 36–67.

Gellhorn, Ernest. "A Justice Breyer May Tip the Court's Balance." *The National Law Journal* (July 4, 1994): A19.

Gillman, Howard. *The Constitution Besieged: The Rise and Demise of Lochner Era Police Powers Jurisprudence*. Durham: Duke University Press, 1993.

Goldman, Sheldon. *Constitutional Law: Cases and Essays*. New York: Harper & Row, 1987.

Goldman, Sheldon. "Bush's Judicial Legacy: The Final Imprint." *Judicature* 76 (1993): 282–297.

Goldman, Sheldon. "Reagan's Judicial Legacy: Completing the Puzzle and Summing Up." *Judicature* 72 (1989): 318–330.

Golick, Toby. "Justice Scalia, Poverty, and the Good Society." *Cardozo Law Review* 12 (1991): 1817–1830.

Gould, Carol C. *Rethinking Democracy: Freedom and Social Cooperation in Politics, Economy, and Society.* New York: Cambridge University Press, 1988.

Graber, Mark. *Transforming Free Speech: The Ambiguous Legacy of Civil Libertarianism.* Berkeley: University of California Press, 1991.

Greenawalt, Kenneth. *Speech, Crime, and the Uses of Language.* New York: Oxford University Press, 1989.

Greenhouse, Linda. "Souter: Unlikely Anchor at Court's Center," *New York Times* (July 3, 1993): A1.

Greenhouse, Linda. "Scalia Tightens Policy on Death Penalty Appeals." *New York Times* (May 6, 1991): A1, A20.

Greenhouse, Linda. "Supreme Court Dissenters: Loners or Pioneers?" *New York Times,* (July 20, 1990): B8.

Greenhouse, Linda. "Justices Find a Right to Die, But Majority Sees Need for Clear Proof of Intent." *New York Times* (June 26, 1990a): A19.

Greenhouse, L. "Name-Calling in the Supreme Court: When the Justices Vent Their Spleen, Is There a Social Cost?" *New York Times* (July 28, 1989): B10.

Grossman, Joel B. and Richard S. Wells. *Constitutional Law and Judicial Policy Making.* 3rd ed. New York: Longman, 1988.

Guinier, Lani. *The Tyranny of the Majority: Fundamental Fairness in Representative Democracy.* New York: The Free Press, 1994.

Halberstam, Malvina. "The Use of Legislative History in Treaty Interpretation: The Dual Treaty Approach." *Cardozo Law Review* 12 (1991): 1645–1652.

Hart, H.L.A. *The Concept of Law.* New York: Oxford University Press, 1961.

Hartz, Louis. *The Liberal Tradition in America.* New York: Harcourt Brace Jovanovich, Inc, 1955.

Hayek, Friedrich A. *The Constitution of Liberty.* South Bend, Indiana: Gateway Press, 1960.

Heck, Edward V. and Melinda Gann Hall. 1981. "Block Voting and the Freshman Justice Revisted." *The Journal of Politics* 43: 852–860.

Hellerstein, Walter. "Justice Scalia and the Commerce Clause: Reflctions of a State Tax Lawyer." *Cardozo Law Review* 12 (1991): 1763–1788.

Hengstler, Gary. "Scalia Seeks Court Changes." *American Bar Association Journal* 73 (April 1, 1987): 20.

Herz, Michael. "Textualism and Taboo: Interpretation and Deference for Justice Scalia." *Cardozo Law Review* 12 (1991): 1663–1684.

Hoffmann, Joseph. "Is Innocence Sufficient? An Essay on the U.S. Supreme Court's Continuing Problems with Federal Habeas Corpus and the Death Penalty." *Indiana Law Journal* 68 (1993): 817–834.

Horowitz, Donald L. *The Courts and Social Policy.* Washington, D.C.: Brookings Press, 1977.

Hovenkamp Herbert. "The Political Economy of Substantive Due Process." *Stanford Law Review* 40 (1988): 379–447.

Hyde, Alan. "The Concept of Legitimation in the Sociology of Law." *Wisconsin Law Review* (1983): 379–426.

Irons, Peter. *The Courage of Their Convictions.* New York: Free Press, 1988.

Johnson, Scott P. and Christopher E. Smith. "David Souter's First Term on the Supreme Court: The Impact of a New Justice." *Judicature* 75 (1992): 238–243.

Johnson, B. "Another Attempt to Eliminate Political Patronage." *Willamette Law Review* 27 (1991): 405–428.

Kairys, David. *With Liberty and Justice for Some.* New York: New Press, 1993.

Kalven, Harry Jr. *A Worthy Tradition: Freedom of Speech in America.* New York: Harper & Row, Publishers, 1988.

Kannar, George. "The Constitutional Catechism of Antonin Scalia." *Yale Law Journal* 99 (1990): 1297–1357.

Kannar, George. "Strenuous Virtues, Virtuous Lives: The Social Vision of Antonin Scalia." *Cardozo Law Review* 12 (1991): 1845–1868.

Karkkainen, Bradley. " 'Plain Meaning': Justice Scalia's Jurisprudence of Strict Statutory Construction." *Harvard Journal of Law & Public Policy* 17 (1994): 401–477.

King, Michael Patrick. "Justice Antonin Scalia: The First Term on the Supreme Court—1986–1987." *Rutgers Law Journal* 20 (1988): 1–77.

Komesar, Neil. "Taking Institutions Seriously: Introduction to a Strategy for Constitutional Analysis." *University of Chicago Law Review* 51 (1984): 366–446.

Kozinski, Alex. "My Dinner with Nino." *Cardozo Law Review* 12 (1991): 1583–1592.

Kramer, Larry. "Judicial Asceticism." *Cardozo Law Review* 12 (1991): 1789–1788.

Ladd, Everett C. *The American Polity: The People and Their Government.* 2nd ed. New York: W. W. Norton, 1987.

Lazarus, Richard J. "Putting the Correct 'Spin' on *Lucas*." *Stanford Law Review* 45 (1993): 1411–1432.

Levinson, Sanford. *Constitutional Faith.* Princeton: Princeton University Press, 1988.

Levitt, Alfred P. "Taking on a New Direction: The Rehnquist Scalia Approach to Regulatory Takings." *Temple Law Review* 66 (1993): 197–222.

Locke, John. *A Letter Concerning Toleration.* Indianapolis: Bobbs-Merrill, 1979.

Lowenstein, Daniel Hays. "A Patternless Mosaic: Campaign Finance and the First Amendment After *Austin*." *Capital University Law Review* 21 (1992): 381–427.

Macpherson, C.B. *The Rise and Fall of Economic Justice and other Essays.* New York: Oxford University Press, 1987.

Maltz, Earl M. "Reconstruction without Revolution: Republican Civil Rights Theory in the Era of the Fourteenth Amendment." *Houston Law Review* 24 (1987): 221–279.

Marcotte, Paul. "Rehnquist's Perspective." *A.B.A. Journal* 73 (April 1, 1987): 19.

Marcus, Ruth. "Waiting Forever on Death Row." *Washington Post National Weekly Edition* (June 18–24, 1990): 11–12.

Marshall, Price. " 'No Political Truth:' The *Federalist* and Justice Scalia on the Separation of Powers." *University of Arkansas at Little Rock Law Journal* 12 (1989–90): 245–264.

Massey, Stephen J. "Justice Rehnquist's Theory of Property." *Yale Law Journal* 93 (1984): 541–560.

Mauro, Tony. "High Court Adjourns for the Summer Intact." *Legal Times* (July 9, 1990): 10.

McConnell, Michael. "Free Exercise Revisionism and the *Smith* Decision." *University of Chicago Law Review* 57 (1990): 1109–1153.

Meaux, J.M. "Justice Scalia and Judicial Restraint: A Conservative Resolution of Conflict Between Individual and the State." *Tulane Law Review* 62 (1987): 225–260.

Meese, Edwin, III. "The Battle for the Constitution." *Policy Review* 9 (Spring 1986): 32–35.

Meese, Edwin III. "The Attorney General's View of the Supreme Court: Towards Jurisprudence of Original Intention." *Public Administration Review* (November 1985): 701–704.

Meiklejohn, Alexander. *Political Freedom*. New York: Oxford University Press, 1965.

Melone, Albert P. "Revisiting the Freshman Effect Hypothesis: The First Two Terms of Justice Anthony Kennedy." *Judicature* 74 (1990): 6–13.

Mezey, Susan G. *No Longer Disabled: The Federal Courts and the Politics of Social Security Disability*. New York: Greenwood Press, 1988.

Mill, John Stuart. On Liberty in *Utilitarianism, Liberty, and Representative Government*. New York: Dutton, 1951.

Milton, John. *Areopagitica*. In *Milton: Political Writings*. Martin Dzelzainis. New York: Cambridge University Press, 1991.

Moore, W. John. "Righting the Courts." *National Journal* (January 25, 1992): 20.

Murley, John A. "School Prayer: Free Exercise of Religion or Establishment of Religion?" in Raymond Tatalovich and Byron W. Daynes, eds., *Social Regulatory Policy: Moral Controversies in American Politics*. Boulder, Colo.: Westview Press, 1988.

Murphy, Walter F. *Elements of Judicial Strategy*. Chicago: University of Chicago Press, 1964.

Myers, Ken. "Scalia Steers Non-Controversial Path During Lecture at Cleveland College." *Akron Beacon Journal* (October 25, 1989): C2.

Nagareda, Richard. "The Appellate Jurisprudence of Justice Antonin Scalia." *The University of Chicago Law Review* 54 (1987): 705–739.

Newland, Sarah. "The Mercy of Scalia: Statutory Construction and the Rule of Lenity." *Harvard Civil Rights–Civil Liberties Law Review* 29 (1994): 197–229.

Note. "Looking It Up: Dictionaries and Statutory Interpretation." *Harvard Law Review* 107 (1994): 1437–1453.

O'Brien, David. *Storm Center: The Supreme Court in American Politics*. 2nd ed. New York: W. W. Norton, 1990.

O'Connor, Joyce. "Supreme Court Journal." American Political Science Association's *Law, Courts, and Judicial Process Section Newsletter* 6 (Spring 1989): 40–47.

Parmet, W.E. and J.O. Brown. "Scalia and Free Speech." *National Law Journal*, (July 27, 1992): 17–18.

Paul, Ellen Frankel. *Property Rights and Eminent Domain*. New Brunswick: Transaction Books, 1988.

Pear. R. "With Rights Act Comes Fight to Clarify Congress' Intent," *New York Times* (November 18, 1991): A1.

Perry, H.W. Jr. *Deciding to Decide: Agenda Setting in the United States Supreme Court*. Cambridge: Harvard University Press, 1991.

Pierce, Richard. "*Morrison v. Olson*, Separation of Powers, and the Structure of Government." *Supreme Court Review* (1988): 1–24.

Pollot, Mark L. *Grand Theft and Petit Larceny: Property Rights in America*. San Francisco: Pacific Research Institute, 1993.

Powe L.A. Jr. *The Fourth Estate and the Constitution*. Cambridge: Harvard University Press, 1992.

Pritchett, C Herman. *The Roosevelt Court*. Chicago: Quadrangle Press, 1969.

Provine, Doris Marie. *Case Selection in the United States Supreme Court*. Chicago: University of Chicago Press, 1980.

Rabkin, Jeremy. *Judicial Compulsions: How Public Law Distorts Public Policy*. New York: Basic Books, 1989.

Radin, Margaret Jane. *Reinterpreting Property*. Chicago: University of Chicago Press, 1993.

Rawls, John. *Theory of Justice*. Cambridge, Mass.: Belknap Press, 1971.

Reid, John Philip. *Constitutional History of the American Revolution: The Authority of Rights*. Madison: University of Wisconsin Press, 1986.

Reisman, D. "Deconstucting Justice Scalia's Separation of Powers Jurisprudence: The Preeminent Executive." *Albany Law Review* 53 (1988): 49–94.

Robel, Lauren K. "Caseload and Judging: Judicial Adaptations to Caseload." *Brigham Young University Law Review* (1990): 3–65.

Rosen, Jeffrey. "Poetic Justice." *The New Republic* (March 8, 1993): 25–27.

Rubin, Thea and Albert P. Melone. "Justice Antonin Scalia: A First Year Freshman Effect?" *Judicature* 72 (1988): 98–102.

"Rude Robes." *Newsweek* October 19, 1992: 5.

Sanders, Alain. "The Marble Palace's Southern Gentleman." *Time* (July 9, 1990): 12–13.

Savage, David G. *Turning Right: The Making of the Rehnquist Court*. New York: John Wiley & Sons, Inc, 1992.

Scalia, Antonin. "Assorted Canards of Contemporary Legal Analysis." *Case Western Reserve Law Review* 40 (1989–90): 581–597.

Scalia, Antonin. "The Rule of Law as a Law of Rules." *The University of Chicago Law Review* 56 (1989): 1175–1188.

Scalia, Antonin. "Judicial Deference to Administrative Interpretations of Law." *Duke Law Journal* 3 (1989a): 511–521.

Scalia, Antonin. "Originalism: The Lesser Evil." *Cincinnati Law Review* 57 (1989b): 849–865.

Scalia, Antonin. C-SPAN Broadcast of Remarks at Washington, D.C. Panel Discussion of Separation of Powers. November 15, 1988.

Scalia, Antonin. "Economic Affairs as Human Affairs" J.A. Dorn, ed. *Economic Liberties and the Judiciary*. Fairfax, Virginia: George Mason University Press, 1987.

Scalia, Antonin. "The Limits of the Law." *New Jersey Law Journal* 119 (1987a): 736–755.

Scalia, Antonin. "Responsibilities of Regulatory Agencies Under Environmental Laws." *Houston Law Review* 24 (1987b): 97–109.

Scalia, Antonin. "A House with Many Mansions: Categories of Speech under the First Amendment" J.B. Stewart ed. *The Constitution, The Law, and Freedom of Expression: 1787–1987*. Carbondale, Illinois: Southern Illinois University Press, 1987c.

Scalia, Antonin "Morality, Pragmaticism and the Legal Order." *Harvard Journal of Law & Public Policy* 9 (1985): 123–127.

Scalia, Antonin. "The Doctrine of Standing as an Essential Element of the Separation of Powers." *Suffolk University Law Review* 17 (1983): 881–899.

Scalia, Antonin. "Regulatory Review and Management." *Regulation* 6 (Jan–Feb 1982): 19–21.

Scalia, Antonin. "The Two Faces of Federalism." *Harvard Journal of Law and Public Policy* 6 (1982a): 19–22.

Scalia, Antonin. "Regulatory Reform: The Game has Changed." *Regulation* 5 (Jan–Feb 1981): 13–15.

Scalia, Antonin. "Back to Basics: Making Law without Making Rules. " *Regulation* 5 (Jul–Aug 1981a): 25–28.

Scalia, Antonin. "The Disease as Cure." *Washington University Law Quarterly* 1 (1979): 147–160.

Scalia, Antonin. "The Legislative Veto: A False Remedy for System Overload." *Regulation* 3 (Nov–Dec 1979a): 19–26.

Scalia, Antonin. "Guadalajara! A Case Study in Regulation by Munificence." *Regulation* 2 (March–April 1978): 23–29.

Scalia, Antonin. "Two Wrongs Make a Right." *Regulation* 1 (Jul–Aug 1977): 38–41.

Scalia, Antonin. "Sovereign Immunity and Nonstatutory Review of Federal Administrative Action: Some Conclusions from the Public Law Cases." *Michigan Law Review* 68 (1970): 867–924.

Scatena, P.C. "Deference to Discretion: Scalia's Impact on Judicial Review in the Era of Deregulation." *Hastings Law Journal* 38 (1987): 1223–1260.

Schlosser, Jay. "The Establishment Clause and Justice Scalia: What the Future Holds for Church and State." *Notre Dame Law Review* 63 (1988): 380–392.

Schultz, David. "Scalia, Property, and *Dolan v. Tigard*: The Emergence of a Post *Carolene Products* Jurisprudence," *Akron Law Review* 29 (1995): 1–34.

Schultz, David. "Supreme Court Articulation of the Politics Administration Dichotomy." In *Handbook of Bureaucracy*. Ali Farazmand, editor. New York: Marcel Dekker, Inc., 1994.

Schultz, David. "Church State Relations and the First Amendment." In *Law and Politics: Unanswered Questions*. David Schultz, editor. New York: Peter Lang Publishers, 1994a.

Schultz, David. "Antonin Scalia's First Amendment Free Speech, Press, and Association Decisions." *Journal of Law and Politics* 9 (1993): 515–560.

Schultz, David. "Antonin Scalia and Expressive Freedom." Unpublished paper presented at the Southern Political Science Association meeting, November, 1993, Savannah, Georgia, 1993a.

Schultz, David. "Judicial Review and Legislative Deference: The Political Process of Antonin Scalia." *Nova Law Review* 16 (1992): 1251–1283.

Schultz, David. *Property, Power, and American Democracy*. New Brunswick: Transaction Books, 1992a.

Schultz, David. "Legislative Process and Intent in Justice Scalia's Interpretive Method." *Akron Law Review* 25 (1992b): 595–610.

Schwartz, Bernard. *The New Right and the Constitution: Turning Back the Legal Clock*. Boston: Northeastern University Press, 1990.

Schwartz, Herman. *Packing the Courts: The Conservative Campaign to Rewrite the Constitution*. New York: Charles Scribners' Sons, 1988.

Segal, Jeffrey A. and Harold J. Spaeth. *The Supreme Court and the Attitudinal Model*. New York: Cambridge University Press, 1993.

Shane, Peter. "Independent Policymaking and Presidential Power." *George Washington University Law Review* 57 (1989): 596–626.

Shiffrin, Stephen. *The First Amendment, Democracy, and Romance*. Cambridge: Harvard University Press, 1990.

Shockley, John, and David Schultz. "The Political Philosophy of Money as Articulated in the Dissents in *Austin v. Michigan Chamber of Commerce*." *St. Mary's Law Review* 24 (1992): 165–196.

Siegan, Bernard. *The Supreme Court's Constitution*. New Brunswick: Transaction Books, 1987.

Slawson, W. David. "Legislative History and the Need to Bring Statutory Interpretation Under the Rule of Law." *Stanford Law Review* 44 (1992): 383–427.

Smith, Christopher E., Joyce Baugh, Thomas R. Hensley, and Scott Patrick Johnson. "The First-Term Performance of Justice Ruth Bader Ginsburg." *Judicature* 78 (1994): 74–80.

Smith, Christopher E. and Scott Patrick Johnson. "The First-Term Performance of Justice Clarence Thomas." *Judicature* 76 (1993): 172–178.

Smith, Christopher E. *Courts and Public Policy*. Chicago: Nelson-Hall, 1993a.

Smith, Christopher E. *Justice Antonin Scalia and the Supreme Court's Conservative Moment*. Westport, Conn.: Praeger, 1993b.

Smith, Christopher E. and Kimberly A. Beuger. "Clouds in the Crystal Ball: Presidential Expectations and the Unpredictable Behavior of Supreme Court Appointees." *Akron Law Review* 27 (1993): 115–139.

Smith, Christopher E. "Justice Antonin Scalia and Criminal Justice Cases." *Kentucky Law Journal* 81 (1992–93): 187–212.

Smith, Christopher E. "Supreme Court Surprise: Justice Anthony Kennedy's Move Toward Moderation." *Oklahoma Law Review* 45 (1992): 459–476.

Smith, Christopher E. and Linda Fry. "Vigilance or Accommodation: The Changing

Supreme Court and Religious Freedom." *Syracuse Law Review* 42 (1991): 893–944.

Smith, Christopher E. "Justice Antonin Scalia: Contradictions in the Opinions and Behavior of the Supreme Court's Institutional Guardian." Unpublished paper presented at the April 1991, Midwest Political Science Association annual convention, Chicago, Illinois, 1991a.

Smith, Christopher E. "Justice Antonin Scalia and the Institutions of American Government." *Wake Forest Law Review* 25 (1990): 783–809.

Smith, Christopher E. *United States Magistrates in the Federal Courts: Subordinate Judges*. New York: Praeger, 1990a.

Smith, Christopher E. and Scott P. Johnson. "Presidential Pardons and Accountability in the Executive Branch." *Wayne Law Review* 35 (1989): 1113–1131.

Smith, Christopher E. "Bright-Line Rules and the Supreme Court: The Tension Between Clarity in Legal Doctrine and Justices' Policy Preferences." *Ohio Northern University Law Review* 16 (1989a): 119–137.

Smith, Christopher E. "Jurisprudential Politics and the Manipulation of History." *Western Journal of Black Studies* 13 (1989b): 156–161.

Smith, Christopher E. "Assessing the Consequences of Judicial Innovation: U.S. Magistrates' Trials and Related Tribulations." *Wake Forest Law Review* 23 (1988): 455–490.

Smith, Christopher E. "Federal Judges' Role in Prisoner Litigation: What's Necessary? What's Proper?" *Judicature* 70 (1986): 144–150.

Stock, Arthur. "Justice Scalia's Use of Sources in Statutory and Constitutional Interpretation: How Congress Always Looses." *Duke Law Journal* (1990): 160–192.

Strauss, David A. "Tradition, Precedent, and Justice Scalia." *Cardozo Law Review* 12 (1991): 1699–1716.

Strauss, Peter L. "Comment: Legal Process and Judges in the Real World." *Cardozo Law Review* 12 (1991): 1653–1662.

Stumpf, Harry P. *American Judicial Politics*. San Diego, Calif.: Harcourt Brace Jovanovich, 1988.

Sunstein, Cass. "Constitutionalism After the New Deal." *Harvard Law Review* 101 (1987): 421–510.

Sunstein, Cass. *Democracy and the Problem of Free Speech*. New York: The Free Press, 1993.

Tate, C. Neal. "Personal Attribute Models of the Voting Behavior of U.S. Supreme Court Justices: Liberalism in Civil Liberties and Economics Decisions, 1946–1978." *American Political Science Review* 75 (1981): 355–367.

Taylor, Stuart. "Scalia Proposes Major Overhaul of U.S. Courts." *New York Times* (February 16, 1987): 1, 12.

Taylor, Stuart. "Season of Snarling Justices." *Akron Beacon Journal* (April 5, 1990): A11.

Taylor, Stuart. "Blackmun Provides a Peek Under Those Robes." *New York Times* (July 25, 1988): B6.

Terry, D. "Decision Disappoints the Victims of Cross-Burning," *N.Y. Times* (June 23, 1992): A10.

Tribe, Laurence H. *Constitutional Law*. Mineola: Foundation Press, 1987.

Tushnet, Mark V. "Scalia and the Dormant Commerce Clause: A Foolish Formalism?" *Cardozo Law Review* 12 (1991): 1717–1745.

Van Alstyne, William. *First Amendment: Cases and Materials*. Mineola: Foundation Press, 1991.

Van Horn, Carl, Donald Baumer, and William T. Gormley, Jr. *Politics and Public Policy*. Washington, D.C.: Congressional Quarterly Press, 1989.

Wasby, Stephen L. *The Supreme Court in the Federal Judicial System*. 3rd ed. Chicago: Nelson-Hall, 1988.

Wechsler, Herbert. "Towards Neutral Principles of Constitutional Law." *Harvard Law Review* 73 (1959): 1–35.

White, Welsh S. *The Death Penalty in the Nineties*. Ann Arbor, Mich.: University of Michigan Press, 1991.

Wildenthal, Bryan H. "The Right of Confrontation, Justice Scalia, and the Powers and Limits of Textualism." *Washington and Lee Law Review* 48 (1991): 1323–1392.

Willwerth, James. "Invitation to an Execution." *Time* (November 22, 1993): 46–47.

Wilson, James G. "Justice Diffused: A Comparison of Edmund Burke's Conservatism with the Views of Five Conservative, Academic Judges." *University of Miami Law Review* 40 (1986): 913–975.

Wilson, James G. "Constraints of Power: The Constitutional Opinions of Judges Scalia, Bork, Posner, Easterbrook, and Winter." *University of Miami Law Review* 40 (1986a): 1171–1266.

Witt, Elder. *A Different Justice: Reagan and the Supreme Court*. Washington, D.C.: CQ Press, 1986.

Wizner, Stephen. "Judging in the Good Society: A Comment on the Jurisprudence of Justice Scalia." *Cardozo Law Review* 12 (1991): 1831–1844.

Wright, Benjamin F. *The Growth of American Constitutional Law*. New York: Reynal & Hitchcock, 1942.

Yackle, Larry. "The Habeas Hagioscope." *Southern California Law Review* 66 (1993): 2331–2431.

Young, L. Benjamin, Jr. "Justice Scalia's History and Tradition: The Chief Nightmare in Professor Tribe's Anxiety Closet." *Virginia Law Review* 78 (1992): 581–622.

Zeppos, Nicholas S. "Justice Scalia's Textualism: The 'New' New Legal Process." *Cardozo Law Review* 12 (1991): 1597–1644.

Cases

Adkins v. Children's Hospital, 261 U.S. 525 (1923)
Airline Pilots v. O'Neill, 111 S.Ct. 1127 (1991)
Airport Commissioners of Los Angeles v. Jews for Jesus, 107 S. Ct. 2568 (1987)
Alabama v. White, 496 U.S. 325 (1990)
Alexander v. United States, 125 L.Ed. 2d 441 (1993).
Allegheny County v. American Civil Liberties Union 492 U.S. 573 (1989)
Allgeyer v. Louisiana, 165 U.S. 578 (1897)
Arizona v. Fulminante, 111 S.Ct. 1246 (1991)
Arizona v. Hicks, 480 U.S. 321 (1987)
Arizona v. Roberson, 486 U.S. 675 (1988)
Arkansas Writers Project v. Garland, 107 S.Ct. 1722 (1987).
Armstrong v. United States, 364 U.S. 40 (1960)
Austin v. Michigan Chamber of Commerce, 110 S. Ct. 1391 (1990)
Austin v. United States, 113 S.Ct. 2801 (1993)
Baker v. Carr, 369 U.S. 186 (1962)
Barnes v. Glen Theater, Inc., 111 S.Ct. 2456 (1991)
Block v. Meese, 793 F.2d 1303 (D.C. Cir. 1985)
Board of Directors of Rotary International v. Rotary Club of Duarte, 107 S. Ct. 1940
    (1987)
Board of Trustees of SUNY v. Fox, 109 S.Ct. 3028 (1989)
Board of Education of Kiryas Joel v. Grumet, 114 S.Ct. 2481 (1994)
Boos v. Barry, 108 S.Ct. 1157 (1988)
Booth v. Maryland, 482 U.S. 496 (1987)
Bounds v. Smith, 430 U.S. 817 (1977)
Bowen v. Kendrick, 487 U.S. 589 (1988)
Bowsher v. Synar, 478 U.S. 174 (1986)
Bradwell v. Illinois, 83 U.S. 130 (1873)
Branti v. Finkel, 445 U.S. 507 (1979)
Bray v. Alexandria Women's Health Clinic, 113 S.Ct. 753 (1993)
Brown v. Board of Education, 347 U.S. 483 (1954)

223

FCC v. League of Women Voters of California, 468 U.S.164 (1984)
FEC v. National Right to Work Committee, 103 S.Ct. 552 (1982)
Federal Election Commission v. Massachusetts Citizens for Life, 107 S. Ct. 616 (1986)
First English Evangelical Lutheran Church of Glendale v. The County of Los Angeles, 96 L.Ed. 2d 250, 107 S.Ct. 2378 (1986)
Florida v. Riley, 488 U.S. 445 (1989)
Flynt v. Falwell, 108 S.Ct. 876 (1988)
Forsyth County v. the Nationalist Movement, 112 S.Ct. 2395 (1992)
Frazee v. Illinois, 109 S.Ct. 1514 (1989)
Freytag v. C.I.R., 115 L.Ed.2d 764 (1991)
Frisby v. Schultz, 108 S.Ct. 2495 (1988)
Furman v. Georgia, 408 U.S. 238 (1972)
FW/PBS v. City of Dallas, 110 S.Ct. 596 (1990)
Gideon v. Wainwright, 372 U.S. 335 (1963)
Goldblatt v. Town of Hempstead, 369 U.S. 590 (1962)
Goldman v. Weinberger, 475 U.S. 503 (1986)
Grady v. Corbin, 495 U.S. 508 (1990)
Green v. Bock Laundry Machine Co., 109 S.Ct. 1981 (1989)
Griffin v. Wisconsin, 483 U.S. 868 (1987)
Harmelin v. Michigan, 111 S.Ct. 2680 (1991)
Harte-Hanks Communications v. Connaughton, 109 S.Ct. 2678 (1978).
Hazelwood School District v. Kuhlmeier, 108 S.Ct. 562 (1988).
Helling v. McKinney, 113 S.Ct. 2475 (1993)
Herrera v. Collins, 113 S.Ct. 853 (1993)
Hirschey v. F.E.R.C., 77 F.2d. 1 (D.C. Cir. 1985)
Hitchcock v. Dugger, 481 U.S. 393 (1987)
Hodel v. Irving, 481 U.S. 704, 107 S.Ct 2076 (1987)
Holland v. Illinois, 110 S.Ct. 803 (1990)
Holmes v. Securities Investor Protection Corporation, 112 S.Ct. 1311 (1992)
Houston v. Hill, 107 S.Ct. 2502 (1987)
Hudson v. McMillian, 117 L.Ed.2d 156 (1992)
Hutto v. Finney, 437 U.S. 679 (1978)
I.N.S. v. Cardoza Fonseca, 107 S.Ct. 1207, 1224 (1987)
Illinois v. Rodriguez, 497 U.S. 177 (1990)
Illinois v. Krull, 480 U.S. 340 (1987)
Immigration and Naturalization Service v. Chadha, 462 U.S. 919 (1983)
In re Reporters Committee for Free Press, 773 F.2d 1325 (D.C. Cir. 1984)
International Society for Krishna Consciousness v. Lee 112 S.Ct. 2709 (1992)
International Society for Krishna Consciousness v. Lee, 112 S.Ct. 2701 (1992)
Johnson v. Texas, 125 L.Ed.2d 290 (1993)
Johnson v. Transportation Agency, Santa Clara County, 480 U.S. 616 (1987)
Johnson v. Mississippi, 486 U.s. 578 (1988)
Jones v. Thomas, 491 U.S. 376 (1989)

Index

About the Authors

David A. Schultz teaches at the University of Minnesota and is President of Common Cause Minnesota. He is the author of numerous articles on Justice Scalia that have appeared in *The Journal of Law and Politics, Akron Law Review, Nova Law Review,* and *Saint Mary's Law Review.* He has published widely on land use, regulatory takings, and eminent domain; First Amendment free speech and religious freedoms; discrimination law; plant closings; and on assorted topics in legal history and judicial politics. His writings have appeared in the *American Journal of Legal History, Suffolk Law Review, Journal of Employee Ownership Law and Finance, Nichols on Eminent Domain,* and in many other law reviews. He is also the author of several books, including *Law and Politics: Unanswered Questions* (1994), *Property, Power, and American Democracy* (1992), and *A Short History of the United States Civil Service* (1991).

Christopher E. Smith is an Associate Professor in the School of Criminal Justice at Michigan State University. He has published fifty scholarly articles on courts and law, including works on the Supreme Court and constitutional law which have appeared in such journals as *Syracuse Law Review, Oregon Law Review, Wake Forest Law Review,* and *Political Research Quarterly.* His most recent books on the Supreme Court and constitutional law include *Justice Antonin Scalia and the Supreme Court's Conservative Moment* (1993), *Critical Judicial Nominations and Political Change* (1993), and *Courts and Public Policy* (1993).